POST-MARXIST ALTER

Also by Nicos P. Mouzelis

*BACK TO SOCIOLOGICAL THEORY: The Construction of Social Orders
   (forthcoming)
*MODERN GREECE: Facets of Underdevelopment
 ORGANISATION AND BUREAUCRACY: An Analysis of Modern Theory
*POLITICS IN THE SEMI-PERIPHERY: Early Parliamentarism and Late
   Industrialism in the Balkans and Latin America

Also published by Macmillan

Post-Marxist Alternatives

The Construction of Social Orders

Nicos P. Mouzelis

Reader in Sociology
The London School of Economics and Political Science

MACMILLAN

First published 1990

Published by
THE MACMILLAN PRESS LTD
Houndmills, Basingstoke, Hampshire RG21 2XS
and London
Companies and representatives
throughout the world

Typeset by Footnote Graphics,
Warminster, Wiltshire

Printed and bound in Great Britain by WBC Ltd, Bristol and Maesteg

British Library Cataloguing in Publication Data
Mouzelis, Nicos P. (Nicos Panayiotou), *1939–*
Post-Marxist Alternatives: The Construction of Social Orders.
1. Social systems
I. Title
301

ISBN 0–333–53156–6

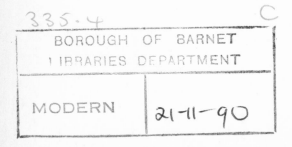

To Claire

Contents

Contents

Acknowledgements

I would like to thank the following persons who have, in a variety of ways, contributed to the shaping of the views developed in this book: George Dertilis, Nikiphoros Diamandouros, Nendis Dimitrakos, John Hall, Vasilis Kapetanyiannis, Joe Llobera, Christos Lyrintzis, Mick Mann, Spilios Papaspiliopoulos, Ian Roxborough, Anthony Smith, Alan Swingewood, Constantine Tsoukalas, Thanos Veremis and Costas Vergopoulos. I would also like to acknowledge my debt to Ellen Sutton for her very prompt and excellent editing.

Nicos P. Mouzelis

Introduction

Marxist theory has been plagued from its very inception by economic reductionism.[1] This has been a prominent feature of classical Marxism and, despite recent attempts to overcome the theoretical impasse into which it leads, still constitutes a major, perhaps *the* major, theoretical weakness of the Marxist paradigm. This deficiency has become ever more conspicuous in the course of the last years as, especially on the Continent, Marxist theory has undergone a period of severe crisis and internal disarray. In fact, I would argue that the present decline of Marxism is related, although by no means due, to its failure to deal in an intellectually satisfactory manner with the issue of economic reductionism.

This work, by focusing on the economy-polity relationship, examines various dimensions of the theoretical impasse into which economic reductionism has steered Marxist analysis; it also proposes a tentative solution to this dilemma. The major arguments underlying and unifying the work as a whole are:

(1)   that Marxism cannot overcome economic reductionism by merely proclaiming the 'relative autonomy' of the state or of ideology, while continuing to conceptualise political and cultural phenomena in economic or class categories;

(2)   that the only effective way of overcoming reductionism is to create new concepts for the analysis of the political and cultural spheres; and

(3)   that a post-Marxist conceptual framework can be constructed that retains certain basic dimensions of Marxism while avoiding economic reductionism.

From this perspective there are two major themes that sustain the present book. The *first* stresses that it is high time to deal with the work of Marx and his disciples in exactly the same way that successful contemporary social analysis deals with the works of Weber, Durkheim and their followers. This means drawing more or less freely, though not arbitrarily, on the wealth of their insights without too much concern for the dogmatic, sectarian or pedantic preoccupations that often mark the orientations of modern Marxists *vis-à-vis* the corpus of classical Marxism; preoccupations such as agonising over whether or not a specific application or utilisation of Marxist concepts

1

is 'really' Marxist, whether or not it conforms with the spirit or letter of the Master's 'sacred texts', whether or not it is inspired by 'bourgeois' values that render it 'unscientific', and so on. In other words what I am arguing is that it is high time to stop setting Marx apart from other classical social theorists, either for purposes of glorification or vilification. It is high time, at least insofar as sociological theory is concerned, to assess the conceptual tools that Marxism is offering for studying macro-historical transformations by using as the main criterion their heuristic utility rather than their contribution to the salvation or damnation of the modern world.

A flexible, non-dogmatic approach to Marxism is not new, of course. It has marked the empirical work of several sociologically-minded historians (for example, E. J. Hobsbawm and F. Braudel) and historically-oriented social scientists (B. Moore, R. Bendix). Such writers have used Marxist concepts creatively without overmuch concern for labels, confessions of loyalty, and suchlike. What the present work tries to do is to spell out more explicitly some of the conceptual tools that can be derived from the Marxist paradigm and which, with proper modification, can be useful in macro-historical, comparative studies of the kind so successfully undertaken by the above-mentioned writers.

I call such an approach *post-Marxist* because, for one thing, it rejects certain fundamental tenets of historical materialism (such as the primacy of the material base); it also makes the cleanest possible break with the time-consuming and often strenuous debates over whether specific Marxist-influenced writings should be considered as belonging to the core, periphery or outer regions of the marxist canon.

On the other hand, as I hope to demonstrate in the chapters to follow, the conceptual framework proposed is quite different from the kind of post-Marxism that rejects outright everything related to Marx – a rejection which often maintains the religious ardour of past commitments by simply transforming the fervent believer into an equally fervent non-believer. Perhaps here is the place to state that I did not have in the past, and do not have in the present, any moral or existential commitments to Marxism as a *Weltanschauung* or as an intellectual tradition that cannot or ought not to be superseded. In consequence I am not particularly concerned with compulsively rejecting Marxism *in toto* (as some post-Marxists do nowadays), nor in feverishly trying to 'save' it from the growing number of its critics and detractors.

My position towards Marxism is entirely pragmatic in the method-ological, heuristic sense: I find that, in the way in which it is used by certain writers in their analyses of long-term societal transformations, it still provides very useful tools for the examination of how whole societies are constituted, persist, and change. I happen to think that these tools can be improved, and some of Marxism's serious method-ological shortcomings rectified, if Marx's holistic logic (which suc-cessfully combines an agency/causal and a systemic/functionalist approach) is extended from the economic sphere to that of politics and culture. As far as the polity is concerned – the major focus of this volume – I believe that this extension has to take seriously into account some of Weber's insights into the issues of political domina-tion. In other words, what I am advocating is a theoretically worked out synthesis of Marx's balanced agency/system holism with Weber's anti-economistic orientation to the study of political domination.

The *second* broad theme of this work is an attitude which, for lack of a better term, I call theoretical pragmatism. This attitude posits that the most fruitful way of assessing the worth of a conceptual framework, such as the one proposed here, is neither to put the major emphasis on its philosophical, epistemological underpinnings, nor to demonstrate its logical consistency. Although both these tasks are important in themselves, what really matters is heuristic utility: the ability of a conceptual framework satisfactorily to solve method-ologically and theoretically recalcitrant social-science issues, as well as to assist in the empirical investigation of concrete problem areas. Given the above, theoretical pragmatism is critical of the philosophical, epistemological turn in the contemporary social sciences, as well as of the wholesale adoption of paradigms used in such disciplines as linguistics, semiotics, or psychoanalysis.

Concerning the first tendency, I would argue that it is indeed both useful and necessary for social scientists to be aware of their ontological and epistemological presuppositions about the nature of the social and the possible modes of knowing it. However, the propensity to philosophise has quite often meant that, in both the Marxist and non-Marxist social sciences, philosophical analysis has tended to displace social and sociological theory proper. By the latter I mean the kind of conceptualising which, rather than giving ready-made solutions to empirical problems, opens up fruitful enquiries and suggests useful ways of looking at social life. This type of theory (which Althusser has called Generalities II) is quite different from philosophical analysis proper, in the sense that it has its own logic and its own specific modes of constitution and validation. In these circumstances, any attempt to try to solve problems of sociological theory by reference to epistemological, ontological ones is likely to lead to conclusions that are neither good philosophy nor good social theory.

In order to make this as clear as possible and to show what I mean by the relative autonomy and specificity of sociological theory, chapter 1 takes a critical look at Gregor McLenan's examination of certain developments in Marxist epistemology that are supposed to overcome some of the social-theoretical problems arising out of Marxism's econcomic reductionism.

Concerning the second orientation towards which theoretical pragmatism takes a critical stand, this refers to the marked tendency in current social theory to search frantically for solutions to its problems in such adjacent disciplines as linguistics, literary criticism and psychoanalysis, disciplines that have experienced important theoretical breakthroughs in the past decades. Here as well, however, preoccupations with such new developments have often led, not to an attempt at careful translation and assimilation of the new insights into the existing body of sociological theory, but to a wholesale rejection of the old and an uncritical adoption of the new. I consider the adoption uncritical in the sense that those who espouse these new conceptual tools are often less concerned with what utility they may have for solving specific problems, and more with their newness or their congruence with prevailing intellectual fashion.

To show this kind of tendency at work, chapter 2 takes a look at a debate between, on the one side, Ernesto Laclau and Chantal Mouffe, two ex-Marxist theorists who, in the light of recent philosophical and theoretical developments, reject Marxism in its entirety and provide a post-Marxist paradigm primarily based on linguistic analysis; and, on the other side, Norman Geras, who makes a distinction between vulgar and sophisticated Marxism, defending the validity of the latter's major orientations. My objection to Geras is that present-day Marxism, however sophisticated and flexible, cannot overcome certain serious theoretical difficulties unless some of its fundamental premises are rejected and new tools created. My objection to Laclau and Mouffe is that it is both possible and desirable to put forward a post-Marxist framework which, unlike the one they are proposing, does not throw out the baby with the bathwater; a conceptual framework that judiciously rescues some of the profound insights obtained by Marxism in its quest for understanding the long-term transformation of whole social formations.

Another way of looking at chapters 1 and 2 (which partly consist of already published articles) is to consider them as a plea against two types of reductionism that, although effectively overcome by the founding fathers, have, under different guises, re-emerged at the present time. In fact, two very positive elements that one finds in Marx, Weber and Durkheim are (1) their successful attempt to separate sociology from philosophy, and to study the societies in which they were living in a less philosophico-metaphysical and a more socio-historical manner; and (2) their emphasis on the specificity of the social and its irreducibility to, for example, the study of psychology or biology. I feel that, to some extent, these two fundamental achievements are put at risk today by social theories that try either to conflate philosophical (particularly epistemological) and sociological analysis, or to reduce the study of the social life to that of language, signs, or the unconscious. Both cases are a denial of the specificity of social analysis and a regression to pre-sociological modes of thought.

If Part I (consisting of chapters 1 and 2) delineates in broad terms the problems to be studied, Part II attempts to provide a tentative solution. This is done by elaborating a post-Marxist conceptual framework capable of dealing with the complex relationships between economy and polity in non-reductive fashion (chapter 3); and by showing the utility of the proposed framework for dealing with specific theoretical and research difficulties that Marxist historians and social scientists are facing in their analysis of concrete historical developments in the 19th- and early 20th-century Greece (chapter 4).[2] Concerning the application of my framework, I had to choose between two strategies: either to provide several empirical examples as I went along developing my various theoretical points, or to develop the whole conceptual framework and then try to use it in the empirical analysis of a single case. I have opted for the latter solution in my belief that looking at a single case in depth allows one to compare in a more systematic way the heuristic utility of the conceptual tools proposed with that of the existing alternatives.

Finally, a couple of appendices add two already published articles, which extend further, or give a broader theoretical background to the problems discussed in the main text. So Appendix I endeavours, on the basis of a system/agency distinction, to differentiate between types of reductionism to be found in the voluminous literature on the Marxist theory of the capitalist state. Appendix II deals with Ernesto

Laclau's attempt, prior to his total rejection of Marxism, at formulating a non-reductive theory of politics.

Before closing the introduction, it may be appropriate to say a few words about the style and presentation of the arguments to be developed. Against a rapidly spreading trend in social theory today – a post-modernist trend that glorifies ambiguity, and delights in the production of elliptical or obscure statements – I have tried very hard to avoid neologisms or unnecessary jargon, as well as to forsake as little as possible the use of conventional social-science categories. Also, as I have tried to safeguard the relative self-containment of each chapter and particularly of the two Appendices, I was not always able to avoid a certain overlapping or repetition of arguments. Finally, in order to make the exposition of the major themes as straightforward as possible, the footnote section contains not only bibliographical references, but also historical information and theoretical comments with only indirect relevance to the central issues discussed in the text.

NOTES

1. By the term reductionism I do not merely mean, of course, the ordering or reduction of complexity that any successful theory brings to a researcher's 'raw' data or unprocessed theoretical material. I mean the methodologically illegitimate practice which consists of dealing with a certain order of phenomena in such a way that their possible distinctiveness and internal dynamic is ignored or under-emphasised in a prioristic fashion. Although this is rather vague definition, the arguments developed below against economic reductionism will make the meaning of the term clearer.

2. Although I take Greece as an example, as the reader with a knowledge of the Marxist theory on development will realise, the same theoretical and research difficulties appear with monotonous regularity in Marxist analyses of other capitalist countries – particualrly those which started their industrialisation relatively late.

Part I
Setting the Problem

1 On the Crisis of Marxist Theory*

1. INTRODUCTION

After the impressive revival of interest in Marxist writings during the 1960s and early 1970s, both sympathisers and opponents recognise and discuss a certain theoretical malaise and disillusionment with Marxist theory. Gregor McLennan's basic argument in *Marxism and the Methodologies of History*[1] is that recent epistemological developments in Marxist philosophy of science, if taken seriously, can contribute considerably to the resolution of the present theoretical difficulties.

What is interesting and refreshing about this contribution is that its author, in developing his major arguments, does not limit himself to abstract theorising; he examines in an erudite and subtle – albeit elliptical – manner a wide range of works in epistemology, philosophy of history, historical methodology and historiography. More precisely, he examines the complex links between three types of writings situated at different levels of abstraction:

(1)   recent *philosophical debates* on the nature of historical materialism and the dialectic, on realism as a theory of knowledge and its affinity to Marxism, on functionalist explanations and their relationship to Marxist tendential 'laws', on the relevance of the analytic philosophy of history for Marxist theory, and so forth;

(2)   historians' *methodological manifestos*, as these emerge or are related to specific historiographical traditions (those of social history, labour and feminist theory, the 'Annales' School);

(3)   *specific historical works* on concrete issues. In this context McLennan examines critically Marx's and Engels' historical writings on France, Soboul's work on the French Revolution and the complex debate on the Labour Aristocracy theory from Lenin onwards.

Given the wide range of topics treated in this highly dense book, I will limit myself to an assessment of the broad themes which underpin the structure of the more detailed arguments.

*This is a modified version of an article which appeared in the *British Journal of Sociology*, Vol. 35, No. 1.

(A)   The first theme running through the whole book is the unobjec-
tionable idea that philosophy in general, and epistemological considerations in particular, cannot be easily separated from substantive
historical research and that the attempt by empiricist historians to
impose a rigid division of labour and to ban epistemological questions
form their specialised fields of interest is self-defeating. McLennan's
argument becomes more interesting and more controversial when he
goes on to claim that a certain type of realist epistemology, which
underlies Marx's work and which has been more explicitly and
systematically developed recently by Marxist philosophers of science
(Roy Bhaskar, David-Hillel Ruben and others)[2] can help to avoid the
teleological, essentialist accounts of historical development which
abound in the Marxist tradition. Moreover, according to the author,
this avoidance of essentialism can be achieved without falling back on
atheoretical, empiricist accounts of the social world: that is, without
abandoning the basic framework of historical materialism.

For McLennan realist epistemologies are usually linked with
empiricist, positivistic views of social knowledge. Social knowledge
is supposed to derive inductively through direct observation and
measurement and to lead to statistical generalisations; it is also
supposed to reflect or mirror faithfully regularities between events or
other social phenomena. The typical response to this type of realism/
positivism is a kind of humanistic realism which looks with suspicion
at all types of social science generalisations, considering them as
social scientists' constructions.

According to McLennan, the post-empiricist, neo-realist epistemology, particularly as developed by Roy Bhaskar, manages to avoid
both empiricism and relativism. It shows that a realist epistemology
can be compatible with a clear anti-empiricist stand. For social
phenomena can only be explained if one goes beyond statistical
regularities and discovers the underlying *generative mechanisms*
which, although *real*, are not empirical (empirical in the sense of
being directly accessible to our senses).[3]

It is these 'non-transparent' but real generative mechanisms which,
despite their qualitative differences,[4] both the natural and the social
sciences are trying to discover.

Now according to McLennan one can find in certain of Marx's
writings an underlying epistemological position which is very near to
the type of anti-empiricist realism mentioned above. For 'Marxism
postulates generative mechanisms at the level of the mode of
production, which help to explain the nature and development of

historical and empirical problems or phenomena. Social forms, conjunctures, and strategies are to be understood in terms of theoretically expressed tendencies that have a real structural status but are not empirically transparent.[5]

(B) This, as already mentioned, does not mean that essentialist and empiricist elements are absent from the writings of Marx and his disciples. But developing further the anti-empiricist realism that one finds in some versions of Marxism can discourage the tendency towards essentialist explanations. Thus the emphasis on *tendencies* which, although not immediately transparent, have a real structural status, discourages the explanation of historical developments in terms of unfolding essences or 'iron laws', or by the establishment of '... functional relationships upheld without reference to empirical complications'.[6] According to the author, one finds such essentialist elements not only in the *Communist Manifesto* but also in Marx's more historically-oriented analyses as well as, of course, in many Marxist-oriented historians. Soboul, for instance, in his classic study of the French Revolution[7] frequently uses arguments which verge on essentialism: objective outcomes are effortlessly transformed, in a retroactive manner, into the 'objectives' of the bourgeoisie (often portrayed anthropomorphically), all forces or groups are identified as representing specific class interests; and, more generally, the inner essence or 'logic' of the transition from the feudal to the capitalist mode of production – rather than specific structural tendencies and social conflicts – seems to be the major motor driving things forward.

However, McLennan thinks that historical materialism can avoid essentialism without losing its specificity and without any serious reformulation of its basic tenets. It is from this perspective that the author examines various interpretations of historical materialism with the aim of assessing which one avoids both essentialism and empiricism. He distinguishes between interpretations which put the primary emphasis on the forces of production (for instance, G. Cohen's fundamentalist reformulations of historical materialism)[8]; those which, following the Lukacsian tradition, emphasise relations of production; as well as various structuralist interpretations (for example, Althusser's, Poulantzas'):

> which have produced a variety of formulations aiming to secure an even-handed 'articulation' of forces and relations, and in so doing attempt to fight clear of both Soviet diamat and the 'humanist' reaction to it.[9]

McLennan opts rather uneasily for the 'structuralist' interpretation, although his emphasis on the importance of agency and the necessity to combine functionalist with causal analysis differentiates his position clearly from Althusser's portrayal of collective actors as mere 'bearers of structures'.

2. NEO-REALIST EPISTEMOLOGY AND HISTORICAL MATERIALISM

(A)   Having given a very short summary of what I consider to be McLennan's main positions, I would like first to focus on the author's basic contention that a realist epistemology which is hostile to both essentialism and empiricism is highly compatible with historical materialism – or rather with the broad, even-handed interpretation of historical materialism that the author gives us.

The difficulty with the above position becomes apparent when one attempts, within a Marxist framework, to study political and cultural phenomena in a way which respects their 'relative autonomy' and specificity. Take, for instance, the author's contention that functional analysis in terms of compatibilities/incompatibilities and structural tendencies must always be complemented by a causal analysis in terms of agency, actors' strategies, accident, and so on. Can structural/functional analysis be applied to each institutional sphere of a social formation (economic, political, cultural) or is it more appropriate on the economic level?

If one adopts the latter position (as the author and many Marxists anxious to establish the 'material' nature and 'primacy' of the economic base do), then the tendency is invariably to more or less equate on the one hand *structural* with *material* and on the other hand, agency, accident, conjuncture with non-material or ideal. And when the distinction is applied on the level of a complex social formation and its institutional spheres, structures and their tendencies are located at the level of the economic base, whereas analysis in terms of agency is relegated to the political and ideological levels.[10]

This way of establishing the primacy of the economic is highly dubious, however. I can see no good reason which can justify the limitation of structural analysis to the level of the economy or of the mode of production. Are there not structural tendencies specific to the polity? Why can we not, for instance, speak about the structural tendencies of a *mode of domination* in the same way that one talks about the tendential laws of modes of production? If the answer is that we cannot because somehow economic structures and constraints are more 'real' or 'material' than political constraints, one still has to show in what precise ways the latter are less real or material than the former. In what sense, for instance, are military or administrative technologies less material or less limiting than economic ones? Or in what sense are structural tendencies towards state expansion or the concentration of the 'means of administration' at the top less constraining or enabling than tendencies towards the concentration of the means of production? Do not the former constrain/enable agents as much as the latter? Any attempt to restrict the idea of structural tendencies or constraints to the level of the economy is unacceptable. If one accepts the structure/agency distinction, it is quite obvious that one can apply it to both economic and non-economic spheres. In other terms, in all institutional spheres one can identify structural tendencies which both limit and create opportunities for agents' projects.

(B) McLennan can argue, of course, that the above position, although not spelled out in his book, is not incompatible with historical materialism. After all, both Althusser and Poulantzas have adopted it: they identify, on the economic, political and ideological levels, specific structural constraints and contradictions the overall configuration of which determines agents' practices.[11]

However, such a position creates other types of complication. Leaving aside the problem of the puppet-like portrayal of agents in Althusserian Marxism, the acceptance of specific contradictions in the political and ideological spheres do not lead us very far, insofar as there is no means of conceptualising such contradictions in non-economic terms. For instance, if the mode of production idea provides a set of concepts (for example, forces, relations of production) with the help of which one can identify structural cleavages and 'tendential laws' on the level of the economy, are there equivalent concepts on the level of politics and the State?

The answer is that there are not. Although one finds hints and intimations both in Marx's work and in that of some more recent theorists,[12] there are not any fully worked out tools within Marxism with the help of which one can study political phenomena in a manner which respects their specificity and internal dynamic. The unbroken tradition from Marx onwards is to conceptualise political structures in economic terms. Thus, the State is either conceived in terms of mode of production requirements for reproduction and expansion or in terms of classes. And whenever Marxists, sensitive to the 'relative autonomy' issue, argue against 'instrumentalist' notions of the State, or against the 'logic of capital' approach, they either put nothing in their place, or end up with conceptualisations which do not escape the economic straitjacket.[13] Thus, for instance, Poulantzas has tried to overcome the crude instrumentalist version of the State as the managing committee of the bourgeoisie by arguing that the State needs 'autonomy' *vis-à-vis* specific capitalist interests because its task is to secure the overall reproduction of the capitalist mode of production. And when, in a later work, he has to avoid both instrumentalist and 'reproduction requirements' definitions of the State, he ends up with yet another economic conceptualisation: the capitalist State is neither an instrument/object nor a subject but an arena in which class contradictions and antagonisms are reproduced in a condensed manner.[14] However ingenious the formulations and the reformulations, they are all based on categories derived from the economic spheres (classes, mode of production). Political and cultural spheres are never conceptualised in their own right; they are invariably seen as the 'conditions of existence' of the economic base. One never poses the problem the other way round, one never enquires about the conditions of existence of political structures, one never conceptualises political groupings and interest groups in terms of the reproductive requirements or contradictions of the political system proper.

Given this glaring gap, this empty space in the Marxist theory of politics, *it is impossible to avoid the essentialism-empiricism dilemma, whatever the epistemological position adopted*. To put it in another way, insofar as neo-realist epistemology has a strong anti-essentialist and anti-empiricist orientation, it is *incompatible* with present versions of historical materialism – however flexible these are. For either one has to go on conceptualising the State in terms of class or mode of production requirements – in which case one falls into the essentialist trap; or one rejects economic conceptualisations altogether but without putting anything else in their place – in which case one faces the empiricist impasse.

(C) In order to make my position more concrete, I will discuss briefly a few of the examples that McLennan himself provides. G. V. Taylor, the historian, argues that, contrary to Soboul's Marxist interpretation of the French Revolution as 'bourgeois', it was primarily a *political* revolution with social consequences favourable to the development of capitalism.[15] According to McLennan: 'Only for Soboul's class essentialism is this notion difficult to accept. "Political Revolution" can be translated as "revolution with no direct class determination" without loss.'[16] But if one assumes that the French Revolution was primarily a political upheaval with 'no direct class determination', the question then arises as to the conceptual tools available to historical materialism for a non-empiricist examination of the structural contradictions and struggles which are *directly* related to its emergence.

Let us take another example related to the complex issue of the political representation of classes. McLennan thinks that Soboul, in a class-reductionist manner, often ignores the heterogeneous class positions of those involved in a political party and quite straight-forwardly labels political formations (heterogeneously composed from a class point of view) as representing the interests of a whole class. He argues, for instance, that the Girondins were the representatives of the bourgeoisie – although 'many critics find no empirical difference between Montagnards and Girondins'.[17] Moreover, both political forces contain elements of all classes within their ranks. And the same is true of the sansculottes which were 'a heterogeneous, internally divided political force'.[18]

Now for McLennan historical materialism can avoid Soboul's essentialism by acknowledging the existence of a variety of class factions within a single political organisation, or 'the ramifications of political differences within a class'.[19] But to point to class factions contained in the *Gironde* or the *Montagne* can hardly help us to explain the basic cleavage between them. If we assume (and this is an empirical question which I do not have the expertise to discuss) that the structural base of the cleavage between these two major political forces has a more directly *political* rather than economic foundation, to resort to a class faction analysis – although useful in itself – does not help us very much.

Insofar as one finds factions of all classes on both sides of a major political divide, either one has to accept the conventional historian's empiricist position on the purely conjunctural foundation of this divide or one has to look for structural explanations not only in the economy, but in the non-economic spheres. It is to this latter alternative that both conventional historians and Marxists turn a blind eye. McLennan, in particular, by identifying structural and material with the 'economic' constantly presents the reader with a false dichotomy: either empiricism or acceptance of historical materialism's emphasis on forces and relations or production. The idea that *non-economic structural* tendencies can provide a non-conjunctural, non-empiricist analysis of certain political developments is entirely disregarded.

3. MONISM VERSUS PLURALISM

Moving now to a related but analytically distinct problem, the lack of an adequate conceptualisation of non-economic spheres within Marxism explains to a great extent why McLennan (as well as many other Marxists) discusses the monism-pluralism dilemma in a rather misleading fashion. According to him neo-realist epistemology, by avoiding essentialism and empiricism, helps the student to avoid both the monism of those interpretations of historical materialism which view history as the unfolding of a single cause, as well as the causal pluralism of non-Marxist empiricists whose explanation of historical phenomena consists of an interminable laundry-list of factors or causes. The author argues that:

> Structural principles must be complemented by, or even include, notions of individual action, natural causes and 'accidental' circumstances. Historical outcomes depend on them, too. Nevertheless, material and social relations can be long-term, effective real structures that set firm limits to the nature and degree of practical effect that accident and even agency have. It is not true, therefore, that historiography can sustain either a single causal explanation or an infinite number of them.[20]

This compromise between monistic and pluralistic explanations is not as satisfactory as it appears at first sight. First of all, many non-Marxist social scientists and historians do not subscribe to the belief that historiography 'can sustain an infinite number of explanations'. Marxism certainly does not have a monopoly of the rejection of both monism and pluralism (as defined by McLennan). Weber, for instance, would not object to the idea of structural constraints setting limits to possible courses of action. He would only object to Marxist attempts to identify, in an exclusive manner, structural constraints with economic ones. When Weber insists that not only the means of production but also the means of coercion and of administration set severe structural constraints on courses of action, he definitely does not support the type of mindless causal pluralism to which McLennan refers. He simply makes the point that one cannot postulate *a priori* that economic contradictions and class struggles should occupy a privileged explanatory status in all complex societies, irrespective of time or space.

As a matter of fact McLennan, in a manner which clearly contradicts his general position *vis-à-vis* historical materialism, seems to accept the Weberian position when he refers approvingly to Anthony Giddens' contention that forces and relations of production and class struggles based upon them are more relevant for understanding the dynamics of capitalist rather than pre-capitalist societies.[21] According to McLennan,

> his terms [that is, Giddens' – NM] may not be the most appropriate, but he does make a substantial point. In early civilisation, 'authority had primacy over allocation' in the sense that neither technical advance in the tools of production, nor control of property were of primary importance in this ... authoritarian division of labour.[22]

Now such a position, which undermines historical materialism's faith in the universal primacy of the forces/relations of production, does not necessarily lead to the 'infinite number of causes' type of pluralism to which McLennan refers. It does not rule out a ranking of causes or even a structural analysis which emphasises the primacy of certain types of constraints/enablements (economic, political, military) in specific kinds of societies, or at specific points of their development. What it does rule out is the idea that the forces and relations of production constitute the basis and provide the primary principle of explanation in a universal, trans-historical manner. This position need not lead to empiricism or to the acceptance of an 'infinite number of causes'. It may easily derive from a conceptual framework which conceptualises the relationship between economic and non-economic spheres in such a way that the primacy of the former (however ingeniously interpreted) is not built into the very definition of the latter. In other terms, I think that one should reject McLennan's false dilemma (either one accepts the 'primacy' thesis or one has to accept an infinity of causes approach); for one can avoid empiricism and 'causal pluralism' without having to accept the types of context-less, trans-historical generalisations that the primacy of the forces and relations of production implies.

In conclusion, the crisis of Marxist theory with which *Marxism and the Methodologies of History* is concerned and to whose resolution it claims to contribute cannot be resolved by a mere recourse to epistemology. Epistemology, although relevant, is not and will never become an adequate substitute for sociological theory proper – that is, for the systematic attempt to construct logically coherent conceptual tools useful for the empirical investigation of social structures and actors.

Of course, for some theorists, to the extent that Marxism's theoretical crisis has to do with its economistic, reductive character, there is no remedy whatsoever. The *illness is in fact terminal*: Marxism cannot overcome economic reductionalism without resorting to empiricism or without abandoning those of its features which give it a distinctive profile. This is a position which I will discuss in the next chapter.

NOTES

1. Gregor McLennan, *Marxism and the Methodologies of History*, London: Vergo, 1987.
2. See R. Bhaskar, *A Realist Theory of Science*, Sussex and New Jersey: Harvester Press, 1978; see also his *The Possibility of Naturalism*, Brighton: Harvester Press, 1979; and D. H. Ruben, *Marxism and Materialism*, Brighton: Harvester Press, 1979.
3. See Bhaskar, *A Realist Theory of Science*, op. cit., p. 13.
4. For some differences between the social and the natural sciences, see R. Bhaskar, *The Possibility of Naturalism*, pp. 54 ff.
5. McLennan, op. cit., p. 32.
6. Ibid., p. 67.
7. A. Soboul, *The French Revolution 1787–1799: From the Storming of Bastille to Napoleon*, 2 vols, London: New Left Books, 1974.
8. G. A. Cohen, *Karl Marx's Theory of History: A Defence*, Oxford: Oxford University Press, 1978.
9. McLennan, op. cit., p. 46.
10. McLennan seems to adopt such a position: 'Revisionist Marxists attempt to register the specificity of political and cultural formations, and so object to the harder Marxist arguments. But structural explanations – *to do with the tendencies of the capitalist mode of production* are indispensable to the revised position, though they are further in the background', (p. 231, italics – NM).
11. See Nicos Poulantzas, *Classes in Contemporary Capitalism*, London: New Left Books, 1975.
12. For an attempt to conceptualise political contradictions in a non-economic manner, see E. Laclau, *Politics and Ideology in Marxist*

Theory, London: New Left Books, 1977. For a critique of his approach, see below, Appendix II.

13. For a critical assessment of various types of reductionist interpretations of the State in contemporary Marxism, see Appendix I.

14. See Nicos Poulantzas, *State, Power, Socialism*, London: New Left Books, 1978.

15. George V. Taylor, 'Non-Capitalist Wealth and the Origins of the French Revolution', *American Historical Review*, 1972, 1966–67.

16. McLennan, op. cit., p. 193.

17. Ibid., p. 188.

18. Ibid., p. 190.

19. Ibid., p. 189.

20. Ibid., p. 234.

21. See A. Giddens, *A Contemporary Critique of Historic Materialism*, Vol. 1, London: Macmillan/Berkeley: University of California Press, 1987.

22. Ibid., p. 56.

2 Marxism Versus Post-Marxism*

1. INTRODUCTION

Given the general anti-Marxist climate of the 1980s, among those Marxists who have taken the 'reductionism versus empiricism' dilemma seriously, most have rejected the Marxist paradigm *in toto*, as a theory which – by its very construction – leads to a deterministic, essentialist view of the social world and/or to authoritarian attitudes in politics.

On the other hand, among those Marxists who have chosen not to abandon Marxism, the dominant strategy is to face the growing number of critics by stressing the distinction between vulgar/mechanistic and voluntaristic/humanist versions of Marxism – arguing that the latter still provide an indispensable tool for the study of total societies and their long-term development.

The position that I will try to defend in this part of the book lies somewhere between the two strategies mentioned above. Against the strategy which indiscriminately rejects everything 'Marxist', I will argue that there are certain dimensions of the Marxist paradigm which, when properly developed, can overcome some of its re-ductionist tendencies and provide useful guidelines for the study of social phenomena. Against the non-vulgar Marxist strategy, as I have already made clear in the previous chapter, I do not believe that the more flexible, less deterministic forms of Marxism are enough in themselves (that is, without radical restructuring and the creation of new concepts) to overcome Marxism's reductive features.

In this chapter I will try to make my position more clear by intervening in a debate between, on the one hand, Ernesto Laclau and Chantal Mouffe, whose *Hegemony and Social Strategy (HSS)* [1] adopts a post-Marxist, discourse analysis approach which rejects the whole Marxist framework as inherently deterministic and teleo-logical; and, on the other hand, Norman Geras whose lengthy criticisms of Laclau's and Mouffe's work leads to an impassioned defence of non-mechanistic Marxism. [2]

* A modified version of this chapter appeared in *New Left Review* , No. 167, Jan.-Feb. 1988.

Let us start with the post-Marxist position. *HSS's* major thesis is that the core of all Marxist theory is based on a necessitarian, deterministic logic which emphasises laws, strict succession of stages, the inevitability of the proletarian revolution, and so on. This logic reduces complexity and leads to an essentialist view of the social and to a closed, monistic type of theoretical discourse. For Laclau and Mouffe all attempts from Marx onwards to soften Marxism's deterministic core by stressing indeterminacy, complexity, the importance of agency, the relative autonomy of the political and so forth are simply *ad hoc* additions to a theoretical edifice which, in its foundations, remains irretrievably monistic. In other terms when Marxists, past and present, try to avoid determinism, they unavoidably fall into the trap of 'dualism' or eclecticism.[3] Therefore deterministic closure or eclecticism/dualism is the grim dilemma of all Marxist theory.

For Geras what Laclau and Mouffe see as the core of Marxism is simply a caricature, a systematic distortion of a theoretical tradition which, in the works of its most successful representatives, has managed to avoid reductionism and monistic closure without resorting to eclecticism or empiricism. Whether one looks at Marx's work or at the writings of Luxembourg, Lenin or Gramsci, one finds an emphasis on the fundamental importance of structural determinations emanating from the economy, these determinations operating not as an all-encompassing monistic cause leading to total closure, but as a framework both enabling and setting limits to what is possible on the level of politics and culture. Moreover, on the level of the whole social formation, the ideas of primacy of one type of structure over other structures or, to use Althusser's expression, the idea of a hierarchy of causalities of uneven weight is neither monistic nor eclectic. It is only Laclau and Mouffe's conceptual manicheism which present us with the 'deterministic/eclecticism' pseudo-dilemma.

What I would like to argue here is:

(1)   that one can defend some key aspects of the Marxist paradigm against the idea of monistic closure not only by reference to the empirical work of specific authors, but also, or rather more appropriately, by looking at the logical status and mode of construction of certain fundamental Marxist concepts, such as the mode of production;

(2)   that the authors of *HSS* replace the one-sided necessitarian logic that one sees in *dogmatic* Marxism with an equally unacceptable

one-sided contingency logic, and that whenever they try to
mitigate their one-sidedness, they are led to dualism/
eclecticism;

(3)   that contrary to Geras' position, there is a type or reductionism
      which is inherent in all Marxist discourse – although this
      reductionism is not as incapacitating as Laclau and Mouffe
      imply.

2.   'CORE' MARXISM: CLOSED OR OPEN?

In order to deal with my first point one has to start by distinguishing
as clearly as possible a substantive theory from a conceptual framework, the latter, rather than providing a set of empirically verifiable
and knowledge-producing statements on some specific issue, simply
'maps out the problem area and thus prepares the ground for its
empirical investigation'.[4] This distinction between conceptual framework and substantive theory corresponds more or less to Althusser's
distinction between Generalities II and Generalities III: Generalities
II consists of conceptual tools which, when applied to 'raw' theoretical material (Gen. I), lead eventually to the production of full-blown
substantive theories (Gen. III).[5]

Now it seems to me that the issue of whether or not core Marxism
is fundamentally a closed or an open system can only be settled in a
satisfactory manner on the level of Generalities II. For, given that, as
Geras argues, in the Marxist tradition one finds both open and closed
substantive theories (on the development of capitalism, for instance),
the problem is to ascertain whether it is the open or closed ones which
are more congruent with the basic conceptual tools of the Marxist
discourse. Contrary to Laclau and Mouffe's position, I will argue that
if one looks carefully at these conceptual tools, *and particularly if one
compares them with equivalent non-Marxist ones*, one will have to
conclude that it is the closed rather than the open substantive
discourses (Gen. III) which do violence to Marxism's fundamental
conceptual apparatus (Gen. II).

In fact Marxism, more than any other paradigm in the social
sciences, can suggest very fruitful ways of studying social formations
from the point of view of both agency and institutional structure,
both as a configuration of collective actors struggling over the control
of scarce resources, and as a systemic whole whose institutionalised
parts or 'sub-systems' can be more or less compatible or incompatible

with each other. As David Lockwood has pointed out long ago, Marxism combines a *system* and a *social* integration view of social formations.[6] As I will argue more extensively in chapter 3, it encourages, *without resorting to dualism* , the examination of incompatibilities between systemic parts or institutional ensembles (for example, that between forces and relations of production) as well as the ways in which such incompatibilities lead or *fail to lead* to the development of class consciousness and class conflict. To use, as much as it is possible, Laclau and Mouffe's terminology, Marxism can help the student to raise questions about the impact of articulatory practices, struggles, antagonisms on *subjects' positions as well as the reverse*: that is, to raise questions about how subject positions (or roles in non-Marxist sociology) cluster into larger institutional wholes, these wholes both shaping and setting limits to subjects' practices. In a nutshell Marxism allows the serious and systematic study of both the practice → subject position and the subject position → practice relationship.

Thus, unlike Laclau and Mouffe's post-structuralist approach, as well as various action-oriented sociological theories (symbolic interactionism, ethnomethodology, exchange theory, conflict theory) *subjects or agents in Marxist theory do not operate in an institutional vacuum*; their strategies or practices have to be seen within specific structural constraints, within institutional ensembles of whose often incompatible organising principles agents may or may not be aware. On the other hand, in contrast to Parsonian functionalism, Marxism does not conceptualise agents as mere puppets of the system. Its conceptual apparatus is such that it leads one to look at collective actors not only as products but also as producers of their social world. Since Parsonian sociology, particularly in its macro-sociological dimensions, is based on a conceptual framework which *encourages* closure, it will be useful to develop further the comparison between this highly influential paradigm in the non-Marxist social sciences with Marxism. This will make more clear in what sense Marxist conceptual tools lead necessarily neither to monistic nor to dualistic types of empirical analysis.

As has frequently been noted, Parsonian action theory (despite its label), systematically underemphasises the voluntaristic dimension of social life, portraying human beings as the passive products of the social system.[7] In strictly Durkheimian fashion it keeps pointing out how society's core values, through their institutionalisation into normative expectations and internalisation into need-dispositions, shape human conduct – without showing the opposite process: how actors, and particularly collective actors, constitute and change society. The direction of influence is always from the system/society to the actor, never the other way round.

This is amply illustrated by the way Parsons conceptualises society as a system. One need only consider his famous AGIL scheme, the fourfold sub-system typology (adaptation, goal achievement, integration, latency) with the help of which he analyses the functioning of all social systems. Each of these sub-systems corresponds to one of the four basic functional requirements that any system has to solve in order to survive as such. The adaptation sub-system, for instance, roughly corresponds on the level of society as a whole to the economy and consists of all processes contributing to the solution of the adaptation requirement – that is, to securing all the resources necessary for a society's survival. These processes are often dispersed among a variety of social groups and collectivities. What brings them together in the 'adaptation' box is that they have one characteristic in common: that of contributing to the same functional requirement or system need. The adaptation sub-system, therefore, is a strictly systemic category, in the sense that it is not founded upon and does not correspond to a concrete collectivity or agency. As a concept it is radically different from such agency concepts as a social movement, a formal organisation, or an interest group. It is true, of course, that sometimes Parsons treats sub-systems as if they were collective actors,[8] ascribing to them characteristics proper only to decision-making units.

The reason Parsons often treats institutional sub-systems or even whole societies and their core values as mysterious anthropomorphic entities deciding and regulating everything on the social scene is, of course, that his functionalist scheme leaves no conceptual room for collective agencies as producers of their social world. In fact, each of his sub-systems is further divided into four sub-sub-systems, and the process of the fourfold systemic division goes on *ad infinitum*. Within this bewildering onion-like scheme of systems within systems, *collective* actors are not merely portrayed in a passive manner – they vanish altogether. There are simply no conceptual tools allowing for their serious examination. As one moves from the individual role player with his/her need-dispositions and role expectations to a macro-level of analysis, agency concepts are displaced by system concepts.

In the light of the above it will have become quite clear in what respects the Marxist paradigm provides more adequate tools of analysis. Marxists too, of course, like Parsonian sociologists, sub-divide whole social formations into sub-systems or institutional parts. For example, the threefold sub-division into the economic, the political and the ideological, are system rather than agency categor-ies. There is, however, a crucial difference between Parsonian and Marxist sub-systems: Marxism conceptualises the economic sphere in such a way that its institutional components do not lead, *à la* Parsons, to further systemic sub-divisions. Insofar as Marxism views the economy as an articulation of modes of production and insofar as the relations of production constitute the major feature of every mode, this key concept provides a bridge between a systemic/institutional and an agency/action approach. In fact the relations of production concept leads quite 'naturally', that is, without any *ad hoc* switch between conceptual planes, from problems of institutional analysis to those of 'strategic conduct' and vice versa.[9] For it requires no mental acrobatics to move from an analysis of how the technical and social division of labour allocates agents into different locations/positions within the sphere of production, to an investigation of the type of practices and struggles to which such structural positions lead or fail to lead. The sharper the focus on the way in which agents react to their class locations by trying to maintain or transform their situation *vis-à-vis* the means of production (or the means *in* production), the sharper the focus on issues that *exclusively* concern Laclau and Mouffe: such as the manner in which subjects' identities and their perceptions of their 'real interests' are formed, the manner in which such self-identities and perceptions are fixed into 'nodal points', or subverted by the emergence of new struggles or antagonisms. The sharper, on the other hand, the focus on how subject positions or class locations cluster together to form larger institutional complexes, the more considerations of strategic conduct are 'bracketed' and the more institutional analysis comes to the fore, the type of analysis that is totally lacking in *HSS* .

By 'bracketing' in this context is meant the temporary suspension of considerations pertaining to actors' skills, strategies, forms of consciousness and the like – a suspension which is necessary in order to deal in a non-cumbersome manner with the analysis of whole institutional orders and their inter-relationships. In other terms, 'bracketing' does not imply an ontological belief in the thing-like character of institutional structures. It is simply a heuristic device for examining properties of the social which cannot be grasped by exclusive and direct reference to agency concepts.[10]

Of course, the balance between agency and institutional structure that Marxist concepts encourage has not always been maintained within Marxism. It has been broken either by ultra-voluntaristic class theories that end up by explaining all social developments in terms of the Machiavellian machinations of a dominant class; or, at the other extreme, by theories stressing structural constraints and contradictions to such an extent that actors are reduced to mere 'bearers of structures'. But despite all this, if one considers Marx's work as a whole, as well as the mainstream Marxist tradition, it does provide the conceptual means for looking at societies both in terms of actors' collective strategies *and* in terms of institutional systems and their reproductive requirements.

This is precisely why historians and social scientists influenced by Marx's work have produced more interesting and convincing accounts of long-term historical developments than those influenced by Parsonian functionalism or other brands of non-Marxist social theory. Leaving aside conventional historians who tend to turn their backs on all social theory, what insights has Parsonian functionalism or non-Marxist sociology to offer in the problem area of how complex societies are transformed? What contributions can be compared favourably with those of such Marxist-influenced writers as Barrington Moore, Hobsbawm or Braudel?[11] If, for instance, one puts the historical investigations of the above writers side by side with those of Parsons, Eisenstadt or Smelser,[12] the substantive superiority of the former is so obvious that no further elaboration is necessary.

3.   THE DISPLACEMENT OF INSTITUTIONAL ANALYSIS

Of course, for Laclau and Mouffe the distinction between subjects' practices and institutional structures is a spurious one. Among other things, they would point out that institutional structures do not emerge from nowhere. Like anything else pertaining to the social, they must be viewed in a non-essentialist manner: they too are the result of discursive practices taking place in a plurality of political and social spaces which are characterised by openness, fragility, contingency and so on.

However, the dismissal of the agency/institutional structure distinction, which one finds not only in Laclau and Mouffe's work but in various structuralist and post-structuralist discourses, creates more problems than it solves. For it either brings in through the backdoor (that is, without acknowledging or without conceptualising properly) the notion of institutional complexes and the way in which they limit/ enable social action; or it consistently ignores them at the price of being totally unable to deal seriously with problems related to the constitution, persistence and long-term transformation of global social formations.

Let me elaborate this point further. To start with, despite Laclau and Mouffe's emphasis on the intrinsically fragile, open, contingent and discontinuous character of the social, they do refer to cases where these characteristics hardly seem to apply: 'In a medieval peasant community the area open to differential articulation is minimal and, thus, there are no hegemonic forms of articulation: there is an abrupt transition from repetitive practices within a closed system of differences to frontal and absolute equivalences when the community finds itself threatened. This is why the hegemonic form of politics only becomes dominant at the beginning of modern times, when the reproduction of the different social areas takes place in permanently changing conditions which constantly require the con- struction of new systems of differences'. [13] So unless one considers a medieval peasant community as not pertaining to what the authors of *HSS* call the 'social' (which would be absurd), then their ontological remarks on its openness and fluidity obviously refer to the 'modern' rather than the 'traditional' social. And even if one focuses on the former, it is not always as precarious or fragile as Laclau and Mouffe portray it. One does not have to adopt an essentialist position in order to stress the obvious fact that from the point of view of specific subjects situated at a specific historical time and social space there are always institutional arrangements which are easily affected by their practices and other institutional arrangements which are not. Of course, in so far as Laclau and Mouffe do not identify discourse with language (and I think, contrary to Geras, that they do not), then I agree with their view that *all* institutional arrangements, whether durable or not, are discursively constructed. *But there is absolutely no reason why one should link discursive construction with fragility and precariousness* – labelling any reference to institutional durability as essentialist. For a social formation's core institutions often portray such a resilience and continuity that their overall, extremely slow transformation can be seen only in the very *longue durée* , needing to be assessed in terms of centuries rather than years or shorter timespans.

Consider, for instance, the strict separation of the ruler's or the civil servant's public position from his/her private fortune.[14] This institutional separation of the 'private' from the 'public' within the Western European State took centuries to be firmly consolidated and today *seems pretty well irreversible*. To all intents and purposes, therefore, this structural feature, together with other structural features of equal durability and resilience (for example, the institution of private property, of markets, of money, the institutional separation between management and ownership in modern corporations and so on) constitute a core which enters the subjects' social milieu not as something to be negotiated or radically transformed, but as an incontrovertible given, as a relatively unshakeable, durable institutional terrain[15] which both limits and makes possible specific articulatory practices – practices the intended or unintended consequences of which may seriously affect more malleable and fragile institutional arrangements. The fact that laypersons and even social scientists tend sometimes to reify a social formation's durable institutional orders (that is, tend to forget that they are discursively constructed and reproduced) does not make them less durable; on the contrary, the 'natural attitude' towards them enhances further their institutional resilience.

Now what conceptual tools do Laclau and Mouffe offer which can help us to explore in a *systematic manner* the more resilient, slow-changing institutional features of modern capitalist societies? The plain answer is that the authors of *HSS* do not provide us with any such tools.

Of course, on a highly philosophical/ontological level they do admit that contingency, openness and fragility have their limits. They do talk, for instance, about necessity existing 'as a partial limitation of the field of contingency',[16] about the fact that 'neither absolute fixity nor non-fixity is possible'[17] and so on. But these highly abstract attempts to redress the balance are rather decorative, in the sense that they are not translated into the construction of specific conceptual tools (Gen. II) for the systematic analysis of those aspects of the social which pertain to 'necessity' and 'fixity'. In fact, on the level of Gen. II the only serious theoretical effort is to reconstruct the concept of hegemony and to show how articulatory practices, constantly construct and deconstruct self-identities, subject positions, nodal points, social and political spaces, and so on. But the conditions of existence of such practices, the way in which practices are both sustained and limited by the more permanent institutional structures of capitalism are never spelled out. The closest Laclau and

Mouffe come to delineating an overall context within which articulatory practices and subject positions are situated is when they talk
about 'discursive formations' and the more general 'field of
discursivity'. [18] But these notions are so vague and inadequate to deal
with the institutional complexities of modern capitalism that the
authors of *HSS* do not use them in any serious, systematic manner. In
fact, when obliged to refer to the broad features of capitalist
formations and their long-term transformations they revert, as Geras
has rightly pointed out, [19] to such conventional Marxist concepts as
exploitation, commodification, the labour-process, civil society,
capitalist periphery and the like – even the dreaded concept of
'society' slips in from time to time! How are the above concepts,
which Laclau and Mouffe freely use, connected with discourse
analysis? The connection is never made clear and the gap between
the two types of concept creates a dualism which is much more
glaring than that found in the Marxist texts that Laclau and Mouffe so
vehemently criticise.

Needless to say, all these conceptual inadequacies have serious
consequences on the way in which *HSS*, on a more empirical level,
deals with concrete issues of social strategy. [20] For instance, the
authors of *HSS* do not have the *theoretical means* to raise the problem
of whether certain articulatory practices are more central than others
and have therefore more chances in hegemonising a certain political
space. For them, as Geras has pointed out, there is nothing one can
say in advance about the relative importance of certain subject
positions, as far as socialist transformation is concerned. The justification they give for this type of agnosticism is that any attempt to
privilege certain positions or practices leads unavoidably to essentialism. For Laclau and Mouffe the crucial limitation of the traditional
left is that 'it attempts to determine *a priori* agents of change, levels
of effectiveness in the field of the social and privileged points and
moments of rupture'[21] But what the authors of *HSS* do not seriously
consider is the possibility of assessing the centrality of certain
positions within a social formation without resorting to essentialism
and without ascribing ontological or epistemological privileges to
specific subjects. One can, of course, wholeheartedly agree with
Laclau and Mouffe on the fact that there are no iron laws of history,
no historical necessity for a proletarian revolution, no 'special
mission' for the working classes, and the like. But this does not mean
that everything goes, and that one has to view, for instance, all social
movements on a par with regard to their chances of playing a

hegemonic role in struggles aiming at a socialist transformation of capitalism.

To make a very obvious comparison, it is not difficult to see that the working class movement, however fragmented or disorganised, has greater transformative capacities and therefore better *chances* of playing a leading role in a hegemonic contest than, say, the sexual liberation movement. The reason for this has to do less with political initiatives and articulatory practices and more with the more central structural position of the working class in capitalist society. This centrality can be assessed in a non-essentialist manner through an analysis of the way in which the major institutional spheres are articulated within capitalism or through a macro-historical, comparative analysis focusing on systematic structural/institutional differences between capitalist, pre-capitalist or non-capitalist social formations.[22]

Now to be fair, Laclau and Mouffe seem to retreat from total agnosticism by admitting that not every articulatory practice is possible: 'This logic of the symbolic constitution of the social encountered precise limits in the persistence, at a morphological level, of the economistic conception of history. Once this has been dissolved, the overflowing of class bounds by the various forms of social protest can freely operate (*Freely*, that is, of any *a priori* class character of struggles or demands – obviously not in the sense that *every* articulation is possible in a given conjuncture.)'[23]

But if every articulation is not possible, how do we assess degrees of possibility, what makes certain articulations more possible than others? Here again *HSS* provides no answer whatsoever. The problem is neither posed nor answered. *And this is because Laclau and Mouffe do not have the conceptual tools for raising such questions*. To repeat, for such questions to be raised one needs a conceptual framework which guides the student to focus on the relatively stable institutional structures of capitalism and the complex ways in which such structures both set limits to, and provide opportunities for, strategic conduct.

To conclude, given the emphasis that Laclau and Mouffe put on articulatory practices, their position is in a sense the exact opposite of the Parsonian/Durkheimian approach that I criticised in the previous section. The latter is exclusively concerned with how the Social System and its core values shape and limit role players' practices, whereas the former deals with how practices constitute as well as constantly subvert the social. Parsonian functionalism, because of its neglect of collective actors, portrays institutional structures as reified entities regulating everybody on the social scene; Laclau and Mouffe, because of their excessive fear of reifying institutional structures, go to the other extreme and analyse practices in an institutional vacuum. The unresolved tension between the institutional system and practice/action oriented approaches to the social is not, of course, new in the non-Marxist social sciences. The over-reaction to the essentialism to be found in certain types of teleological functionalism (including the Parsonian one) have a very long history in sociology. From this point of view *HSS* , although in some crucial respects different,[24] has a lot in common with those interpretative sociologies (symbolic interactionism, phenomenological sociology, ethnomethodology) whose excessive fear of essentialism or reification have led them away from what should be a central concern of all social analysis: that is, of how total social formations are constituted, reproduced and transformed. It is precisely because Marxist conceptual tools, when flexibly used, can help the student to avoid the schizophrenic split between system-blind action theories and teleologically-oriented system ones that Marxism still has something vital to offer on issues of long-term societal transformation.

4. THE RELATIVE AUTONOMY OF THE POLITICAL

But if Marxism can help the student to avoid the reduction of institutional analysis to an analysis of strategic conduct (and vice versa), it is much less successful in avoiding another type of re-ductionism: the reduction of non-economic spheres to the economy – and this despite repeated Marxist statements about the relative autonomy of the state, the political, the ideological and so on. Here it seems to me that Laclau and Mouffe are right and Geras is wrong: whenever considerations of the 'relative autonomy' of the political or the cultural are introduced into the Marxist discourse, this is done in such a manner that we do have a type of conceptual dualism – although I see this dualism and its eventual resolution in a different manner from the authors of *HSS*.

I will elaborate this point by focusing on the way in which Marxism conceptualises the relationship between the economic and the polit-ical (most of my arguments, however, could apply to other institu-tional spheres as well). At the risk of over-generalisation I would argue that present-day Marxist theories put forward two equally unsatisfactory views of this relationship.

The first of these consists of a straightforward reductionist approach whereby political phenomena are explained in terms of either the reproduction requirements of capital, or the interests and projects of the economically dominant classes. Where the emphasis is on classes, the politically dominant groups are considered to be merely the instruments of the bourgeoisie, the political institutions being fashioned by the Machiavellian designs of that same class. Where the emphasis is on the reproduction requirements of the capitalist system, political agents and institutions are again conceptualised exclusively in terms of economic categories: at best they are viewed as conditions of existence of the capitalist economy, at worst their development is teleologically explained in terms of the changing requirements of the capitalist mode of production. Since this type of reductive thinking has been extensively discussed and criticised in the relevant literature,[25] I shall concentrate on the second approach, which sets out to by-pass the reductionism of the first by laying particular stress on the 'relative autonomy' of the political sphere. Here the Marxist strategies for upholding the 'primacy of the economic' thesis, as Laclau and Mouffe correctly point out, are twofold: *either* one ends up with a sophisticated monism by introducing 'determination in the last instance' type of clauses; *or* one avoids monism by falling into 'dualism'. In this latter case the political sphere is considered as ontologically different from the economic one – in the sense that whereas structural determinations operate on the economic level, agency/conjunctural considerations prevail on the level of the polity. Therefore in this case the economy is not determining political developments directly, but merely delineates what is possible on the level of the superstructure. What, according to this view, is going to emerge within these set limits depends on the *political conjuncture* – and this leaves no more room for a theorisation of specifically political structures and contradictions.[26]

Now this approach subjects the political sphere to a subtle and sophisticated down-grading. For while it is conceded that economic constraints or forces can no longer be regarded as the direct determinants of politics, it is proposed that political phenomena, although relatively autonomous, are not amenable to the same kind of analysis as economic ones. On the one hand, economic phenomena can be accounted for in terms of the structural tendencies of the capitalist mode of production. On the other hand, as far as political phenomena are concerned, given their fluid, transient, or less 'material' character, structural analysis must be entirely replaced by a study of the political conjuncture.

Therefore here we do have a qualitative, ontological difference between the economic and the political sphere and *this ontological dualism has consequences on the level of Gen. II.* For the 'relative autonomy' emphasis does not lead to the creation of specific conceptual tools for the study of the political sphere proper. *Instead politics and the state continue to be defined in class/economic terms.* So what is being given with the one hand on the level of substantive statements on the relative autonomy of the state for instance, is taken away with the other on the methodological level by the insistence that the State *must* be conceptualised in economic, class terms.

It is not surprising therefore that a century after Marx's death, with some significant exceptions, Marxists still have very little to show in terms of a non-reductive theory of politics. In contrast, for instance, to Parsonian functionalism (which has generated a sophisticated, albeit unsatisfactory corpus of concepts for the study of political development in the works by Almond, Deutsch, Apter, Nettl, Eisenstadt and others), Marxism has no conceptual armoury of this type. For what we usually call the Marxist theory of the capitalist State is not in fact a theory of the State *per se*, but rather a theory of how the State contributes or fails to contribute to the reproduction requirements of capitalism. [27]

The argument here is *not* that one cannot establish systematic relationships between political struggles and class contradictions or that the State in capitalist societies is entirely autonomous from the economy. Neither is the argument that predominantly political or other non-economic struggles (ethnic, generational, gender-based) are systematically more important than class struggles. Rather the argument is that Marxism, having failed to elaborate specific conceptual tools for the study of politics, *builds the alleged primacy of the economic into the definition of the political.* In that sense it is unable to study the complex and *varying* relationships between economy and polity, in a theoretically coherent and at the same time *empirically open-ended* manner.

Now Laclau and Mouffe deal with the type of dualism just discussed in a very simple way: they reject the economy/polity distinction altogether. For them, given that politics in the broad sense of the term permeates all social spaces (there is a 'politics' of production, of the family, of the school and so on); and given that all distinctions between institutional spheres are discursively constructed, to start the analysis with a 'pre-constituted' economic and political sphere in order to examine their alleged interrelationships, is to fall again into the essentialist trap. Therefore politics for them should be seen not as 'a determinate level of the social but as a practice of creation, reproduction and transformation of social relations'.[28]

The above solution to the dualism problem might be elegant but not very convincing or useful. First of all the well-trodden idea that there is a *political* dimension in all social interaction (idea which in *HSS* is put into 'discourse' terms) is not reason for ignoring or even denying the existence, in all capitalist societies, of a differentiated set of institutional structures which have a *predominantly* political character: that is, which are geared to the production and repro-duction of the overall system of domination. The core institutional features of such a system (political parties, state bureaucracy, legislative and judiciary bodies and so on) can, both analytically and concretely, be distinguished from the core institutional features of the capitalist economy. The fact that we often use the term politics to refer both to a differentiated institutional sphere and to the 'political' as an inherent dimension of all social situations is no good reason for rejecting the former in favour of the latter.

Moreover, as I have already pointed out, the fact that the distinction between the economy and the polity in capitalist forma-tions is discursively constructed and reproduced, by no means implies that it is not extremely durable and that it does not constitute one of the fundamental features of advanced capitalism. In that sense it is not at all true that the frontiers between the economic and the political are in constant flux, being the unpredictable results of articulatory practices. I would rather argue that the separation between the economic and the political (in the *specific* sense that in capitalist formations the economy is 'insulated' from *direct* political control), as well as the specific way in which the state massively intervenes in the economy in order to maintain the above separation and to boost the accumulation process, constitute permanent features of all advanced capitalist societies.[29] And one can argue this not on the basis of any essentialist notions of what capitalism really is, but on the basis of comparative-historical research establishing in what specific ways capitalist formations are distinct from non-capitalist ones.

If the post-Marxist solution to the dualism problem that *HSS* provides is unsatisfactory, can there be a more satisfactory solution within Marxism? Can there be a way of avoiding economic reductionism (or monism in Laclau and Mouffe's terms) without falling into empiricism (or dualism)? In other terms, can Marxism overcome the 'monism versus dualism' dilemma while retaining a distinctive theoretical profile?

As I have already pointed out in the previous chapter, for some theorists the idea of a non-reductionist Marxist theory of politics is a contradiction in terms – since a conceptual framework which deals with the political sphere in a non-economistic manner ceases *ipso facto* to be Marxist. For others, a non-reductionalist theory of the polity is possible, provided one creates new conceptual tools which:

(1) try to conceptualise non-economic institutional spheres in a way that does not build into their very definition (and hence excludes from empirical investigation) the type of relationship they are supposed to have with the economy;

(2) try to avoid economism without falling into the compartmentalisation of the political and economic spheres to be found in neoclassical economics and in non-Marxist political science, that is, without abandoning some fundamental features of the Marxist paradigm such as its holistic, political economy orientation and its agency-structure synthesis.

I think that this latter position, whether considered Marxist or post-Marxist, should be seriously explored, particularly since, at the present moment at least, there is no alternative macro-sociological paradigm which can deal in a more satisfactory manner with the complex ways in which whole societies are transformed within the context of the world economy and polity.

In a way Laclau's previous work, particularly his *Politics and Ideology in Marxist Theory*[30] (*PIMT*), was a serious attempt to create such new conceptual tools within the Marxist tradition. For instance, his interesting distinction between *class* and *popular* interpellations and antagonisms was an important step toward elaborating, in a theoretically coherent manner, the idea that not all political struggles should be conceptualised in class terms. However, already in *PIMT* the specifically political-institutional context within which popular interpellations and antagonisms were embedded was systematically ignored. Thus, while in this work the mode of production constituted the structural basis of class interpellations and antagonisms, the structural basis of popular interpellations was the social formation as a whole.[31] What was missing in the *PIMT* analysis was an *analytic* concept which could operate on the level of the polity in a way analogous to that of the mode of production concept on the level of the economy: for instance, the notion of a *mode of domination*, consisting of an articulation of specific political technologies (forces of domination) and specific ways of appropriating such technologies (relations of domination), if theoretically developed, could provide the conceptual means for studying the complex linkages between the economic and the political in a logically coherent and empirically open-ended manner. This type of anti-reductionist strategy, which would consist in analytically distinguishing not only political from class agents but also political institutional structures from economic ones, was not taken in *PIMT*. And of course in *HSS* not only the institutional context of macro-politics but also economic institutional structures recede into the horizon as articulatory practices come to occupy the centre stage. In *HSS* therefore the balance between the institutional system and agency is totally broken as Laclau and Mouffe end up by joining all those action-oriented theorists whose excessive fear of essentialism or reification leads them to turn their backs on any serious examination of how global institutional orders persist and change.

5. METHODOLOGICAL HOLISM AND AUTHORITARIANISM

I would like to close this chapter by discussing briefly another major criticism against Marxism which one finds in a mild form in *HSS* and in a more extreme one in many ex-Marxists who have espoused various libertarian political positions: this is the idea that Marx's notion of totality and his holistic orientation to the study of social phenomena is not only indissolubly linked with essentialism, but also with an authoritarian or even totalitarian approach to politics.

That authoritarian conclusions can be drawn from Marx's varied oeuvre is undeniable. It is true, for instance, that in his more positivistic, deterministic writings society, as *HSS* points out, is portrayed as a totality the essence of which unfolds according to strict economic laws, these laws giving unity and firm direction to the social formation as a whole. Within this scheme of things the role of human agency is minimised, since the unity of the proletariat and its revolutionary role is inscribed in its very position within the division of labour, and guaranteed by the very laws of motion of the capitalist mode of production.

It is also true that this deterministic, mechanistic conception of social development can easily be linked with a *scientistic* view of the social, a view which tends to reduce moral and political problems to technical ones by naively asserting that there is a single 'scientific', and therefore 'indisputable', solution to every social conflict and antagonism. The under-conceptualisation of the political sphere proper, and Marx's vision of a future stateless communist order immune against class antagonisms, only reinforce this type of pseudo-scientific bias which has provided fertile ground for all sorts of authoritarian and totalitarian ideologies and practices among Marx's epigoni.[32]

However, neither the deterministic/mechanistic nor the scientistic/authoritarian elements can be considered as representing the core of Marx's thought; and, what is more important from our point of view, *none of these elements are intrinsically linked with a holistic conceptual framework*. In fact it is generally accepted that, unlike other 19th-century evolutionist theories, Marx's evolutionist scheme of stages – which emphasises the importance of class struggles as a fundamental mechanism of transition from one stage to the next – provides the conceptual means for avoiding a strictly unilinear, deterministic view of development of the kind that is set out in the evolutionist writings of Comte, for instance. Moreover, the very way in which the Marxist stages are constructed, with each stage being predominantly conceptualised in terms of the prevailing relations of production rather than of the quantitative growth of the forces of production, again indicates the extent to which the Marxist categories point to the importance of struggles, to the divisional/appropriative rather than merely to the technological aspects of social life.

The best proof of this lies of course in Marx's own historical writings, where classes and class fractions neither play a secondary role, nor are presented as following the 'logic of capital', puppet fashion. In fact the prominence of the relations of production in Marx's conceptual scheme is a strong guarantee against technicist-neutralist views of the social. And while it is true that the 'political' disappears in Marx's communist utopia, it is also true that his major contribution to classical political economy was precisely the system-atic introduction of a *historical* and *political* dimension in the analysis of economic phenomena. It was the assertion that what most eco-nomists had hitherto considered as the natural, eternal laws of the market were in fact regularities based on historically specific struggles leading to specific forms of exploitation.

One could go on *ad infinitum* debating what weight should be attached to those aspects that underemphasise agency and stress structural determinations, the laws of motion of capital and so on. Yet it is of less consequence whether Marx's overall work is labelled deterministic or not, or whether or not a radical break is discovered between his early and late work. What is indeed of more importance is that Marx's overall work provides the *conceptual means* for looking in a theoretically coherent manner at social formations and their overall reproduction/transformation from both an agency and a structural/institutional point of view. This type of balanced holism does not *necessarily* entail a deterministic, essentialist orientation to the study of the social; neither does it *necessarily* lead to authoritarian political attitudes. Methodological holism in itself is not indissolubly linked with assertions about the ontological nature of the social, nor with the degree of relatedness or non-relatedness of social institutions, nor with the type of political controls that do or should prevail in any specific social whole. At its best, a holistic framework merely proposes an anti-atomistic strategy of investigation: it attempts to provide conceptual tools that guard against the study of economic, political and cultural phenomena in a compartmentalised, context-less, or *ad hoc* manner. It provides, in other terms, a language which, instead of erecting barriers, facilitates the study of the complex ways in which global societies are constituted, reproduced and transformed.

NOTES

1. E. Laclau and C. Mouffe, *Hegemony and Social Strategy: Towards a Radical Democratic Politics*, London: Verso, 1985.

2. N. Geras, 'Post-Marxism?', *New Left Review*, No. 163, May-June 1987. The debate between Laclau/Mouffe and Geras continued with the former answering Geras' criticisms in 'Post-Marxism without Apologies', *New Left Review*, No. 66, Nov.-Dec. 1987, and with the latter's rejoinder, 'Ex-Marxism without Substance: Being a Real reply to Laclau and Mouffe', *New Left Review*, No. 169, May-June 1988. Since the two last articles do not in anyway affect my critical remarks of Laclau/Mouffe's and Geras' basic theoretical positions, I have not directly dealt with them in the present chapter.

3. The term *dualism*, as used by Laclau and Mouffe, implies a conceptual incongruity between Marxism's fundamental categories, which are based on a deterministic and economistic view of the social, and the

various *ad hoc* additions (like the relative autonomy of the political) which try to mitigate its economism. In that sense the above authors' dualism or eclecticism is quite similar to the way in which I use the term *empiricism* in chapter 1.

4. See S. F. Nadel, *The Theory of Social Structure*, Vol. I, London: Routledge, 1962, p. 1.

5. See L. Althusser, *For Marx*, London: Allen Lane, Penguin, 1969, pp. 183–90 and p. 251. It has to be admitted that it is not always easy to distinguish between conceptual framework (Gen. II) and substantive theory (Gen. III) in the sense that all statements contain both substantive and metatheoretical/methodological elements. However, depending on where the emphasis lies, a distinction can and must be made between theories whose predominant preoccupation is with how to look at the social world, and theories which try to tell us something we do not already know about its functioning and structure.

6. D. Lockwood, 'Social Integration and System Integration' in G. K. Zollschan and W. Hirsh (eds), *Explorations in Social Change*, London: Routledge, 1964. See also N. Mouzelis, 'Social and System Integration: Some Reflections on a Fundamental Distinction', *British Journal of Sociology*, Dec. 1974.

7. See *The Social System*, New York: Free Press, 1957.

8. See on this point Stephen Savage, *The Theories of Talcott Parsons: The Social Relations of Action*, London: Macmillan, 1987.

9. For an elaboration of the distinction between institutional analysis and a 'strategic conduct' approach, see A. Giddens, *The Constitution of Society*, London: Polity, 1984, pp. 289 ff. From the perspective adopted here, Giddens' distinction between institutional analysis and analysis in terms of strategic conduct is similar to Lockwood's distinction between system and social integration. For Giddens, however, given that he uses the system/social integration dichotomy differently from Lockwood, the two dichotomies do not coincide. For a critical discussion of Giddens' view of the concepts of social and system integration, see N. Mouzelis, 'Restructuring Structuration Theory', *Sociological Review* (forthcoming).

10. It is precisely this type of bracketing that Laclau and Mouffe are rejecting as essentialism. For them (as well as for ethnomethodologists and other phenomenologically-oriented social theorists) any reference to concepts leading to structural/systemic rather than practice/agency considerations means *ipso facto* a reification of the social. However, as I will argue below, the price they have to pay for their excessive fear of reification is the incapacity to deal systematically with the overall institutional context within which specific articulatory practices are embedded.

11. See, for instance, B. Moore, *Social Origins of Dictatorship and Democracy*, Boston: Beacon Press, 1966; E. J. Hobsbawm, *The Age of Revolution: Europe 1789–1848*, London: Weidenfeld & Nicolson, 1962; F. Braudel, *The Mediterranean and the Mediterranean World in the Age of Philip II* (2 vols), London: Fontana, 1973.

12. See, for instance, T. Parsons, *Societies in Evolutionary and Comparative Perspectives*, Englewood Cliffs: Prentice Hall, 1966; S. Eisenstadt,

The Political Systems of Empires, Glencoe, Illinois: Free Press, 1965; N. Smelser, *Social Change and the Industrial Revolution*, Cambridge: Cambridge University Press, 1959.

13. *HSS*, p. 138.
14. On the differentiation between State and royal household in Western Europe, see Otto Hintze, *Staat und Verfassung*, Gottingen, 1962, pp. 275–320.
15. Needless to say, the use of topographical metaphors when reference is made to durable institutional arrangements does not necessarily entail, as Laclau and Mouffe claim, any essentialist connotations. As I have already argued, the only thing it entails is a *temporary* methodological bracketing of considerations pertaining to the skills and awareness of subjects.
16. *HSS*, p. 111.
17. *HSS*, p. 121.
18. *HSS*, p. 134.
19. See 'Post-Marxism?', p. 74.
20. See *HSS*, pp. 149–94.
21. *HSS*, pp. 178–9.
22. Such an attempt can be seen, for instance, in Marx's *Grundirisse*. One can see it as well in M. Mann's *The Sources of Social Power*, Vol. 1, Cambridge: Cambridge University Press, 1986; and Giddens, *A Contemporary Critique of Historic Materialism*, Vol. 1, London: Macmillan, 1987, and *The Nation-State and Violence: Vol. Two of a Contemporary Critique of Historic Materialism*, London: Polity Press, 1985.
23. *HSS*, p. 86.
24. It is different, for instance, in terms of its exclusive focus on discourse analysis, its structuralist 'decentring' of the subject, its post-structuralist emphasis on the discontinuous, disorderly character of the social and so on.
25. For a systematic discussion of different types of reductionism in Marxist political theory, see Appendix I.
26. For the adoption of such a theoretical position in the study of third world capitalist countries cf. John Taylor, *From Modernisation to Modes of Production: A Critique of the Sociologies of Development and Underdevelopment*, London: Macmillan, 1979, pp. 132 ff. For a more specific application to Latin America cf. D. Portantiero, 'Dominant Classes and Political Crisis', *Latin America Perspectives*, Vol. 1, No. 3, 1974. For a somewhat different approach which also leads to an empiricist treatment of politics, cf. P. Hirst, 'Economic Classes and Politics' in A. Hunt (ed.), *Class and Class Structure*, London: Lawrence and Wishart, 1977; cf. also A. Cutler *et al.*, *Marx's Capital and Capitalism Today*, London: Routledge & Kegan Paul, 1977.
27. See A. Przeworski, 'The Ethical Materialism of John Roemer', *Politics and Society*, Vol. 4, No. 3, 1982, p. 290.
28. *HSS*, p. 153.
29. See on this point C. Offe and R. Volger, 'Theses on the Theory of the State', *New German Critique*, Vol. 6, 1975.

30. Ernesto Laclau, *Politics and Ideology in Marxist Theory (PIMT)*, London, 1977.
31. *PIMT*, p. 166. For a critical review of this position, see Appendix II.
32. For a detailed analysis of such connections, see I. Balbus, *Marxism and Domination*, Princeton, N.J.: Princeton University Press, 1982.

Part II

The Economic and the Political: Towards a Non-Reductive Framework

3 Technology, Appropriation, Ideology: Beyond the Base/ Superstructure Dichotomy

Historic materialism's conceptualisation of society as an economic-material infrastructure and a legal, political, ideological super-structure has been extensively criticised by both Marxist and non-Marxist social theorists. Most of the former (fundamentalists apart) nowadays consider the crude topographical analogy increasingly untenable, an analogy that views society as a two-storey house, the upper floor of which is a poorly designed, jerry-built addition to the lower one. Among those who categorically reject the base/superstructure dichotomy there are some who hold that such rejection *ipso facto* implies a denial of Marxism *tout court*; others maintain that Marxism does not stand or fall on the issue of the base/ superstructure conceptualisation, and that this famous distinction does not constitute a *sine qua non* condition of historic materialism.

In this chapter I shall argue that for the latter position it is not enough merely to reject the base/superstructure dichotomy and leave it at that. It is necessary to go further and to create new *tools* that can help provide a conceptualisation of a whole social formation which (1) avoids some of the major drawbacks of the base/superstructure dichotomy, and (2) retains some of the distinctive features of the Marxist paradigm. I shall try to show that such a conceptualisation, which, for reasons already explained I call post-Marxist, is indeed possible.

1. HISTORIC MATERIALISM: FROM PHILOSOPHICAL TO HISTORICAL ANALYSIS

Marxism has typically linked technologies and the mode of their control with the idea of society's material or economic base – where 'material' and 'economic' are for the most part[1] used interchangeably. To understand why this should be so, a few words are needed about the problematic way in which Marx and subsequent Marxists

45

have moved from philosophical considerations about social being and consciousness, or about Man (capital M) and his ideas, to more historical sociological considerations concerning different institutional spheres and their interconnections.

Let us take as an example philosophical, ontological distinctions, such as Man's 'material existence' and his ideas about that existence. On a societal level these are more or less automatically seen as corresponding to the distinction between the economy on the one hand, and political, religious, kinship institutions on the other. The economy, or more specifically the forces and relations of economic production, are regarded as the material infrastructure, and all other institutional spheres are relegated to the 'less material' super-structure.[2] The dichtomy of infrastructural-material versus super-structural-non-material has been associated with a variety of other dichotomies, such as non-normative/normative, structural/conjunc-tural, objective/subjective, and so on.

Once all or some of these highly dubious parallels are accepted, it becomes easy to use arguments or images from the philosophical debate for bolstering the economic-primacy thesis on the institu-tional, societal level. For example, Feuerbach's idea of man project-ing his powerlessness and lack of control over the natural forces into the sky and so creating a fictitious image of an omnipotent and domineering god can be taken to show not only the illusory character of religious *beliefs*, but also the lack of 'materiality' of religious *institutions*. More generally, the quite plausible statement that there is a difference between what men say or think they do and what they actually do is used to demonstrate the primacy of economic produc-tion over legal, political, or ideological superstructures.

It is not my intention here to discuss the legitimacy of philosophical distinctions between matter and ideas, or between being and con-sciousness; neither do I wish to consider the complicated problems involved in passing from philosophical to more historical, sociological levels of analysis. Leaving all that aside and assuming that the distinction (for instance) between what men do and what they say they do[3] can indeed give us some useful hints on how to study whole societies, it seems to me that it would make more sense to apply that distinction *within* specific institutional spheres or orders rather than *between* them.

So within the political sphere one can easily distinguish between how the ruling groups control the means of domination and coercion, and how they conceive or justify such controls. That is to say, one can distinguish between the *actual* way in which power is distributed between rulers and ruled, and the way in which *political* ideologies present that distribution. (There is, for instance, a vast literature in political science showing precisely the discrepancies between the prevalent myths and ideologies concerned with the democratic, 'open' character of Western parliamentary regimes, and the frequently restrictive, authoritarian manner in which power is in fact exercised in those polities.)[4]

Similar distinctions can be applied in all other institutional spheres. To take one which Marxists are all too ready to dump as 'mere ideas' or ideologies, the religious institutional sphere also has certain techniques of indoctrination or socialisation. One need only think for example of the formidable bureaucratic and legal machinery of the Catholic Church, and the armoury of ritual and dogma with the help of which it tries to maintain and expand its message.[5] Moreover, there are certain institutionalised ways of controlling such techniques. So in the Catholic Church the technologies of indoctrination are controlled in a highly autocratic manner by the Vatican-based curia headed by the Pope.[6] In consequence, it is perfectly possible to speak in this so-called non-material, ideological sphere of *technologies or forces* and *relations* of indoctrination that generate specific cleavages, and of struggles between those who do and those who do not control the means of indoctrination. Also, of course, as in all other major institutional spheres, it is easy to identify within that of religion certain *dominant ideologies* that set out to justify or present an idealised and distorted picture of how the means of indoctrination are controlled.

I think enough has been said to show that distinctions such as between what men do and what they think or say they do make more sense in the context of specific institutional spheres than when applied in such a way that the whole social formation is divided into an economic-material infrastructure and a less material, more ideal superstructure. However one may conceive of the infrastructural, material elements (whether in terms of technologies, in terms of actual relations as against ideal ones, in terms of social processes governed by structural rather than conjunctural determinations, and so forth), one will find them playing a prominent role not only within the sphere of economic production but in all major institutional orders.

The gist of my argument here is that neither should the concepts of technology and its mode of appropriation/control be confined to the sphere of economic production, nor should the concept of ideology be relegated to the superstructural, non-material spheres – and so be

made into a residual category referring in blanket fashion to kinship,
religious, and other 'secondary' institutions. Human beings do more
than merely produce economic goods for their physical survival. They
also produce, with the help of specific tools and technologies, the
political order that makes organised life in complex societies possible;
as well as the cultural order that enables them to relate meaningfully
to each other and to the non-human worlds surrounding them. Each
major sphere of production – whether economic, political, or cultural
– implies specific technologies and appropriation of these technologies; it also implies specific ideologies with the help of which those
who profit most from the prevailing control and appropriation
arrangements try to justify the status quo.

Marxists can argue, of course, that in all societies it is economic
production that in certain ways is more important than other types of
social production. Even if one were to accept this (I personally do
not), it would still be no reason for conceptualising non-economic
spheres in such a way as to define right out of existence their *specific*
technologies, the mode of their control, and the corresponding
dominant ideologies. In order to make this fundamental point quite
clear, it is important to distinguish between two analytically separate
levels for discussing the validity and utility of historic materialism: a
methodological level and a substantive one.

2.   HISTORIC MATERIALISM: SUBSTANTIVE AND METHODOLOGICAL ISSUES

On the *substantive* level, historic materialism proclaims privileged
status for the forces and/or relations of production if there is to be any
attempt at understanding the constitution, functioning, and long-
term transformation of societies. This primacy of the material base
vis-à-vis its political, legal, and ideological 'superstructure' is either
seen to apply across the board to all human societies past and
present; or, in a drastically attenuated interpretation of the doctrine,
it is supposed to apply above all to capitalist social formations.[7]
According to the latter view, in pre-capitalist societies non-economic
institutional spheres may dominate the economic one, but even so the
economy maintains its primacy since 'in the last instance' it is always
the economy that determines which of the non-economic spheres can
acquire such dominance.[8]

On the methodological, conceptual framework level, the primacy thesis, however formulated, has resulted in a refusal to create conceptual tools that can seriously take into account the specificity and relative autonomy of non-economic institutional spheres. As I have mentioned already, it has invariably led to attempts at defining political and cultural phenomena in economic categories – in terms of their relevance and contribution to the reproduction requirements of the dominant mode of production, or to the interests of the exploiting classes. The argument in justification of this strategy has been that the overriding dynamic of the material base ultimately imposes its logic on all superstructural spheres, and so brings the whole of the social formation together in a unity that makes the creation of separate, non-economic conceptual tools quite unnecessary. It is by considerations such as these that the substantive thesis about the overriding importance of the material, economic base leads to a methodological position, or rather to a conceptual framework that refuses to theorise the cultural or the political in any terms other than their contribution to the economic. Given this situation it is not surprising that, as I tried to show in the previous chapters, when Marxists stress the 'relative autonomy' of non-economic institutions, their emphasis (in the absence of specific conceptual tools for the study of such spheres) remains an empty gesture, a mere rhetorical flourish.[9]

The major point I wish to make, however, is that the substantive and methodological implications of the primacy thesis *need not be indissolubly linked*. Even if Marxists, for whatever reason, refuse to abandon their faith in the universal primacy of the forces and relations of production, *on the level of conceptual tools there is no reason why this faith must be translated into a refusal to conceptualise the sphere of politics and culture in non-economic terms*. After all, rejection of the current methodological implications of the primacy thesis does not logically entail rejection also of the substantive propositions of historic materialism: it involves no inconsistency at all to accept the latter while rejecting the former. For even if it is agreed that in all capitalist societies, or in all societies *tout court*, it is the forces and relations of production that constitute the basic motor for social change, this substantive proposition does not imply any obligation to accept the methodological straitjacket of conceptualising non-economic spheres in economic terms. It does not, in other words, exonerate the Marxist researcher from finding a way of theoretically conceptualising for instance the economy and the polity without building the alleged primacy of the first into the very definition of the second.

Having taken this position, I do not find it necessary to discuss in any detail the complex debates over the substantive propositions of historic materialism. [10] So as not to give the impression that I am trying to avoid taking sides on the substantive level, it is sufficient to say here that I consider any attempt to identify a material base (however defined), which is *universally* somehow more important than other institutional spheres – like all transhistorical, contextless generalisations in the social sciences – can only lead to substantive statements that are either wrong or trivial. If, on the other hand, the primacy thesis is limited to capitalist societies in comparison with pre-capitalist ones, then it becomes both more plausible and more interesting. Yet this interpretation too runs into difficulties when one comes to consider the late-late industrialising societies of the capitalist periphery and semi-periphery. [11] For my present purposes, however, it is enough to bracket all substantive arguments and simply to put forward the proposition that, irrespective of which institutional sphere is dominant or determining in a given social formation, one cannot properly study complex, differentiated societies without a non-economic conceptualisation of the political and the other so-called superstructural spheres. I would also argue that one can indeed achieve such a conceptualisation, by applying to the non-economic institutional spheres some of Marx's powerful insights on the *technological, appropriative*, and *ideological* dimensions of social life.

3. TECHNOLOGY

(A)   Giving, as Marxism does, a central place to the notion that men collectively transform themselves and nature through the creation and application of tools can be of help when one looks at society as an ongoing human construct, rather than as a given, unexplained, taken-for-granted reified entity. Furthermore, the constructionist, anti-reification connotations of the technology concept are enhanced when one goes beyond the base/superstructure distinction and acknowledges that forces or technologies of production do not have to refer exclusively to economic production.

To take the political sphere as an example, it is not difficult (as noted already) to identify *political* technologies that play a crucial role in the constitution, reproduction, and transformation of the polity and of society in general. Let me develop this point in some depth.

Political technologies or 'forces of domination' could refer to the complex ways in which political power is produced. In relatively differentiated state societies, it would refer, for instance, to the intricate means by which the state not only imposes order, but also extracts resources and mobilises or demobilises those under its jurisdiction. I have in mind here not merely the type of disciplinary, surveillance micro-technologies that Michel Foucault has so brilliantly examined,[12] but also what Weber has called *means of administration and coercion*,[13] that is, the macro-institutional, organisational ensembles that, on the level of the *whole polity*, link rulers and ruled (for example, types of state administrative or military apparatuses, techniques of taxation, of national accounting, of mass mobilisation and so forth). Closer to contemporary political sociology, I also have in mind the techniques used by political leaders to bring into the political arena all those who, for one reason or another, have been left outside the sphere of active politics – techniques such as the populistic and clientelistic forms of political incorporation that play such a prominent role in Third-World politics (a point developed more extensively in the next chapter).

Now the similarities between all the above technologies and those of economic production are quite striking. Even if one accepts G. Cohen's interpretation of what Marx meant by forces of production (to wit: labour power, the instruments of labour, and the knowledge that makes their construction possible – all these seen *in isolation from* the work and property arrangements within which they are always embedded),[14] it is still easy to see that there is a similar dimension in the politico-military sphere. Here we have first of all *means of destruction*, which are as concrete and material as economic tools and machines. Like their economic counterparts, they too can be combined in various ways with manpower in order to produce violence or the threat of violence. Moreover, just as economic technologies are both analytically and concretely detachable from specific social and organisational arrangements (by portraying a limited neutrality[15] that allows their being transplanted from one type of relations of production to another), so military technologies too can be transferred and made to operate in contexts characterised by radically different relations of domination. It is less obvious but nevertheless tenable that not only military technologies but also administrative technologies of political rule portray a quite similar type of transferability. So techniques of accounting or mass propaganda, for instance, are also based on the application of a certain kind of knowledge, they also entail (if to a lesser degree) material tools for their operation, and they too can be transplanted from one political system to another.

Moreover, even if the forces of production are taken to refer to not only material tools and the knowledge of their production, but also to the work arrangements or processes that more or less strictly 'correspond' to them,[16] one can still draw interesting analogies between economic and non-economic technologies. Let me give an example. In the same way that there is what may be called elective affinity between types of economic technology and types of work organisation,[17] so there are similar affinities in the military sphere:

> The development of infantry armed with muskets went along with the introduction of systematic drill. Given the general unreliability of aim and of firing mechanisms, guns were effective only if fired in unison. Since they took considerable time to reload, armies were organised into ranks firing in staggered order. The Dutch army in the 1590s introduced systematic firing and reloading drills, along with marching in step, which made for much better discipline in battle ... The organisation of military drill spread by diffusion and emulation, just as the hardware did.[18]

In short, the argument here is that in almost every respect[19] the technologies or forces of domination in the politico-military sphere evince characteristics similar to those of the forces of economic production.

(B)   In view of the above, we may speak of the development of the forces of domination, just as on the economic level we speak of the development of the forces of production. Both tend to have a 'progressive', cumulative character, in the sense of more efficient technologies of domination/coercion *tending* to replace less efficient ones – although, as in the case of economic technologies, this process is never irreversible.[20]

In any case, there can be no doubt that with the advent and dominance of Western capitalism the development of both economic and political technologies acquired an unprecedented momentum, and in that sense one can justifiably speak of a process of growing rationalisation in both the economic and political fields. Concerning the latter, the type of growing political rationalisation which, from very different perspectives, of course, has been the focus of Weber's work on bureaucracy and Foucault's on 'bio-power', can fruitfully be seen as a process indicating the extraordinary development of the forces and technologies of domination in post-feudal European societies. To quote from Foucault:

> If the economic take-off of the West began with the techniques that made possible the accumulation of capital, it might perhaps be said that the methods of administering the accumulation of men made possible a political take-off in relation to the traditional, ritual, costly, violent forms of power, which soon fell into disuse and were superseded by a subtle calculated technology of subjection. In fact, the two processes – the accumulation of men and the accumulation of capital – cannot be separated; it would not have been possible to solve the problem of the accumulation of men without the growth of an apparatus of production capable of both sustaining them and using them; conversely, the techniques that made the cumulative multiplicity of men useful accelerated the accumulation of capital.[21]

Although he hardly acknowledges it, Foucault's analysis of the large-scale spread of disciplinary techniques in 19th-century Europe, which resulted in the more efficient management and control of whole populations and in the concomitant growing regimentation of the individual, can very well be taken as a deepening of Weber's insights into the spread of bureaucratic, rational-legal principles and forms of organisation in the West (forms of organisation that have led to the production of 'mutilated' personalities operating as cogs in huge bureaucratic machines).[22] For Weber, technique or technology (in German, *Technik* is used for both) refers to

> every rule or system of rules that permits reliably reproducible action, whether methodical or customary, that can be predicted by participants in interaction and calculated from the perspective of the observer.[23]

Here *customary* action implies that one can achieve predictability and calculability in highly traditional forms of social organisation; whereas the term *methodical* refers to consciously planned rules and procedures, that is, to bureaucratic ones.[24]

For Weber, as is well known, bureaucratic principles of organisation tend to become dominant in modern times not only in public administration, but in all institutional orders (economic, religious, educational, and so on). This implies the separation of the direct 'producers' not only from the means of economic production, but also from the means of administration, coercion, indoctrination, and the like. In all these areas, therefore, the 'means' tend to be concentrated at the top. This connotes increases in both formal and substantive rationality on the one hand,[25] and on the other the undermining of the autonomy of subordinate organisational levels and an overall decrease in individual initiative and freedom:

> Sociologically speaking, the modern state is an 'enterprise' (*Betrieb*) just like a factory: this exactly is its historical peculiarity. Here as there the authority relations have the same roots. The relative independence of the artisan, the producer under the putting-out system, the free seigneurial peasant, the travelling associate in a *commenda* relationship, the knight and vassal, rested on their ownership of the tools, supplies, finances and weapons with which they fulfilled their economic, political and military functions and maintained themselves. In contrast, the hierarchical dependence of the wage worker, the administrative and technical employee, the assistant in the academic institute, as well as that of the civil servant and the soldier is due to the fact that in their case the means indispensable for their undertakings and for their economic existence are in the hands of the entrepreneur or the political ruler . . . This all-important economic foundation: the 'separation' of the worker from the material means of operation – from the means of production in the economy, from the means of war in the military, from the means of administration in public administration, from the means of research in universities and laboratories, and from financial means in all these cases – is the common and decisive basis of the modern state in its political, cultural and military operations and of the private capitalist economy.[26]

Needless to say, the amazing spread of bureaucratisation, the fact that both economic and non-economic organisations acquire increasingly a uniform, calculable, *machine-like* character, makes even more imperative the broadening of our focus of analysis and the study of modern technology as a fundamental dimension of all institutional spheres.

Finally, although both Weber's and Foucault's views on growing rationalisation refer to forms of domination and/or subjugation that are not limited to the political and economic spheres, what is important from our perspective is that both theorists make a clear distinction between economic and political technologies, and rightly emphasise the crucial importance of both for understanding Western development. Their insights are useful, therefore, for developing the concept of technology, not merely as a means of economic goods production but, among other things, as a means of political power production. When that has been done it will become possible to examine the intricate relationship between means of production and means of domination in a more rigorous and systematic manner.

(C) If it is accepted and seriously taken into consideration that there are technologies of political production just as there are technologies of economic production, then proving the primacy of the infrastructure by stressing its 'materiality' makes very little sense. Whether the concept of the forces of production is interpreted in Cohen's restricted sense or in a broader fashion (as including not only material tools but also 'technical', organisational work arrangements), it can justifiably be argued that political technologies portray as much materiality as do economic ones – whatever one's definition of materiality. In consequence, historic materialism must either drop the primacy thesis altogether, or it must shift its focus from the primacy of the *economic* to the primacy of the *technological*,[27] in which case it will have to admit that a society's technological base is by no means exclusively located in the economic or material base.

At this point I would like to have it understood that my major aim is not to produce yet another interpretation of the primacy thesis, this one based on the paramount importance of technologies as a means of social construction. For me, the utility of rejecting the base/superstructure straitjacket and the strictly economistic conceptualisation of the 'technological' is not to rescue the primacy thesis, but rather to shift the attention in the ongoing debates on historic materialism from substantive to *methodological* issues; from sterile attempts at establishing in contextless, transhistorical manner universal laws about the primacy of this or that factor or dimension, to attempts at constructing *useful conceptual tools* for the study of how complex societies are constituted, reproduced, and transformed.

From that angle, broadening the concept of technology so that it can be applied to an examination of the non-economic institutional spheres can help us look at society as an ongoing accomplishment, as a construction, rather than as an opaque, preconstituted, given fact. It can help us, in other words, break away from the Durkheimian/Parsonian tradition that tends to portray society as a reified, omnipotent deity that in some mysterious fashion pulls all the strings behind the social actors' backs. Moreover, it can do this without going to the other extreme, as phenomenologically oriented theorists do: without reducing macro-institutions and collective actors to the intersubjective understandings and interpretative practices of individual actors.

In fact, the Marxist emphasis on the technological dimension of social existence can, if adequately reformulated, constitute a useful methodological device; it can lead to interesting questions about the complex ways in which social actors, in their efforts to create and appropriate/control economic, political and cultural technologies contribute more or less unintentionally to the constitution and transformation of whole social orders. This type of investigation, absolutely central to any serious attempt at understanding concrete societies, is conspicuously absent in the major non-Marxist social science paradigms. For instance, the Parsonian/functionalist and the phenomenological/hermeneutic theoretical traditions both fail, though for opposite reasons, to conceptualise collective actors and their relationship to the means of economic, political, and cultural production, (that is, to *the means of social construction*). Parsonian functionalism does not do so because of its one-sided systemic emphasis, which results in an underconceptualisation of the voluntaristic dimension of social life in general and of collective action in particular; the latter paradigms fail because of their incapacity to move from the micro-worlds of actors' intersubjective understandings to the macro-worlds of collective actors and their struggles. From this point of view, therefore, a reformulated Marxist paradigm – drawing attention to the obvious fact that human beings, in their collective capacity of creating economic and non-economic technologies, are both products and producers of their social world – can contribute significantly to the revitalisation of the social sciences. This point will, I hope, become clearer from my discussion of the second major dimension of the Marxist conceptual framework, that of appropriation.

4. APPROPRIATION

Let us move on now to the fundamental notion of Marxism that technologies are controlled not by 'Society' or by 'Man' in general, but by specific groups, and that this differential control of the means of production creates cleavages that are relevant to an understanding of both societal stability and change. In this area again the Marxist paradigm, when freed of its economic shackles, has much useful methodological insight to offer.

To start with, as mentioned in the previous chapter, the centrality of the relations-of-production concept in Marxism is not only a valuable safeguard against technicist/neutral views of the social, but is at the same time an excellent conceptual device for studying societies both from an *agency/action* and from a *systemic/functionalist* perspective – or, to use Lockwood's terminology, it is a device for looking at social wholes both from a *social* and a *system* integration point of view. Since this is a crucial point indeed, I shall develop it further by looking in some detail at the ways in which non-Marxist approaches deal with the system/social integration problematic.

(A)   In Weberian or neo-Weberian theories of class, for instance, the main focus of analysis is not, as in Marxism, on the sphere of production but on the sphere of distribution. The basis for the constitution of social classes is not the relationship of economic subjects to the means of production, but their market capacities, their differential chances of acquiring resources in a market context.[28] This usually leads either to social-stratification studies that reduce class analysis to a construction of statistical boxes; or, more dynamically, to various conflict theories that conceive of classes as groups or quasi-groups competing for scarce resources in the market place.

Let us look first at the social-stratification approach. It consists of the creation of categories (social strata) that group under one umbrella all members of a statistical population who have one or more characteristics in common: income, educational credentials, chances of mobility, and so forth. Such an approach is, of course, useful for mapping out a social system's distributional aspects, for instance, the manner in which various resources or rewards are allocated among the members of that society or of a less inclusive collectivity. To a limited extent it can also show how various distributions correlate with one another.

What it cannot do, however, is to explain them. It cannot tell us how and why such a distribution came about. Neither can social stratification tell us to what extent the characteristics that all members of a social stratum have in common are or should be the basis of what Giddens calls class structuration: the creation of actual group boundaries and the development of group awareness or class consciousness. In other words, the social-stratification approach leads to a nominalistic view of class, where the collective actors and their antagonistic relationships are replaced by categories that are *connected with each other only statistically* (for example, category A has a higher income than category B).[29]

(B) The nominalism portrayed in social-stratification studies, although to some extent linked with Weber's methodological individualism,[30] is not an inherent feature of the Weberian sociological tradition. Weber's concept of social closure, for instance, as developed by Frank Parkin and others,[31] does lead from the analytic/formalistic categories of social stratification to a view of classes as concrete collectivities constituted and reproduced through conflicting strategies of exclusion and usurpation.

According to Parkin, any unequal distribution of resources sooner or later results in the formation of antagonistic groups. The group that is favoured by the prevailing distribution of rewards/opportunities will attempt to consolidate its privileged position through strategies of closure/exclusion; whereas 'negatively privileged' groups will adopt 'usurpation' strategies in an attempt to change the existing distribution of rewards in their favour. Moreover, modes of closure can be based on collectivist or individualist criteria of exclusion. Collectivist criteria single out some generalised attitude of a whole collectivity as the basis for exclusion (for example, race, religion, language), while individualistic criteria focus on specific attributes of individuals (for instance, educational credentials).[32]

Parkin holds that the closure theory of class not only avoids the nominalism and static character of the social-stratification approach, but that it also overcomes a number of difficulties inherent in Marxist class theory. As mentioned already, Marxists are unable to deal in a non-reductionist manner with non-economic cleavages and conflicts. Given the total lack of appropriate conceptual tools, social struggles due to racial, ethnic, or sexual differences are seen either exclusively as factors aggravating or accelerating class conflict, or conceptualised as mere epiphenomena of underlying class antagonisms.

Parkin argues that closure theory is able to overcome Marxist reductionism because it can equally well be applied to situations where the basis for exclusion is not the ownership/control of the means of production, but some other form of advantage or opportunity in the economic, political, or cultural sphere. Moreover, closure theory can uphold a dichotomic model of class conflict without encountering the usual difficulties of such models. The theory rejects, for instance, the Marxist distinction between 'objective' class locations and practices, as well as the sterile exercise of deciding whether certain class locations (such as those of managers or white-collar workers) belong to the exploited or exploiting camp. In closure theory, exploitation can occur not only between, but also within classes. So an excluded group (for example, skilled blue-collar workers) can, in addition to an 'upward'-oriented usurpation strategy, adopt a strategy of exclusion towards less privileged groups (such as unskilled workers).[33]

Parkin's closure theory must be acknowledged as an attempt to avoid the static character of studies that merely measure how rewards are distributed in society, as well as of Marxist theories that, although more dynamic, reduce all social conflicts to a struggle between owners and non-owners of the means of production. However, nominalism and reductionism are avoided only at a price – this being a theory that is not particularly useful in terms of its metatheoretical/methodological guidelines.

Let us take Parkin's rejection of the Marxist distinction between class locations and class practices. Parkin rightly points out that, on the basis of this distinction, Marxists either automatically derive class practices and strategies from 'objectively determined' class locations or, whenever there are discrepancies between class locations and practices, explain them away by the *deus ex machina* intervention of the 'political' or 'ideological' instances – these latter being conceptualised in economic fashion. Parkin thinks he is able to avoid all of the above complications by totally ignoring, or rather dismissing, the 'location' side of the distinction. In his view, class should not be linked with the way the labour contract and the ensuing division of labour allocate positions within production. Class, he says, refers exclusively to practices, to group processes of exclusion and usurpation.[34] This, however, completely ignores the system-integration aspects of society, and portrays classes as antagonistic groups fighting each other in an institutional vacuum. What Parkin advocates is to explain the constitution and development of class conflict purely in terms of the antagonists' strategies, and not at all in terms of the shifting institutional terrain in which their antagonism is rooted.

This one-sided emphasis on agency at the expense of systemic/institutional analysis is not sufficiently remedied by making distinctions between different types of closure, and identifying the ways in which they interconnect and so reinforce or neutralise each other.[35] Although such a tactic is definitely an improvement, it provides no better guidance than the initial theory does to the problem of how more or less overlapping cleavages due to different types of closure are affected by constraints and opportunities that arise from overall institutional incompatibilities on the level of system integration.

In conclusion, because of its one-sided emphasis on agency, Parkin's theory of closure does not provide a useful framework for the study of how various distributions of rewards and opportunities are constituted, maintained, or transformed. Similar objections can be made to most market-oriented theories of class, as well as to the various conflict theories that aim not so much at providing a theory of class as at giving a more general model of social stability and change.[36]

If in Parkin's closure theory social processes are linked up directly with collective actors whose strategies of exclusion/usurpation are central to the analysis, Parsonian functionalism, as mentioned in the previous chapter, goes to the other extreme. In the Parsonian paradigm, social processes are not seen primarily from the point of view of such collectivities as classes or interest groups, but from that of the social system and its functional requirements. Here functional exigencies take the place of strategy concepts, whereas role strains and institutional incompatibilities take the place of class struggles and group antagonisms.

Since I have already dealt with Parsons' system-oriented approach,[37] I shall restrict myself here to mentioning a more positive aspect of Parsonian functionalism. This is that, like closure theory and the social-stratification approach, Parsonian theory manages to avoid the reductionist methodology that one invariably finds in the Marxist paradigm.

It is true, of course, that in his later writings Parsons has ascribed a primacy, giving the cultural system top priority in his cybernetic hierarchy of systems.[38] However, the cybernetic primacy of the cultural system does not have the *methodological* consequences that the primacy of the economic has for historic materialism. This is so because Parsons has always been concerned with providing a common language that avoids both *compartmentalisation* and *reductionism*. He avoids compartmentalisation by theorising the four sub-systems in such a way that their interchanges can be studied without it being necessary to move from one theoretical plane to another (without considering, for example, in the fashion of neo-classical economics, political or cultural factors as mere 'parameters' of the economic-adaptation sub-system). He also avoids reductionism, by providing sub-languages with the help of which each sub-system can be investigated in terms of its own logic and dynamic, as well as in terms of its inter-relationship with the other three sub-systems.

(C) Moving on now to Marxism, the first point I wish to make is that, despite its reductionist tendencies, the Marxist framework does provide conceptual tools that allow one to avoid the schism between systemic and action-oriented theories. As a matter of fact, the concept of relations of production, and the ensuing distinction between class locations and class practices,[39] constitute a *modus operandum* that facilitates both institutional analysis and analysis in terms of strategic conduct. It draws attention to the institutions of capitalist property as they are related to the fundamental division between owners/controllers and non-owners/non-controllers of the means of production, and to their compatibility or incompatibility with other institutional wholes of the capitalist system. At the same time it encourages action questions about the ways in which agents react to the locations in which they are placed, how they form or fail to form a collective awareness of common interests, the degree to which their collective organisation succeeds in defending such common interests, and so on.

To repeat yet again, the more we focus on how agents react to their locations by trying to maintain or transform their structural positions *vis-à-vis* the means of production, the more we are concerned with issues of strategic conduct – with issues concerning the manner in which subjects construct their identities and their views of what constitutes their interests, how they go about promoting them, and so on. The more we focus, on the other hand, on the way class locations cluster together and form larger institutional ensembles, the more we bracket considerations of strategic conduct. We then ask questions about the reproductive requirements of such ensembles, about the circumstances in which they are or are not compatible with each other, whether or not their eventual incompatibilities/contradictions provide favourable conditions for the development of specific forms of struggle, and so on. In other words, as we shift our attention from strategic conduct to the study of society as a system of institutional parts, we are increasingly concerned with the fundamental issues that non-teleological functionalist analysis has always raised. (Those issues persist in disguised form even in the writings of those who, for one reason or another, are hostile to functionalism and no longer use its vocabulary).[40]

Of course, as mentioned in the previous chapter, the balance between agency and institutional structure has often been broken in Marxism; this break having led either to ultra-structuralist theories which portray agents' practices as the 'effects' of structural determinations, or, at the other extreme, to theories emphasising agents at the expense of the institutional framework within which they operate. This latter imbalance has taken the form of ultra-voluntaristic theories of class (where the dominant classes are seen as omnipotent anthropomorphic entities) or, as in 'rational-choice' or analytic Marxism, of theories which tend to reduce the features of macro-social systems to the rational properties of actors.[41] However, the point is that the Marxist paradigm, unlike Parsonian structural functionalism, does provide the theoretical *option* of a balanced agency-system approach, and this is the option that has been chosen and used successfully by several Marxist and Marxisant students of long-term socio-historical transformations.[42]

A second positive point about the Marxist paradigm is that, by locating class antagonisms primarily within the sphere of production, it emphasises the fact that class relationships are not similar to, and cannot easily be equated with, other antagonistic relationships between groups competing for resources in the market place or elsewhere. In fact, class exploitation is a very special type of 'closure', where the resources over which the antagonists are fighting *derive directly from their relationship within the system of production*. Insofar as class exploitation is a matter of the surplus labour extracted by owners from non-owners, there is an intimate link between the antagonists' competitive relationship and the object of their competition. This type of link does not exist where groups are considered as competing in the market over jobs or educational credentials, for instance.[43] From this point of view, class exploitation is not simply group competition over the distribution of rewards; it is a fundamental type of conflict situation, which allows the establishment of quite precise links between the antagonists and the overall institutional context in which their conflict is embedded. This overall institutional context is absolutely necessary for understanding the basic forms of the antagonism between exploiters and exploited, and the complex ways in which it evolves through time.

A final advantage of the relations-of-production concept is that it does not simply avoid the individual/society dichotomy that is so prevalent in the Durkheimian tradition, but replaces it with a much more fruitful dichotomy, that of *macro*-actors and the *macro*-institutional system. The dichotomy between the individual and society unavoidably leads to a crippling imbalance between actors viewed on the *micro*-level of analysis, and society conceived as a *macro*-system of institutional orders. The result is a highly lopsided framework which, like a badly constructed boat, is bound to list heavily on the side of either system or agency, and must capsize in the end. In other words, it inevitably results in either an overemphasis on systemic analysis which, in the manner of Durkheim or Parsons, portrays society/culture as a mysterious entity manipulating individual conduct; or, by way of reaction, to the total rejection of systemic/functionalist analysis and an exclusive concern with inter-subjectivity.

In Marxism, on the other hand, at least as far as its less mechanistic or deterministic versions are concerned, the social formation/macro-agency distinction quite clearly occupies the place of that of society/individual. This makes it possible to deal with societal transformation without reifying society and without abandoning the historical, macro-sociological orientation. If the Durkheimian 'individual' cannot change the macro-structures that encompass his/her existence, macro-actors are able to bring about societal transformations – if by macro-actor we mean any decision-making entity whose decisions entail consequences stretching widely in terms of time and space. This definition would include not only such collective actors as business corporations, political parties, trade unions, governmental agencies, and the like, but also single individuals whose economic, political, or culturally-based power makes the consequences of their action widely felt. (One could use the term *mega-actors* when referring to the latter type of macro-actors.) Seen from the point of view of these definitions, a whole class is never an actor, of course. But neither is it a mere statistical category, as in the social-stratification approach. For in non-vulgar Marxism class locations provide a structural base that, without being mechanistically determining, favours the development of organisations or social movements that aim predominantly at both shaping and promoting class interests.[44]

Another way of making the same point is to argue that Marxism's emphasis on collective actors enables the student to realise that the construction and reproduction of macro-institutional orders is not only the result of 'single' members of society or 'lay persons' reproducing rules routinely by merely using them in everyday micro-interactions. This rather 'populistic' view of how social orders are created and maintained (a view prevailing primarily but not exclusively in the various micro-sociological, hermeneutic approaches), insofar as it fails to stress the *highly unequal* contribution of social actors to the construction, reproduction and transformation of institutional orders, is extremely one-sided and misleading. (It is in fact as misleading as Marxist oriented theories which go to the opposite extreme and view the production/reproduction of institutions as *exclusively* due to the machinations of the dominant classes.)

Consider for instance the institution of marriage. It is true, of course, that rules or norms pertaining to marriage are reproduced as a very great number of men and women 'instantiate'[45] these rules in their day-to-day interactions as husbands and wives. But to explain how such rules came about, how they are maintained, 'repaired' or transformed one has to take into account not only micro-actors or micro-situations, but also a multiplicity of macro-actors and the complex games that they play through time. One has, for example, to take into account such *collective actors* as feminist movements fighting against patriarchal rules, organisations opposed or favouring the use of contraceptives as a means of birth control, anti-and pro-abortion pressure groups, governmental departments and their strategies to enhance or discourage high birth rates, groups of legislators attempting to increase or decrease inheritance taxes, societies for the protection of children against sexual abuse, political parties and their policies on a variety of issues such as family allowance, divorce and so forth. One also has to take into account *mega-actors*, that is, individuals who have the capacity to influence in a considerable manner 'public opinion' in marriage matters, such as media tycoons, persons who are able to set standards of conduct or whose opinions of marriage rules are widely respected, such as spiritual leaders, well-known writers and the like. All the above macro-actors (whether collective or mega-agents) have more access to the 'means of marriage construction/reproduction' than single husbands and wives as isolated couples. When one, for whatever reasons, neglects this vertical/hierarchical dimension of the problem, when one views exclusively 'single members' as the producers and transformers of macro-institutions, one ends up with a highly skewed, 'flat' vision of the social world. It is like trying to explain the construction and maintenance of a complex edifice by focusing exclusively on the bricklayers and ignoring the crucial contribution of planners, architects, engineers, supervisors, managers, maintenance technicians, financial and legal advisers and so on.[46] And as I have already pointed out, the neglect of macro-actors unavoidably leads to *reification* or *reductionism*. In the former case society is anthropomorphised while its 'needs' or reproductive requirements are illegitimately transformed into social causes. In the latter case, following the precepts of methodological individualism, the enormous complexity of macro-institutional spheres and the complex games that macro-actors play within them, are reduced to the attributes of the 'individual', of 'lay persons' or of inter-individual micro-situations.[47]

Marxism, by rejecting the highly misleading 'individual-society' schema, by pointing to the unequal access of agents to the means of production, and by emphasising the importance of collective actors (mainly classes and their organisations), provides conceptual tools which can lead the student away from both reificatory and reductive (in the methodological individualism sense) types of explanation. (Needless to say, as already mentioned, this does not mean that one does not find such explanations in Marxist theories.)[48]

In conclusion, looking at the overall positive aspects of the 'appropriation' notion, it seems to me that successful Marxist analyses of long-term historical transformation of whole societies portray two features which are often absent from non-Marxist approaches: (1) an attempt to view such transformations in an *integrated* fashion by focusing on both institutional (system integration) and strategic (social integration) aspects of social formations; (2) an attempt to deal with institutional structure and agency in a *balanced* manner by insisting that *macro*-institutional contradictions or incompatibilities must in the first instance be related to *macro*-agents and struggles.

(D)   As with the forces-of-production concept, however, the utility of the relations-of-production notion is seriously undermined by Marxism's in-built economistic features, by the fact that the fundamental insights it entails are restricted to the economic sphere. Marxism has no similar conceptual tools to help us examine in non-reductionist fashion the 'appropriation' dimension of the non-economic spheres. For instance, if one looks at the polity again, the idea that it should be possible to identify specific systemic contradictions and social struggles related to the appropriation and control not of the means of production but of the means of domination is alien to and incompatible with Marxism. As already mentioned, the theoretical gaps are plastered over by means of over-extending the relations-of-production concept, by using it to explain all social conflicts directly or 'in the last analysis', irrespective of whether these conflicts are based on political, ethnic, racial, sexual, or generational cleavages. Following this by now well known formula, Marxists either dismiss all non-economic struggles as epiphenomenal, as merely pale reflections of fundamental class struggles; or, whenever these non-economic struggles are too obviously autonomous or crucial for bringing about societal changes, they rebaptise them as class struggles by stretching the concept of class to refer to all types of interest groups.[49] This means that struggles over the control of non-economic technologies are either downgraded, or are completely ignored by means of definitional manipulations that conflate economic and non-economic institutional spheres.

The main point I wish to make here is that, in order to get out of the above theoretical impasse, and make the notion of *appropriation* more fruitful, it is not enough to proclaim the relative autonomy of the 'political' and the 'cultural'. New conceptual tools must be created that can help us study issues related to the control of non-economic technologies in a conceptually-autonomous and open-ended manner. To be more specific: if one wants to express the idea that there are political cleavages which, although indirectly related to economic cleavages, have a logic or a history of their own, one needs to show how these cleavages are independently constituted. So if on the level of the economy the idea of relations of production provides the means for theorising cleavages between exploiters and exploited, an analogous conceptual apparatus is needed for conceptualising political struggles between dominated and dominant groups.

(E) The above can be illustrated by discussing the relations-of-domination concept in greater detail. As I conceive it, this concept points to the manner in which politico-military technologies are controlled, that is to say to the institutionalised ways of regulating the *political* division of labour, the distribution of political power between dominant and dominated groups.

In the same way as relations of production constitute the basis for the formation of exploiting and exploited classes, so the prevailing relations of domination in a polity constitute the structural basis for the formation of politically dominant and dominated groups. In fact, the concept of relations of domination leads us to view the relationship between dominant and dominated groups as analogous to that of exploiting and exploited. In both cases the antagonism that is indicated by the respective concepts is over resources which are *not extraneous but intrinsic* to the relationships themselves. In the case of exploiters-exploited, the antagonism is over the amount of surplus labour that the owners/controllers of the means of production manage to extract from the non-owners; in the case of the dominating-dominated relationship, the antagonism is over the amount of political consent or compliance that the holders of the means of domination can extract from the non-holders.

In other words, both the concepts of relations of production and relations of domination lead away from a social-stratification type of approach, where social subjects are classified into a number of discrete taxonomic categories according to income or how much political power they enjoy. Both concepts focus on a *structural relationship* between subjects differentially situated *vis-à-vis* the control of technologies. Moreover, both concepts allow us to ask questions about the ways in which subjects react to their structural locations within the economic and political division of labour – questions such as to what extent those who occupy underprivileged positions are aware of their disadvantaged situation, in how far they try to organise and react to it collectively, and so on.

What this means is that, just as in class analysis one can distinguish class locations from class practices, so a similar distinction could usefully be made between 'objectively'-determined locations of domination/subordination and the actual practices of political subjects. In the one case we examine how political subjects are structurally situated *vis-à-vis* the means of domination; in the other we look at how political subjects attempt to maintain or change the dominant or subordinate positions within the political division of labour.

A point that cannot be stressed enough here is that the introduction of the location/practice distinction in both the economic and the political spheres leads away from the essentialism entailed in notions like 'real' and 'objective interests' or 'false consciousness'. For in order to understand how subjects conceive of what their economic or political interests are, it must be taken into account how political locations link with economic locations, and how political subjects relate to economic ones. If this is done, then the problem is no longer one of mechanistically deriving political practices from class positions; neither is it a question of explaining discrepancies between 'objective' class interests and class consciousness by the *deus ex machina* intervention of the 'political' or the 'ideological'.[50] Instead, it becomes a matter of examining in a non-essentialist and non-reductionist manner the separate constitution of subjects and their locations both in the economic and the political spheres. Once this is established, the degree of overlapping and, more generally, the complex inter-relationships between the economy and the polity can be assessed in a conceptually coherent and empirically open manner.

5.   IDEOLOGY

(A)   The Marxist notion of ideology has received extensive treat-ment and innumerable reformulations in the course of the past decades. I intend neither to put forward yet another interpretation of what Marx meant by the term, nor to review the voluminous literature on the subject. What I do propose instead is to point out that some useful methodological guidelines for research can be derived from the way both Marx and some of his followers have used the term in their analyses of specific historical situations.

One basic notion which, having been widely accepted, has become something of a platitude, is that those who own and control the means of production will tend to maintain and consolidate their privileged position by promoting or merely accepting discursive and non-discursive practices that:

(1)   give a distorted picture of how the means of production are owned/controlled;
(2)   provide reasons that justify and legitimise the prevailing control/ownership arrangements.[51]

Now both the *distorting* and *justifying* aspects of ideology lead to the more or less intentional concealment of contradictions related to the appropriation of the means of production. This concealment of contradictions, whether it takes the form of hiding structural in-equalities related to the appropriation of the means of production, or to neutralising antagonistic interests by presenting them as mere differences,[52] constitutes the most fundamental and useful dimension of the Marxist notion of ideology.

A second basic proposition related to the Marxist notion of ideology is that, given the dominant position of the owners of the means of production, their ideological views have a good chance of being accepted in one form or another by large sections of the population. This becomes obvious from the fact that certain ideological themes are so subtly all-pervasive that they have come to be part of everyday language, or even part and parcel of the way in which subjects constitute their identities and relate to each other.

To say this differently: the Marxist concept of ideology can be conceptualised not only as a system of abstract ideas, but also as a system of concrete, institutionalised practices entailed by social locations within production; or even, on the level of the personality, as a set of 'socialising' processes that either make the subject more pliable, or more willing to accept the status quo. On these levels it is not only the exploited, but even the exploiting classes that may be unaware of the distorting, justificatory functions of ideologically infused social practices.

Finally, a third characteristic of the ideology concept is that in certain conditions (for instance, when contradictions between forces and relations of production keep growing) the underprivileged may escape from the grip of the dominant ideology and develop counter-ideologies or utopias which, by projecting what the future 'ought to be', challenge the status quo and undermine the 'obvious rightness' of the dominant classes' ideological themes.

In the work of Marx and that of subsequent Marxists (particularly Lukacs and Gramsci) the concept of ideology has, of course, also been used in a much broader sense. Instead of focusing on the notion of concealment or legitimation of the relations of production, it refers to the broader world view or *Weltanschauung* of the dominant or dominated classes, or even more generally to processes positively constituting group identities or human subjectivities.[53] In my own view, and notwithstanding the methodological difficulties entailed in the concealment/legitimation definition of ideology, I consider it the more useful of the two – particularly in cases needing specificity and analytical acuity. If used more flexibly, it could assist with asking systematic questions about the crucial discrepancy between how technologies are controlled in actual fact, and how these controls are viewed by social subjects.

The *demythologising* function of the Marxist concept of ideology becomes even more obvious from the fact that its construction prevents the student from dealing with belief systems in a neutral, free-floating manner. When the Marxist concept of 'dominant ideology' is compared with, for instance, its Parsonian equivalent of society's 'core values', both formulations are seen to share the plausible idea that societal cohesion is, at least partly, based on certain norms and beliefs that are held in common by a large number of social subjects. However, the two formulations differ in how they link or do not link those common norms and values with concrete agents.

In the Marxist paradigm, the concept of ideology is constructed in such a way that we absolutely have to ask *who* questions, that we have to link norms and values to concrete interest groups. In so far as certain values are widely accepted in society, the Marxist paradigm encourages one to ask questions concerning the relations between collective agents and the constitution, reproduction, and transformation of such values: who is behind the dominant belief systems?; who contributed and how to their dominance?; whose interests do they tend to serve?

This type of question is not possible in Parsonian functionalism, where values and norms are conceptualised in a 'disembodied' manner. In fact, as already mentioned, as Parsons shifts his analysis from the *cultural* to the *social* systems, core values become institutionalised into 'role expectations'; and when his analysis moves on from the social to the *personality* system, values are internalised and become the actors' 'need dispositions'. In all this elaborate schematisation, the connection of values with collective agencies capable of having an overall transformative impact on society is never explored. It is not therefore suprising that, in true Durkheimian fashion,[54] Parsons' core-value system resembles a reified, mysterious entity pulling all the strings behind the social actors' backs.

(B)   Again, as in the case of the concepts of forces and relations of production, the heuristic utility of the Marxist concept of ideology is seriously diminished by the base/superstructure distinction. The typical mapping out of the whole social formation in terms of the economic, political, and ideological instances – and the relegation of the two last into the superstructural sphere – means that the 'ideological' becomes a residual category, a blanket term for denoting all non-economic and non-political institutions. So religion, art, education, kinship are all indiscriminately conceptualised as institutional spheres, the main function of which is the generation of a variety of mystificatory, justificatory practices for the purpose of reproducing the prevailing relations of production.[55]

Within this simplistic view, the possibility that educational or religious institutions, for example, may have a logic and historical dynamic of their own is hardly acknowledged, and even if it were, there are no conceptual tools capable of taking their specificity seriously into account. As with the conceptualisation of the state, therefore, the only kind of framework that Marxism provides for the study of the various 'ideological' institutional spheres is one that shows their contribution to the reproduction of the economy. Marxism has no tools for asking questions about the internal constitutions of such spheres, about their internal contradictions and struggles leading to developments that may or may not be directly related to the reproduction of the dominant mode of production.

The above drawbacks of the Marxist concept of ideology can be effectively overcome if one refuses to locate the 'ideological' within a dichotomy of material base versus superstructure, if ideology is seen as a crucial dimension of *every* major institutional sphere. As a matter of fact, in so far as all institutional spheres are partly constructed and reproduced by technologies, and insofar as such technologies are controlled by privileged groups, conditions will be such as to favour the emergence of mystificatory, justificatory practices. At the same time, counter-ideologies will tend to emerge through which, more or less deliberately, underprivileged groups will try to change the prevailing status quo.

In the above formulation, the concept of ideology becomes both broader and narrower. It is broader because ideologies are seen to exist not only in the non-political regions of the superstructure, but in all major institutional spheres, including the economic and political ones.[56] It becomes narrower because, by emphasising that each institutional sphere has its technological, appropriative, and ideological dimensions, it avoids the crude reduction of such complex institutions as those of religion or education to 'mere ideologies' with the reproduction of the dominant mode of production as their major *raison d'être*. Of course, such a reformulation of the ideology concept does nothing to deny the possibility that educational or religious institutions could operate in such a way as to contribute to the reproduction of the prevailing relations of production. What it does do is to stress that:

– *first*, education or religion not only are not 'mere ideologies', but have their own internal dominant ideologies that aim to legitimate the ways in which religious and educational technologies are controlled;

– *second*, that the complex and various ways in which religious and/or educational ideologies are linked with economic ones should be a problem open to empirical investigation;

– *third*, that once specific tools have been created for the study of the internal constitution, reproduction, and transformation of the educational or religious spheres, then these spheres will cease to appear (as far as their internal organisation is concerned) as mere epiphenomena. They can instead be seen as complex, internally articulated institutional ensembles that are amenable to the same kind of structural analysis as economic institutions.

There is a basic objection that could be raised to the above rather obvious, but in my opinion heuristically useful, conceptualisation of ideology. In so far as ideological practices and themes (whether in the economic, political, or cultural spheres) present among other things a distorted picture of the way technologies are controlled, one ends up again with a distinction between 'reality' and 'ideas' that is not so very far removed from historic materialism's material/ideal dichotomy. It might be argued that ideologies are as real as the appropriation and control mechanisms they are trying to depict and legitimate; or conversely, that relations of appropriation, like everything else social, have a symbolic dimension, that they too entail 'ideas', subjects' definition of the situation, and so on.

I believe that this difficulty can be solved by taking into account that although ideologies, as well as the 'social reality' they depict or justify have a symbolic, ideational dimension, this is no reason for not distinguishing between *first-* and *second-order* symbolic levels: a taken-for-granted, socially constructed 'reality' (appropriative arrangements) from a socially constructed discourse about such arrangements.[57] Any analysis that tends to conflate the two levels (by arguing, for instance, that everything social is ideological) transforms the concept of ideology into a blanket term, and by doing so destroys its utility as a demystifying device.

There is a second objection to the concept of ideology. It argues that the emphasis on concealment entails a sharp and objectionable distinction between ideological/'false' and non-ideological/'true' or scientific discourses.[58] This objection implies, of course, complex philosophical questions about what is true and what is not, and the nature of social knowledge. These are not questions to be examined here. The only point – even if it is not altogether persuasive – that I would like to stress is that second-order conceptualisations may be wrong about first-order conceptualisations; the former are, therefore, corrigible. Moreover, it is worth stressing in this context that the social sciences can maintain their critical function only if they operate on the assumption that there are false beliefs in society; and that, with the help of adequate theorising and proper handling of the empirical evidence, it is possible to distinguish between more and less false discourses. From this perspective I would fully agree that

> The main role of the social sciences in respect of the critique of common sense is the assessment of reasons as good reasons in terms of knowledge either simply unavailable to lay agents or construed by them in a fashion different from that formulated in the meta-languages of social theory.[59]

6.   THE MODE-OF-DOMINATION CONCEPT

(A)   The above, necessarily sketchy discussion of the technological, appropriative and ideological dimensions of social orders suggests the possibility of constructing a conceptual framework that would assist in the systematic and theoretically congruent study of the polity's internal organisation as well as its relationships with other institutional spheres.

As will be obvious from the previous section, there is no reason why one should not formulate a *mode of domination* concept to help with the systematic study of the relationships between political technologies, the manner of their appropriation and control, and the way in which such controls are legitimated.

To start with, a mode of domination may be taken to refer to a specific type of production: that of political power. Just as the production of economic goods can be differentiated according to the types of technology used and the manner of appropriation and control, so the production of political power (as a resource) can be differentiated in terms of the political technologies used and the manner of their control. This being so, a mode of domination can be examined in ways quite similar to those applied to the examination of a mode of production. For example, one can study the genealogy of a mode of domination (by tracing the particular history of its basic institutional features), its basic structural tendencies, its conditions of existence, its systemic contradictions, and the kind of political struggles and ideologies that are possible on the basis of such contradictions.

It should be emphasised here that in proposing the construction of a mode-of-domination concept the aim is not a complete isomorphism between the economic and the political spheres. I do not think, for example, that one should try to elaborate on the political level a theory equivalent to the labour theory of value on the level of Marxist economics – quite aside from the fact that Marx's theory of value seems to me neither useful nor tenable.[60] Nor do I think that one should try to establish strict, deterministic relations between political technologies, relations of domination, and political ideologies. As I reject both the substantive and the methodological implications of historic materialism, I consider attempts at establishing the 'primacy' of one of the three dimensions on the level of politics as useless and sterile as are similar attempts at establishing in universalistic manner the primacy of the forces or relations of production within a mode of production or within a social formation as a whole. The same holds true, of course, for the relationship between mode of production and mode of domination.

If I propose a mode-of-domination concept, this is not intended as a *substantive* theory that can provide universal truths on the quintessence of the political or its 'true' relationships with the economy or culture. Instead, the aim is to provide a *conceptual framework* which, rather than offering ready-made universal solutions to the enigmas of social life, allows interesting questions and suggests useful ways for exploring, in theoretically consistent and empirically open-ended manner, the relationships between the technological, the appropriative and the ideological within the polity, as well as the complex relationships between the polity and other institutional orders.

It is in this light that I would like to make a few brief points about the heuristic utility of the mode-of-domination concept. Thereafter I shall move on to show more concretely how the application of the concepts proposed here can help us overcome some of the impasses into which Marxist historiography leads us in the analysis of specific historical developments.

Now I believe that the major advantage of the mode-of-domination concept is that, as with that of the mode of production, it allows the examination of the polity both from a *social integration* point of view, that is, as a configuration of collective actors struggling over the control of the means of domination; *and* from a *system-integration* perspective, that is, as a system of institutions that contribute to the constitution of such struggles.

(B)   Looking at the configuration-of-actors approach, a first step is to focus on the strategies and tactics of dominant and dominated groups, the former trying to consolidate their hold over the means of domination, and the latter attempting to shift the balance of political power in their favour, thus changing the prevailing relations of domination. Of course, a social-integration approach is not concerned only with how the major *political* actors relate to each other. Given the polity's representational functions (which are real enough both in parliamentary and non-parliamentary regimes), it is also concerned with the complex ways in which political actors *represent or fail to represent* the interests of actors in other institutional spheres (economic, cultural, and so on). One of the chief issues that such an approach can raise is the extent to which politically or militarily powerful groups are strong enough to *primarily* pursue their own interests rather than those of economically and culturally dominant groups. It will finally have to be fully acknowledged that there are cases where political developments do not merely reflect class struggles but, on the contrary, political struggles shape and constitute in fundamental ways class and other interests in civil society. Without something like the mode-of-domination concept, Marxism is unable to deal with such cases seriously.[61]

(C) The issues of representation/non-representation are not confined to the social-integration or the action level of analysis; they can and must also be studied from a *system-integration*, institutional angle. For instance, the degree of preponderance of politico-military agents over economic or cultural ones may be due to specific conjunctural conditions, or it may be the result of slowly changing institutional structures that systematically enhance the position of one social group over another.[62]

As I have already pointed out, once the focus shifts to the system-integration level, issues of strategic conduct are bracketed, the analysis focusing primarily on institutional structures, their reproductive requirements/conditions of existence, the systemic incompatibilities/contradictions between institutional ensembles and the like. From this systemic point of view we may consider contradictions or incompatibilities between the polity and the economy as institutional wholes, or we may focus on contradictions within the polity proper.

As far as the former are concerned, the mode of domination framework can help us to avoid the Marxist structuralist view of the State as performing the functions of capitalist reproduction.[63] This reductive view of the state encourages the student either to ignore the obvious fact that the State has reproductive requirements of its own or leads him/her to the view that the needs or reproductive requirements of the capitalist economy are paramount – in the sense that whenever there are systematic incompatibilities between the economy's and the polity's reproductive requirements, the former invariably prevails over the latter. The construction of a mode of domination concept, on the other hand, effectively challenges this reductive view of the state. It shows that it is inadmissibly naive to consider *a priori* that the only or even major function of the State is the fulfillment of the economy's needs or the overall co-ordination of the social formation (as the precondition for expanded economic production).[64] The political system has other major functions and conditions of existence, such as, for instance, the maintenance of its own institutional structures, and particularly the maintenance and enhancement of the prevailing relations of domination. This presupposes policies for strengthening the power position of politically and militarily dominant groups, not only *vis-à-vis* internal opponents, but also *vis-à-vis* oppositional actors on an inter-societal or international level.[65] This being the case, obviously the requirements for preserving the prevailing relations of domination, or enhancing the ruling group's position in the international politico-military arena, may well be more or less incompatible with the polity's 'economic' and 'co-ordination' functions. In cases especially where civil society is weak, as I will try to show in the next chapter, the requirements of preserving the politico-military status quo may easily prevail over the need for the expanded reproduction of capitalism.

Finally the mode of domination concept can help the student to study functional incompatibilities or systemic contradictions not only between the economy and polity as a whole but also within the polity. It provides him or her with the conceptual tools for raising questions about the possibility of systemic contradictions which are specific to the polity proper, contradictions which – even when related to economic developments – are not mere reflections of the latter.

It must be stressed once more at this point that when one speaks about *incompatibilities* between the reproductive requirements of the economy and the polity from a system-integration point of view, or about functional incompatibilities within the polity proper, this always implies *contradictions between institutions* rather than *conflict between actors*. Although institutional incompatibilities/contradictions and group struggles are interrelated, they must be kept analytically distinct, since the one does not automatically beget the other: there may well be institutional incompatibilities that do not lead to the emergence of struggles on the social-integration level of analysis. In cases, for example, where the politically dominant groups are able, through a mixture of ideological and coercive means, to prevent the organisation of politically underprivileged quasi-groups,[66] the growing institutional, systemic contradictions may not be accompanied by a concomitant development of organised opposition to the political status quo. All that the concept of institutional incompatibilities implies, therefore, is that the basic organising principles underlying a set of institutionalised practices are incongruent with the organising principles of a different set of institutional practices.[67] Whether or not the actors involved in this contradictory situation are going to become aware of the incongruity, and whether or not such awareness will lead to collective organisation and action, remains an open question.

If what has been said above is accepted, then with the help of the mode-of-domination concept the problem of the degree of compatibility can be investigated, not only between the economic and the political institutional orders, but also between the forces and relations of domination within the polity. In a manner very similar to that of mode-of-production analysis it can be argued, for instance, that the rapid development of political technologies may lead to growing institutional contradictions within the polity between the forces and relations of domination – and that these institutional incompatibilities in turn are relevant for understanding the type and dynamic of the political ideologies and struggles on the social-integration level of analysis. In normal circumstances, institutional incompatibilities or contradictions generate favourable conditions for the development of anti-status quo ideologies and struggles. The reason for this is that the more such political contradictions grow, the more will the ruling groups find it difficult to keep their hegemonic position intact and to impose their ideological views of the political order on the mass of the ruled. This means that the greater the political contradictions, the better the chances of politically underprivileged groups escaping from the grip of the dominant political ideologies and developing counter-ideologies aimed at the radical transformation of the existing relations of domination.

The mode of domination concept, as schematically delineated above, can help us to eliminate a set of pseudo-dilemmas which are very prevalent not only in Marxist but also in non-Marxist historians and social theorists. This is the notion that if one rejects 'materialist' interpretations of history (that is, interpretations which put the primary emphasis on the development of the forces or relations of production), one is forced to resort either to empiricism (that is, to a mere description of historical events) or to idealism (that is, to an emphasis on 'ideas' as the main driving force of all historical developments).

Since I have dealt with the 'economism versus empiricism' dilemma in previous chapters, I will here try to demonstrate the utility of the mode of domination concept as an effective means of showing the misleading character of the 'materialism versus idealism' dilemma. Consider, for instance, a sophisticated analyst of Marxism like John Roemer. In a recent publication he refers to two major interpretations of Marx's historical materialism: the one, developed by G. Cohen, puts the emphasis on the relatively autonomous dynamic of the forces of production as the motor force of history; whereas the other, developed by R. Brenner in his analysis of the European transition from feudalism to capitalism, considers the relations of production and the related class struggles as the fundamental mechanisms of social transformation. According to Roemer:

> In Cohen's account of historical materialism, a new form of property relations emerges, because it can fit with changes in the productive forces. In Brenner's account, the success of a revolutionary transformation is determined by the power and organisation of the various classes. In these senses both of the variants discussed here offer materialist, as opposed to 'idealist' explanations of revolutionary change. A materialist explanation is one in which the motive forces are competition, scarcity, supply and demand; an idealist one emphasises the role of ideas, usually of certain 'great men', which are taken to be the exogenous driving element . . . Although very few social scientists and historians today would endorse in a wholehearted way either of the two Marxist accounts given here of the evolution of property relations, it is probably the influence of historical materialism that accounts for the almost completely materialist approach to these questions now taken by social scientists and historians . . . Indeed it is questionable what it means to take a specifically Marxist approach to history when the materialist axiom, the cornerstone of the Marxist approach, has become central to almost all contemporary social thought.[68]

Roemer is partly[69] right to argue that a form of materialism has become central to macro-historical analyses of historians and social scientists who are not or do not call themselves Marxist. But neither the 'obviousness' of the materialist approach nor its widespread application is a guarantee of its universal validity or utility. This becomes very clear when one takes seriously into account that when one refuses – in specific historical contexts – to consider the growth of economic technologies or the development of class struggles as the primary forces of historical transformation, one does not have to resort to 'mere ideas' or to a 'great men' account of history. Between the material base and 'mere ideas' there are vast areas of institutionalised life that the materialist-idealist straitjacket makes it impossible to address. The mode of domination concept can be useful not only in dispensing with such 'disembodied' categories as 'ideas', but also in reminding the historian or social scientist that there are political technologies, relations of domination and political ideologies which can be as central or even more central to the explanation of macro-historical transformations than the forces and relations of production. And the same, of course, holds true for cultural technologies, and their mode of appropriation and legitimation. Even more crucially, the concepts of political and cultural modes of social construction can shift the focus of attention from the vacuous problem of the material base's universal primacy to the empirical problem of the causal or functional importance of each mode of social construction in specific types of social formations or in specific types of societal transformations.

7. CONCLUSION

I have argued in this chapter that technologies, their mode of appropriation and control, and the way in which such controls are depicted and legitimated on the ideological level should not be viewed in terms of the base/superstructure dichotomy that tends to locate the first two dimensions in the material, economic base, and the third in the non-material superstructure. Instead, the *technological*, the *appropriative*, and *the ideological should be considered as constitutive elements of all major institutional spheres*. So in highly differentiated societies, and whether one looks at their economic, political, religious or educational spheres, one can always identify:

(1) technological means (means of social construction) through which men and women more or less unintentionally construct, reproduce, and transform their social existence;

(2) patterned ways in which these means of social construction are appropriated/controlled;
(3) a set of dominant ideological themes and practices that both justify and usually give a distorted picture of the ways in which the technologies are controlled.

Any attempt to split up or compartmentalise these three dimensions by locating technological means and their mode of appropriation exclusively within the economy, not only gives a highly distorted and impoverished view of all non-economic institutions; it also makes impossible a theoretically coherent and empirically open-ended investigation of the complex relationships between economic and non-economic institutional orders.

As I have kept emphasising in this chapter, this reformulation of the notions of technology, appropriation and ideology does not aim at providing yet another version of the primacy of the material base, a thesis broadened here to include not only economic but also political, military, and cultural technologies. I have, in fact, rather neglected the (in my view less interesting) question of whether or not a certain dimension (the technological, the appropriative, the ideological) is in a transhistorical, universal sense more important than other dimensions of social existence. Instead, I have focused on the *heuristic utility* of these three dimensions, my argument being that, once they are no longer viewed in the material-base/superstructure straitjacket but as fundamental dimensions of every major institutional sphere, they can provide useful guidelines for those interested in the constitution, reproduction, and transformation of large-scale, differentiated societies. For, as I have argued, the technological dimension leads to an anti-reificatory, constructionist view of institutional orders; the appropriation dimension provides an effective bridge or synthesis between a systemic/functionalist and an agency/causal view of these orders; whereas the ideological dimension enhances the demystifying potential or social analysis.

Finally, analysis of technology-appropriation-ideology as whole configurations identifiable in all major institutional spheres leads to the ideas of modes of non-economic production (mode of domination, mode of cultural production, and so on). Constructing on the level of the non-economic institutional spheres concepts analogous to the mode-of-production concept makes it possible to go beyond the reductionist base/superstructure dichotomy, while putting forward propositions for an alternative post-Marxist conceptual framework.

This framework is holistic – in the sense that it provides isomorphic concepts that allow us to study the economy, polity, and culture in non-compartmentalised fashion – without resorting to economism or to an agency/institutional-system imbalance. In other words, the proposed framework suggests the possibility of a non-reductive mapping of a whole social formation, while retaining some of Marxism's fundamental insights, particularly its potential for a balanced agency-institutional system approach.[70]

I am, of course, aware of the many limitations of the conceptual framework presented in this chapter. Not only have I limited my analysis to the relationships between the economy and the polity (only making scant references to culture), but even within this restricted space, more attention has been given to the three dimensions of technology, appropriation, ideology rather than to their interrelationships or to the overall relations between modes of production and modes of domination. One reason for the latter imbalance has to do with my often repeated belief that the task of sociological theory is not to provide universal substantive generalisations – like, for instance, the establishment of the general dominance of one of the three dimensions or of one of the modes of social construction over the others (any such attempts invariably lead to substantive generalisations which are either wrong or trivial). I rather see the task of sociological theory as entailing the tentative construction of conceptual tools facilitating empirical research either by solving methodologically crippling puzzles, or by suggesting fruitful ways of looking at and raising questions about the social world.

From this perspective I have tried to follow a concept-building strategy which is more Mertonian[71] than Parsonian – in the sense that my aim was not to provide a highly detailed, fully worked out conceptual map meant to be useful for the study of all social systems in all their structural and evolutionary complexities. My task was rather to provide, in as tentative and as *parsimonious* a fashion as possible, a set of interrelated concepts specifically geared to tackle the problem of economic reductionism in Marxism and the unsatisfactory manner in which it deals with the analysis of long-term transformations of capitalist societies[72] – particularly late-industrialising ones.

Therefore the way to assess the conceptualisations elaborated in this chapter is primarily to see to what extent they manage to deal in a more satisfactory and fruitful manner with the above-mentioned problems. This is precisely what I am trying to do in the next chapter, where I show how the application of the mode of domination concept may help to overcome some of the difficulties that Marxism encounters in the analysis of political developments in a concrete historical context.

NOTES

1. For some Marxists though, Marx makes a distinction between the material and the economic sphere; see for instance G. A. Cohen, *Karl Marx's Theory of History: A Defense*, Oxford: Clarendon Press, 1978, pp. 26–37. My general argument holds, however, whether one makes the distinction or not.

2. For works pointing out the problematic nature of the passage from social being/consciousness to the base/superstructure dichotomy, see K. Kosik, *Dialectics of the Concrete*, Boston: Reidel, 1976, pp. 141 ff; J. Larrain, *The Concept of Ideology*, London: Hutchinson, 1979, pp. 63 ff.

3. A less problematic but more awkward way of expressing this distinction would be: discursive and non-discursive practices related to economic production and 'second-order' conceptualisations or theories about such practices. For a more detailed discussion of this point see below Section 5B.

4. A classical example of this type of literature is R. Michels, *Political Parties*, New York: Collins, 1962.

5. Weber, in discussing the nature of Church organisation in the age of capitalism and democracy, writes:

    > Hierocracy has no choice but to establish a party organisation and to use demagogic means, just like all other parties. This necessity reinforces the bureaucratic tendencies, since the hierocratic apparatus must be equal to the task of a party bureaucracy ... The means employed are similar to those of the other mass parties – apart from the highly devotional means that were created by the Counter-Reformation for the purpose of mass agitation.

    From *Economy and Society*, ed. G. Roth and C. Wittich, Berkeley Cal.: University of California Press, 1978, Vol. II, p. 1195.

6. Weber refers frequently to the struggles that led to the concentration of the means of indoctrination at the top:

    > In the Church the most important outcome [of the Vatican Council] of 1870 was not the much-discussed dogma of infallibility, but the universal episcopate (of the Pope) which created the ecclesiastic bureaucracy (*Kaplanokratie*), and turned the bishop and the parish priest, in contrast to the Middle Ages, into mere officials of the central power, the Roman Curia.

    Economy and Society, op. cit., Vol. II, p. 1393.

7. For the adoption of the latter solution in Marx's late work see A. Giddens, *A Contemporary Critique of Historic Materialism*, Vol. I, London: Macmillan, 1981.

8. See on this point L. Althusser and E. Balibar, *Reading Capital*, London: New Left Books, 1970, pp. 216 ff.

9. An obvious exception to this is Althusser's anti-economistic attempt to conceptualise not only economic but also political, ideological, and theoretical practices as distinct productive activities entailing specific raw material, technologies or 'means' and end products. (See L. Althusser, *For Marx*, London: Penguin, 1965, p. 253.) However his attempt to save historic materialism by introducing the 'determination in the last instance' clause and his more general structural determinism, which unavoidably leads to teleological explanations, prevented him from developing further and using these concepts in a constructive manner.

10. See on this point A. Giddens, *A Contemporary Critique of Historical Materialism*, op. cit.

11. See on this point N. Mouzelis, *Politics in the Semi-Periphery: Early Parliamentarism and Late Industrialisation in the Balkans and Latin America*, London: Macmillan, 1986, Chapter 4.

12. See M. Foucault, *Power/Knowledge*, ed. Colin Gordon, Brighton: Harvester Press, 1980; and his *Discipline and Punish: The Birth of the Prison*, London: Penguin, 1977.

13. See M. Weber, *Economy and Society*, op. cit., Vol. II, pp. 956 ff.

14. See G. A. Cohen, *Karl Marx's Theory of History: A Defense*, op. cit., pp. 28–62.

15. I say 'limited neutrality' because, as has frequently been stressed in the relevant literature, technology is never totally neutral, given that certain material technologies imply or favour types of work organisation that may enhance or hinder workers' autonomy or job satisfaction.

16. For such a broader definition of technology see M. Stanley *The Technological Conscience*, New York and London: The Free Press, 1978.

17. See for instance R. Blauner, *Alienation, Freedom and Technology*, Chicago: Chicago University Press, 1964.

18. W. H. McNeil, *The Pursuit of Power: Technology, Armed Force and Society since A.D. 1000*, Chicago: University of Chicago Press, 1982, pp. 125–35. Quoted in R. Collins, *Weberian Sociological Theory*, London: Cambridge University Press, 1986, p. 91.

19. This does not mean, of course, that there are no differences between economic and political technologies. If technology is broadly defined as entailing material tools, know-how, and compatible work arrangements, then as a rule the material-tools component plays a more important role in economic than in political technologies. For more information on these three dimensions of technology see D. Mackenzie and J. Wajeman (eds), *The Social Shaping of Technology*, Milton Keynes: Open University Publications, 1985.

20. Contrary to the claims of orthodox Marxism about the 'uninterrupted'

development of production across time and space, the advance of the forces of both production and domination can indeed be stopped or reversed. This becomes clear when one looks at societies not in terms of *general evolution*, but in terms of their own, specific trajectory. For the concepts of general and specific evolution see M. D. Sahlins and E. R. Service (eds), *Evolution and Culture*, Ann Arbor, Michigan: University of Michigan Press, 1960.

According to Ellen Meiksins Wood, Marx (contrary to many of his disciples) was quite aware that it was rather in capitalist than pre-capitalist societies that the forces of production, through the process of competition, were developing in an uninterrupted, cumulative manner. See her 'Marxism and the Course of History', *New Left Review*, No. 147.

21. M. Foucault, *Discipline and Punish*, op. cit., p. 210.
22. See on this point H. L. Dreyfus and P. Rabinow, *Michel Foucault: Beyond Structuralism and Hermeneutics*, Brighton: Harvester Press, 1982, pp. 132 ff.
23. Quoted in J. Habermas, *The Theory of Communicative Action*, Cambridge: Polity Press, 1987, Vol. II, p. 169.
24. According to Jacques Ellul, both traditional and modern techniques imply a drastic curtailment of individual initiative – which is why techniques, while not necessarily entailing it, make mechanisation possible. For Ellul, modern techniques have not only replaced traditional ones in the industrial societies, but have also achieved a high degree of 'autonomisation', in the sense that considerations of efficiency have displaced all other values. This means that technical rationalisation has acquired an internal logic and dynamic that is virtually unstoppable. See J. Ellul, *The Technological Society*, New York: Vintage Books, 1963
     The marked tendency towards 'technicisation' of the modern world is also stressed by J. Habermas. He views both material and social technologies as the institutional embodiment of instrumental rationality, the latter spreading in all institutional spheres and thus displacing moral-practical and aesthetico-practical rationalities. For a discussion of the three rationalities, see J. Habermass, *The Theory of Communicative Action*, op. cit., Vol. I, pp. 238 ff.
25. For a definition of the two terms see M. Weber, *Economy and Society*, op. cit., Vol. I, pp. 85–96.
26. M. Weber, *Economy and Society*, op. cit., p. 1394.
27. For a distinction between the economic and the technological, see M. Weber, *Economy and Society*, op. cit., pp. 65 ff.
28. See D. Binns, *Beyond the Sociology of Conflict*, London: Macmillan, 1977, chs. 1 and 3.
29. Given this nominalism, it is not surprising that adherents of the social-stratification approach have difficulty in deciding into how many categories to divide a given population. Since no single member's market position is exactly identical with that of another, it is possible in principle to identify an indefinite number of gradations, leading to an indefinite number of social categories.

30. See on this point J. M. Barbalet, 'Principles of Stratification in Max Weber', *British Journal of Sociology*, Vol. 31, No. 3, 1980.

31. For a review and critical analysis of closure theories see R. Murphy, 'The Structure of Closure: A Critique and development of the theories of Weber, Collins, Parkin', *British Journal of Sociology*, December 1984, and his *Social Closure: The Theory of Monopolisation and Exclusion*, Oxford: Clarendon Press, 1988.

32. In ideal typical terms, a fully successful strategy of collectivist exclusion would lead to a *communal* rather than class type of conflict; whereas at the other extreme, a fully successful strategy of individualistic exclusion would give rise to *status* groups rather than classes. Social classes, which for Parkin are situated between status and communal groups, are collectivities with a mode of closure that is based on a mixture of individualistic and collectivistic rules of exclusion. See F. Parkin, *Marxism and Class Theory*, London: Tavistock, 1979, and his earlier work, *Class Inequality and Political Order*, London: Paladin, 1972.

33. See Parkin, *Marxism and Class Theory*, op. cit., pp. 89 ff.

34. Ibid., pp. 3–5, 11–27, 102–115.

35. See R. Murphy, 'The Structure of Closure', op. cit.

36. For a systematic critique of conflict theories, see D. Binns, *Beyond the Sociology of Conflict*, op. cit.
    On the positive side, it can be said that closure and conflict theories overcome the nominalist, static analysis of social-stratification studies, seeing that they refuse to view classes or other interest groups as mere aggregates of individual actors who simply have some social trait in common. Instead, they see them as collective agencies which, in certain conditions, have the capacity to act, to take tactical and strategic decisions in the pursuit of their often antagonistic goals. Moreover, closure and conflict theories do not suffer from the self-imposed, crippling limitations of all those phenomenologically oriented approaches that consider it an illegitimate reification to ascribe goals and decision-making capacities to collectivities. This freedom is precisely why closure and conflict theories are able to move from the micro, intersubjective worlds of the phenomenologists to a macro-level of analysis and can ask questions concerning the overall transformation of societies. From this point of view, the conceptual framework they offer is *holistic* – albeit holistic in a way that stresses strategic conduct at the expense of systemic/institutional analysis. In that respect they are the mirror image of a third major strand in non-Marxist sociology, where the holistic framework leads to the other unacceptable extreme, that of emphasising systemic requirements and institutional incompatibilities to the detriment of collective action. I am thinking here of course of Parsonian functionalism, a paradigm whose major differences with Marxism have already been discussed in chapter 2.

37. See above, chapter 2, section 1.

38. See T. Parsons, *Societies: Evolutionary and Comparative Perspectives*, Englewood Cliffs, N.J.: Prentice Hall, 1966, pp. 11–14.

39. For the distinction between class locations (or places) and class
     practices, see N. Poulantzas, *Les Classes Sociales dans Le Capitalisme
     d'Aujourd'hui*, Paris: Seuil, 1974, pp. 10 ff. For Poulantzas, class
     locations are the 'objective' positions of agents in the technical and
     social division of labour; whereas class practices refer to such things as
     the political organisations or agencies representing a class, and the
     strategies or policies the latter formulate in a concrete conjuncture.
     However, in Poulantzas' work as in that of Althusser, the balance
     between agency and institutional structures is broken, in the sense that
     he shows only how institutional structures shape agents' practices; he
     never attempts to show how practices have an impact on institutional
     structures. See below, Appendix I.

40. For instance, in Anthony Giddens' work the rejection of functionalism
     entails nothing more than the rejection of those teleological misuses of
     the functionalist paradigm that Robert K. Merton criticised so bril-
     liantly several decades ago. Giddens has chosen not to use the
     functionalist terminology any longer. The way in which he attempts to
     overcome some of the more obvious shortcomings of the strictly
     hermeneutic tradition in sociology (by emphasis, for instance, on the
     importance of examining social phenomena not merely in terms of
     agency but also in terms of an institutional analysis, which brackets
     considerations of strategic conduct), unavoidably leads him to re-
     introduce functionalism by the back door. See F. Dallmayr's critique
     of Giddens' structuration theory in A. Giddens, *Profiles and critiques
     in social theory*, London: Macmillan, 1982
     A similar point can be made concerning all those Marxist or post-
     Marxist writers who increasingly speak, for example, about the
     conditions of existence of the capitalist system, rather than of its
     reproductive or functional requirements. This practice simply avoids a
     now unfashionable vocabulary, but adds nothing to the analysis. In so
     far as one accepts a non-teleological version of functionalism (and
     most theoretically informed functionalists do), conditions of existence,
     functional requirements, or reproductive requirements are inter-
     changeable terms. Marxist-influenced writers ignoring this, merely
     present as great innovations theoretical points which, expressed in a
     somewhat different vocabulary, have already been made by non-
     Marxist functionalist sociologists.

41. Since I discuss ultra-structuralist and ultra-voluntaristic theories in
     Appendix I (see Sections 1 and 2), I will here make some comments on
     analytic Marxism's reductive tendencies.
         Analytic or rational-choice Marxism tries to apply tools drawn from
     analytic philosophy and from game theory in an attempt to re-examine
     some fundamental theoretical and substantive issues of the Marxist
     discourse. Up to a certain extent, it has contributed considerably to
     the solution of the above problems by clarifying and demystifiying a
     variety of concepts and theories exclusively operating at the macro-
     level of analysis. By attempting to provide the 'micro-foundations' of
     macro theories – that is, by trying to show what macro-institutional
     structures and class struggles mean in terms of the concrete behaviour

of decision-makers engaged in maximising or optimising activities or games, it has shed considerable light on a variety of issues which are central to Marxism (see, for instance, J. E. Roemer, *Free to Lose*, Cambridge, Mass.: Harvard University Press, 1988; M. Taylor (ed.), *Rationality and Revolution*, Cambridge: Cambridge University Press, 1988; and A. Przeworski, *Capitalism and Social Democracy*, Cambridge: Cambridge University Press, 1985). It has also illuminated aspects of Marx's work which were previously obscure or misunderstood, its clear and lucid analyses providing a salutary antidote to the obfuscating and reifying style of Althusserian Marxism. (See, for instance, Jon Elster, *Making Sense of Marx*, Cambridge: Cambridge University Press, 1985.) However, its exclusive focus on rational choice often leads analytic Marxism either to a neglect of the institutional context within which actors play their rational games, or to the reduction of macro-institutional structures and actors into a mere *aggregate* of micro-actors or micro-games.

For a development of this last point see N. Mouzelis, *Back to Sociological Theory*, op. cit., ch. 5. For a discussion of some other limitations of rational choice theory see J. Elster (ed.), *Rational Choice*, Oxford: Blackwell, 1986, Introduction.

42. See, for instance, B. Moore, *The Social Origins of Dictatorship and Democracy*, London: Penguin, 1967; P. Anderson, *Lineages of the Absolutist State*, London: New Left Books, 1974, and his *Arguments within English Marxism*, London: New Left Books, 1980; E. J. Hobsbawm, *The Age of Revolution 1789–1848*, London: Weidenfeld & Nicolson, 1962, and his *The Age of Capital 1848–1875*, London: Weidenfeld & Nicolson, 1975; E. Wallerstein, *The Modern World System: Capitalist Agriculture and the Origins of the European World-Economy in the Sixteenth Century*, New York and London: Academic Press, 1974.

43. See on this point J. M. Barbalet, 'Social closure in class analysis: A critique of Parkins', *Sociology*, Vol. 16, No. 4, November 1982.

44. For M. Olson Marx was wrong to think that large-scale class organisations can be based on individuals joining them for rational/ instrumental reasons. For Olson an individual acting rationally in such a situation would abstain from joining – since his joining such a large group would make no 'perceptible' difference to its overall performance. Hence his idea that one needs special, additional incentives or the use of coercive means for building up class organisations. (See M. Olson, *The Logic of Collective Action: Public Goods and the Theory of Groups*, Cambridge, Mass.: Harvard University Press, 1965.)

However, Marx was less concerned with the rationality or irrationality of individuals joining class organisations and more with the objective conditions which facilitate or hinder the passage from what Olson calls a latent group to an actual one. For instance, Marx thought that in comparison with the putting-out system, the factory, by bringing many direct producers under a single roof facilitates communications and provides a more favourable environment for the development of class consciousness and the emergence of organised class interests.

    For a discussion of class as agency in the sense adopted here, see G. Therborn, 'Problems of Social Scientific Marxist Analysis', in N. Eisenstadt and H. J. Heller (eds), *Macrosociological Theory*, Beverly Hills, Calif: Sage, 1985, pp. 144 ff.

45.   For the concept of instantiation of rules see A. Giddens, *The Constitution of Society*, op. cit., pp. 16 ff.

46.   For a further development of these arguments see N. Mouzelis, *Back to Sociological Theory: Bridging the Micro-Macro Gap*, op. cit., chs. 2, 4 and 5.

47.   For a reductive approach which sees society not as an aggregate of individuals, but as an aggregate of 'micro situations', see R. Collins, 'Interaction Ritual Claims, Power and Property: The Micro-Macro Connection as an Empirically-based Theoretical Problem', in J. C. Alexander *et al.* (eds), *The Micro-Macro Link*, Berkeley: University of California Press, 1987. For a critique of Collins' 'methodological situationalism' see N. Mouzelis, *Back to Sociological Theory: Bridging the Micro-Macro Gap*, op. cit., chapter 4.

48.   See my critique of analytic Marxism in this chapter, footnote 41.

49.   See above, chapter 2, section 3; see also Appendix I.

50.   For an approach resorting to this type of explanation see N. Poulantzas, *Les Classes Sociales dans le Capitalisme d'Aujourd'hui*, op. cit., and his *Pouvoir Politique et Classes Sociales*, Paris: Maspèro, 1968, pp. 66 ff.

51.   See J. Larrain, *The Concept of Ideology*, op. cit., chapter 2.

52.   On the idea of neutralising antagonistic interests see E. Laclau, *Politics and Ideology in Marxist Theory*, London: New Left Books, 1977. For an extensive critique of Laclau's work, see below, Appendix II.

53.   For a work emphasising the constitutive, meaning-creating aspects of both ideology and utopia, see P. Ricoeur, *Lectures on Ideology and Utopia*, New York: Columbia University Press, 1986. See also L. Althusser, 'Ideology and Ideological State Apparatuses', in L. Althusser, *Lenin and Philosophy and Other Essays*, London: New Left Books, 1971; and G. Therborn, *The Ideology of Power and the Power of Ideology*, London: Verso, 1980.

54.   Durkheim uses the concept of ideology in order to contrast the objective analysis that appertains to science with the distorted, false representation of the social world that appertains to ideology. So while his society's collective representations have ideological dimensions, he makes no attempt *à la* Marx to link these ideological elements to collective actors or interest groups. See on this point J. Larrain, *The Concept of Ideology*, op. cit., chapter 3.

55.   Marx does not always use the concept of ideology as a residual category. He often implies that ideology, as a concealment of contradictions pertaining to the relations of production, constitutes only a part of the superstructure. At other times he treats all non-political superstructural spheres as ideological. See on this point J. Larrain, op. cit., p. 51.

56.   A similarly broad definition of ideology is given by J. B. Thompson, who argues that to study ideology is to examine how a system of meanings or significations sustains asymmetrical power relations (or relations of domination). The modalities through which meanings support asymmetrical power relations are those of legitimation, dissimulation, and reification. See his *Studies in the Theory of Ideology*, Cambridge: Polity Press, 1984, chapter 3. The difficulty with Thompson's definition is that it cannot deal satisfactorily with cases where an unintentional consequence of dissimulation and legitimation discourses is the weakening rather than strengthening of asymmetrical power relations.

57.   Of course, one could well question the distinction between first-and second-order discursive practices by pointing out that the intricate interconnections between the two blur completely what at first had seemed quite distinct levels of discourse. According to Foucault, for instance, the difference between a pre-interpreted social reality and a distorted or false representation of such a reality disappears when it is understood that theories (whether ideological or not) constantly shape the human realities they are supposed to explain, depict, distort, or justify. See A. Foucault, *The History of Sexuality*, London: Penguin, 1979, Vol. I

An answer to this argument is that it emphasises to an absurd degree the capacity of social theories (ideological or not) for radically reshaping the realities they concern themselves with. It does not take into account that in some conditions certain aspects of 'social reality' can be extremely resilient or even impervious to the transformative impact of ideologies or of social-scientific discourses. For instance, where powerful privileged groups conceive it to be in their interest to resist all attempts at radically changing the way economic, political, or cultural technologies are controlled, they may well succeed in fully maintaining the discrepancy between the prevailing actual restrictive controls and the dominant ideology that presents a distorted or idealised picture of those controls.

58.   See M. Morris and P. Patton (eds), *Michel Foucault: Power, Truth, Knowledge*, Sydney: Feral Publications, 1979.

59.   A. Giddens, *The Constitution of Society*, op. cit., p. 339. To support this statement, Giddens distinguishes between credibility and validity criteria

relevant to the critique of reasons as good reasons. Credibility criteria refer to criteria, hermeneutic in character, used to indicate how the grasping of actors' reasons illuminates exactly what they are doing in the light of those reasons. Validity criteria concern criteria of factual evidence and theoretical understanding employed by the social sciences in the assessment of reasons as good reasons.

Ibid., p. 339.

60.   For an effective critique, see A. Cutler, B. Hindess, P. Hirst, and A. Hussain, *Marx's Capital and Capitalism Today*, London: Routledge, 1977, Vol. I.

61.   A final point concerning the issue of political representation on the social

integration level. There is a tendency nowadays, particularly by 'discourse' oriented political scientists, to dismiss the concept of representation on the grounds that it tends to view the interests of the represented in an essentialist manner, as pre-constituted objective realities. I think that the conceptualisation offered here allows one to deal with this objection without rejecting the concept of representation altogether. For if one looks systematically at the relations between economic, political and cultural modes of construction, it is possible to view the interests (economic, ethnic, generational, sexual and the like) of the represented as *social constructions* resulting from a multitude of economic, political and cultural discourses. One can then view the relationship between the socially constructed interests of the represented and the practices of their political representatives as a relation between first and second order discourses – in this way avoiding essentialism and economism while retaining the heuristically useful notion of political representation.

62.   To give a concrete example, the all-powerful position of the Argentinian armed forces during the post-1930 period was not the result of ephemeral circumstances that could easily have been changed by an appropriate civilian strategy; it was due primarily to a set of institutional structures, economic and political, that hindered the formation of a strong conservative party in the countryside. This situation created a power vacuum on the right of the political spectrum that was eventually filled by the army. On the overwhelming power position of the military in Argentina, see A. Rouquié, *Pouvoir Militaire et Société Politique à la République Argentine*, Paris: Seuil, 1978; see also M. Goldwert, *Democracy, Militarism and Nationalism in Argentina 1930–1966*, Austin: University of Texas Press, 1972, pp. 35 ff; and N. Mouzelis, *Politics in the Semi-Periphery: Early Parliamentarism and Late Industrialisation in the Balkans and Latin America*, London: Macmillan, 1986, pp. 99 ff.

63.   See on this point Appendix I.

64.   For a conceptualisation of the State in such terms see N. Poulantzas, *Pouvoir Politique et Classes Sociales*, op. cit.

65.   On the importance of such State functions see M. Mann, 'The autonomous power of the state: its origins, mechanisms and results', *Archives Européennes de Sociologie*, 1984, xxv, pp. 185–213; see also his *The Sources of Social Power*, Cambridge: Cambridge University Press, 1987, Vol. I, pp. 17–33; and T. Skocpol, *States and Social Revolutions: A Comparative Analysis of France, Russia and China*, Cambridge: Cambridge University Press, 1979.

66.   For the notion of quasi-group, as a social category with the potentiality of becoming a group, see R. Dahrendorf, *Class and Class Conflict in Industrial Society*, London: Routledge & Kegan Paul, 1959.

67.   On this point see A. Giddens, *The Constitution of Society*, op. cit., pp. 193–9.

68.   John Roemer, *Free to Lose*, Cambridge, Mass.: Harvard University Press, 1988, p. 124.

69.   I say *partly* because there are of course many historical sociologists and

sociologically minded historians who reject the primacy of the material base without at the same time taking refuge in mere 'ideas'. For instance, the present focus in historical sociology on the fundamental importance of state structures for understanding revolutions and other forms of macro-historical transformations is a good illustration of such an attitude. See, for instance, Theda Skocpol, *States and Social Revolutions*, Cambridge: Cambridge University Press, 1979. See also Peter Evans *et al.* (eds), *Bringing the State Back In*, Cambridge: Cambridge University Press, 1985.

70.   It is possible to present the above argument in a diagram showing in schematic form the theoretical space that the conceptualisation of the political, put forward in this chapter, occupies in relation to the prevailing paradigms in the social sciences.

The new tools for the conceptualisation of the polity (Box 6) reject Marxisms's economistic/reductionist tendencies, while maintaining its 'balanced' and integrated system/agency approach (this means a move from Box 2 to Box 6). Alternatively they draw on Weber's anti-economistic, anti-reductionist political sociology, while rejecting his methodological individualism (this means a move from Box 5 to Box 6); as well as those non-reductionist holistic approaches that one-sidedly over-emphasise systemic analysis at the expense of collective agency (Box 7) or vice versa (Box 8).

	Methodological individualism	Holism I (Action-System)	Holism II (Action<*System*)	Holism III (*Action*>System)
(Marxist Tradition) Reductionist/ Economic	(1)	(2) MARX	(3) Althusserian Marxism	(4) – Ultra-voluntaristic theories of class – Analytic Marxism
Non-reductionist (Weberian Tradition)	(5) WEBER———→(X)↓	(6)	(7) Parsonian Functionalism	(8) – Conflict theories – Phenomenological sociology – Closure theories

FIGURE 1   *General Methodological Orientation*

71.   What I have in mind here is not so much Merton's rather unsatisfactory ideas about 'middle range' theories, but his much more successful attempt to construct a series of interrelated concepts (for instance latent functions, functional alternatives, dysfunctions, and so on)

which made possible the distinction between methodologically accept-able and unacceptable forms of functional analysis. (See R. K. Merton, *Social Theory and Social Structure*), Glencoe: Free Press, 1963). As I have already mentioned, I think that his contribution to the debate on functionalism is still relevant today; for those who reject functionalism as inherently teleological only manage to avoid its by now 'unfashionable' terminology, while still being obliged to use *its logic* in any serious attempt to explain macro-historical developments (see above, chapter 3, section 4C).

72.   By limiting my scope to capitalist societies, I want to stress that the extension of this framework to non-capitalist societies will obviously entail a series of problems not tackled here. Thus the idea of the economy and polity entailing specific and distinct technological, appropriative and ideological dimensions can make sense in societies where there is a clear differentiation between the economy and polity (that is, to capitalist societies). To try to apply the framework, without serious modifications, to non-capitalist industrial societies, to pre-industrial or, even worse, to stateless societies would of course be quite self-defeating.

In fact it is even problematic whether the concepts of society and social formation (interchangeably used in this book) could or should apply to such macro-configurations as pre-industrial empires or multi-state civilisations which, unlike nation-states, do not have a *unitary* character. For a discussion of this last point see Michael Mann, *The Sources of Social Power*, Cambridge: Cambridge University Press, 1986, pp. 11 ff.

4 Application: Socio-Political Transitions in 19th- and Early 20th-Century Greece

The reductionist features of the Marxist paradigm prove to be particularly restrictive when Marxist methodology is applied to the study of late industrialising capitalist societies – societies where the state played an exceptionally vital role in the process of industrialisation, and where very often the struggles and contradictions within the politico-military sphere proper seem to be crucial for understanding overall societal transformations.

Trying to show the utility of the mode-of-domination concept in some depth, I shall concentrate my attention on Greece as a late-industrialising capitalist society, whose political institutions are roughly comparable to those of the parliamentary democracies of the capitalist centre. By way of introduction I shall take a brief look first at how Marxism sets out to analyse and explain socio-political developments in the capitalist periphery and semi-periphery.

1. MARXISM AND THE SOCIOLOGY OF DEVELOPMENT

(A) Marxism (as explained already in the previous chapter), when viewed not as a set of laws but as a conceptual framework more or less useful for the analysis of specific situations, presents several advantages over competing approaches. Two of these advantages are particularly pertinent in the present context.

First, unlike neo-classical economic theory, which views phenomena in a compartmentalised fashion, Marxism is well equipped for the holistic examination of social formations. Seeing development as an overall societal transformation, the Marxist political-economy approach investigates how contradictions and struggles within the economy are systematically related to changes in the political and cultural spheres. *Second*, unlike other paradigms in the social sciences,

93

Marxism can suggest useful ways of looking at societies from the point of view of both agency and institutional structure, so leading to a properly *balanced* synthesis of causal and non-teleological functionalist modes of explanation.

Needless to say, a balanced action/structure holism is indispensable for the study of development. It would be pretty well impossible to account for long-term developments without a conceptual scheme that is both holistic and at the same time sensitive to group struggles as well as to systemic, institutional contradictions and mechanisms of change. It is not surprising, therefore, that any theory trying to account for long-term societal transformations in more than purely descriptive terms tends to be influenced by Marxism. Neither is it surprising that, despite the present crisis of the dependency model in development theory, and of Marxism in general, nothing has emerged to replace it as a tool for the systematic study of how whole societies are constituted, persist, and change.

(B) What has just been said must not, however, be allowed to obscure the fact that, as stressed already, the holism of Marxist theory has been achieved at the price of a reductive treatment of the political and cultural spheres. This reductionism has particularly grave consequences in the development field. Limiting the discussion again to a consideration of the polity, it can be said that, in spite of its ritualistic emphasis on the relative autonomy of the political, Marxism continues to define third-world politics and the state in class, economic terms.

To repeat a point made earlier: if the State in capitalist formations is defined as an instrument of the economically dominant classes, or as performing the function of capital, this automatically rules out of court the investigation of cases where the economically dominant groups are the passive creatures of policies initiated by militarily or politically dominant groups; or cases where state policies hinder rather than promote the enlarged reproduction of capitalism. Such cases are, of course, very common in the capitalist periphery, where civil society in general and classes in particular are weak, and where very often the reproductive requirements of the polity are quite incompatible with those of the economy – when the economy must often give way.[1]

For example, the large-scale political patronage on which big business depends in many Third-World countries may benefit specific capitalists, but not necessarily the development of capitalism *per se*.

Given that the criteria for state intervention in the economy are most often not based on the 'general interests of capital' but on the particularistic interests of political favourites, it is quite misleading to build into the definition of the State the idea that, even when relatively autonomous from the pressures of economically dominant groups, it is structurally bound to serve their overall interests. Against this criticism it might well be argued that, in as far as capitalist relations of production remain dominant, the State, by definition and irrespective of its specific economic policies, contributes to the maintenance of capitalism, and in that sense does help the general interests of capital. If such a watered-down version is adopted, then it is perfectly true that all states that do not systematically set about destroying capitalist relations of production are *ipso facto* helping capital. But this is a banality that adds absolutely nothing to an understanding of the nature of the State in the capitalist periphery.

In these circumstances it is not surprising that Marxists do not take very seriously the obviously negative, obstructionist role (*vis-à-vis* the expanded reproduction of capitalism) that the State is playing in many Third-World countries. Consider, for instance, Marxist writings that view Third-World formations as an articulation of modes of production within which the capitalist mode dominates but takes a 'restrictive form' (in the sense that non-capitalist forms persist on a large scale). In trying to account for this ubiquitous characteristic of Third-World formations, the role of the State in 'restricting' capitalism has hardly been considered. The marked persistence of pre-capitalist or non-capitalist forms in the Third-World has been explained at one time or another in terms of the interests of metropolitan capital,[2] in terms of indigenous capital profiting in various ways from the persistence of non-capitalist forms,[3] or in terms of the nature of Third-World pre-capitalist economies.[4] What has not been given any serious thought is the extent to which at least the internal obstacles to the expanded reproduction of capital in the Third-World are more political than economic. The same neglect has obscured the fact that the way in which the Third-World State is organised, and the way in which it intervenes in the economy, frequently strangles rather than encourages capitalist expansion; and that the few success stories of 'late-late' capitalist development (that is, the Southeast Asian type of capitalist trajectory) were possible only due to the atypical structure of the polity and its remarkable capacity for massive and selective intervention in the economy, without this intervention killing private initiative.

In respect of these latter cases it is worth quoting extensively from an analysis which is unblinkered by either Marxist economism or neo-classical market-orientated theories of growth:

> In terms of mainstream economics, it is paradoxical that the East-Asian financial systems have both more control and more market-determination than those of many other countries. The reason why the financial controls do not produce the disasters that mainstream economics predicts is that the public-sector-in-general is more effective in these countries than in many others: more effective in promoting a competitively-oriented will to produce. So my argument does not conclude that most other developing countries should attempt to institute the same pattern of financial controls as in East Asia. The same controls in many other countries, with less effective public sectors, could be confidently expected to have the adverse consequences that mainstream economics predicts, with no noticeable beneficial ones.[5]

It may be objected that if neo-classical economists do not take the political dimension seriously, it is otherwise with Marxism whose holistic, political-economy approach attempts precisely to combat the compartmentalisation of economic and political phenomena that is found in the textbooks of conventional economics. But, as pointed out already, Marxist holism is achieved at the price of seeing the whole in terms of categories drawn exclusively from the economic, and this leads to a political-*economy*, rather than to a *political-economy* or to a *political*-economy approach. If, therefore, neo-classical economists deal with the political as a relevant 'parameter' but leave it outside their main field of investigation, Marxists similarly devise a variety of ingenious conceptual tricks for acknowledging, and simultaneously refusing to deal seriously with the political dimension.

Given all the above, it is not at all surprising that Marxist analyses are much more successful when they focus on the long-term historical transformation of Western societies (where the capitalist mode of production has more or less imposed its logic on the whole social formation), than when they refer to the capitalist societies of the periphery (where more often than not it is the State's logic and dynamic that predominate). I do not think, for instance, that it is entirely by chance that in the Marxist oriented centre-periphery development literature Emmanuel Wallerstein's scholarly work is the most representative contribution among studies focusing on the 'centre' part of the divide,[6] whereas André Gunder Frank's highly schematic-formalistic writings[7] are considered the most representative work on the periphery's capitalist trajectory. Neither is it accidental that there is no writer who has analysed the various developmental trajectories of the so-called Third World in a way which is at all comparable with the penetrating and insightful manner in which B. Moore, for instance, has traced the developmental routes of early modernisers. In other terms, what I am suggesting is that if Third World studies do not have yet their B. Moore or Wallerstein, this might have something to do with the fact that Marxist theory, which has been quite dominant in the field, has not adequate conceptual tools for studying social formations in which struggles over the means of domination/coercion are often more important than struggles over the means of production.[8]

Some of the above general points will, I hope, become more concrete in the following sections, which deal specifically with the Greek case.

2. GREEK MARXIST HISTORIOGRAPHY AND THE DILEMMAS OF CLASS ANALYSIS

Greece, like several other Balkan and also Latin American societies, acquired its national independence at the beginning of the 19th-century, soon afterwards adopting Western parliamentary forms of rule. These forms functioned in a relatively stable, albeit restricted manner, during the second half of the 19th century, a period during which, despite the adoption of universal male suffrage, a handful of notable families were practically monopolising state power. Their virtually exclusive powerhold was broken in 1909 by a military intervention. This opened up the way for a wider system of political participation, based less on oligarchic 'coteries of notables' and more on relatively centralised but clientelistic political parties. Given that most attempts at going beyond a merely descriptive account of long-term historical developments in Greece are based on some version of Marxism, I shall try to show how Marxist-oriented historians and social scientists have dealt with the early 20th-century transition from oligarchic to post-oligarchic politics.

(A) Marxist historians have conventionally explained the early 20th-century transition from oligarchic to post-oligarchic politics in

Greece as a *bourgeois revolution*: as the consequence of a late 19th-century conflict between a 'rising' bourgeoisie and a 'declining' feudal landowning class.[9] Behind this early and very crude class analysis of what is conceived of as the 1909 'revolution' lies, of course, the evolutionist idea that Greece and other peripheral and semi-peripheral capitalist societies will go through the same developmental stages that Western European countries experienced a hundred years earlier.[10]

Now leaving aside the very serious difficulties inherent in Marxist class analyses of Western European 'bourgeois revolutions',[11] the early Marxist account of the 1909 transition simply took explanatory schemes developed for the analysis of Western European development and transposed them mechanistically to a country which had had a radically different historical trajectory. A very obvious difference between the Western and the Greek developmental route is that, whereas in the former the development of industrial capitalism and the formation of an industrial bourgeoisie and proletariat preceded the break-up of oligarchic politics, in late industrialising societies like the Greek one, the process was reversed: the demise of oligarchic parliamentarism and the broadening of political participation did not follow but preceded the large-scale development of industrial capitalism. In other words, in Greece (as well as in several other semi-peripheral, late industrialising parliamentary democracies) the opening-up of the political system and the transition from political 'clubs of notables' to organised parties occurred in a predominantly pre-industrial context, with the industrial classes still weak in both numeric and organisational terms.[12]

It could well be argued that even in Western Europe it is very difficult, if not impossible, to establish a *direct* link between the rise of an industrial bourgeoisie and proletariat, and the broadening of political participation. But there can be no doubt that, in a variety of more or less *indirect* ways, both the industrial classes have generally played an important role not only in bringing about the demise of oligarchic politics, but also in directing the political development towards a type of parliamentary democracy which, in the late 19th century, was characterised by a relatively strong civil society, by predominantly non-clientelistic political parties, and by a legal-bureaucratic state apparatus.[13]

There is also no doubt that in Greece, as I shall try to show below, the absence of large-scale capitalist industrialisation, as well as of other favourable preconditions for the development of a well-functioning parliamentary democracy, meant that the early post-oligarchic political system was marked by the persistence of particularistic, clientelistic politics and by a quasi-patrimonial[14] authoritarian state apparatus that controlled in vertical, incorporative manner civil-society interests and associations. Therefore, whatever one may call the 1909 military intervention, it was certainly not a bourgeois revolution in the sense in which the term has been used by Marxist and non-Marxist historians in their analysis of 19th-century Western European socio-economic and political developments.

In defence of the Marxist interpretation of 1909 as a bourgeois revolution it can be said that if late 19th-century Greece did not have an important industrial bourgeoisie, it did have a merchant class that fulfilled a task similar to that of the industrial bourgeoisie in Western Europe a century earlier. However, this argument presents a number of difficulties.

The development of merchant capital can very easily coexist with, and even reinforce non-capitalist modes of production and exploitation. It is only when capital *enters the sphere of production* (whether in industry or agriculture) that it has revolutionary consequences for the whole of the social formation, and tends to create acute social antagonisms on the level of both production and circulation.[15] This being so, the absence of any serious antagonism between landowners and merchants in pre-industrial Greece is not at all surprising. One should remember, moreover, that in a great many cases the division between merchant and landowner was not clear-cut, Greek landowners often being involved in both internal and external trade operations. And although occasional parliamentary debates centred on tariff protection for the big wheat growers of the North (debates reminiscent of the English parliamentary struggles over the Corn Laws), I shall show below that such class issues were not dominant in 19th-century Greek political life.[16]

(B)   This brings us to the issue of what specifically political role, if any, the Greek landowning classes were playing in the 19th century. The Marxist notion of a Greek 'feudal' landowning class holding a monopoly of state power in the period before 1909 is highly misleading. The plain fact is that the big landowners in Greece never managed to acquire the kind of economic and political dominance that their counterparts enjoyed in several 19th- and early 20th-century Latin American societies, for instance. The historical reasons for this have to do with the fact that after the Greek War of Independence, most of the ex-Turkish lands were taken over by the State, becoming 'national lands'. The State refused to sell them by auction, and the Dotation Law of 1835 gave the peasant families actually cultivating these lands the opportunity to purchase their small plots with low annual payments over a 36-year period.[17] This trend towards the formation of small private landholdings was accentuated by the Agrarian Law of 1871, which led to the break-up of the national lands and their large-scale distribution to peasant families. Therefore, at least in the Peloponnese – the political core region of the early Greek kingdom – peasant smallholdings became the dominant, although not exclusive, form of land ownership and cultivation.[18]

In the regions that were incorporated into the modern Greek state later, the Turkish landlords did not have to withdraw as abruptly as in the Peloponnese (and were granted special safeguards for their lands), and so managed to sell their estates, mainly to rich diaspora Greeks resident in Alexandria, Constantinople, and Smyrna.[19] But these relative late-comers never succeeded in wielding the type of political influence which, for instance, Argentinian or Chilean landlords could exercise in 19th-century Latin America. Whereas the latter had been active participants in shaping the early post-independence state apparatus, their Greek counterparts appeared on the social and political scene only when the State had already been usurped, as it were, by the so-called *tzakia*. These were a number of highly influential patrician familes whose origins can be traced precisely to those chieftains and local notables (*proestoi*) who had played a crucial role during the Greek War of Independence. Given that the road via landowning was relatively closed, the *tzakia* notables sought power and prestige by turning to the State, by becoming tax farmers, academics, top bureaucrats, politicans, and the like. Ultimately, the 'state budget itself became their principal economic base'.[20]

In view of the above, it is highly misleading to see a 'rising bourgeoisie' behind the transition from oligarchic to post-oligarchic politics in early 20th-century Greece. It is just as misleading to regard those who were exercising oligarchic power in late 19th-century Greece as a landowning class.[21]

(C) Now given this *relative* autonomy of the holders of political power from both commercial and landowning interests, Greek Marxist historiography has been faced with the problem of how to account for the class character of the 19th-century political oligarchy in Greece. For here we have an all-powerful political group (or quasi-group)[22] that seems to be neither an 'instrument' nor a *direct* representative of the interests of merchants, industrialists, or the relatively weak landowning classes. In view of the Marxist methodological imperative that politically dominant groups *must* be entirely accounted for in class terms, the problem could only be solved by creating a new class category, that of the *state bourgeoisie*. The *tzakia* families, therefore, have been seen as a state bourgeoisie by authors who were critical of the naïve evolutionism of earlier Marxists.[23]

However, the term state bourgeoisie (used extensively in Marxist analyses of countries where the State seems stronger than civil society) is highly confusing. At best it is a simple contradiction in terms, at worst it implies prefabricated, aprioristic notions of the economy-polity relationship. It suggests that there is an affinity between state-power holders and other non-state bourgeoisies; or that the former represent an important fraction of the 'overall' bourgeoisie; or, finally, that the 'real' bourgeoisie has 'delegated' part of its powers to state officials, and so on. Whatever the interpretation, there is no doubt that conceptualising those who have state power as a distinct class, or even as a class fraction, conflates the economic and the political spheres; it stretches the concept of class to such an extent that it becomes extremely difficult to examine empirically the relationship between those who control the means of production and those who control the means of domination. This handicap becomes particularly crippling in situations (very frequent in peripheral societies) where the interests between economically and politically dominant groups are antagonistic; or in cases where the conditions of existence of the mode of domination are not congruent with those of the dominant mode of production.

The mode-of-domination concept overcomes the above difficulties, as will be shown below, by allowing an examination of the economy-polity relations from either an agency or a systemic point of view, that is, in terms of both *social* and *system* integration. It sets up for empirical investigation the problem of the complex and changing relationships between holders of means of production and holders of means of domination; as well as the analytically distinct problem of the compatibility or incompatibility between the economy's and the polity's conditions of existence.[24] In consequence, it is capable of making sense of the (from a Marxist point of view) paradoxical situation where politically dominant groups adopt policies hostile to their class of origin, or policies that systematically subvert rather than encourage capitalist development.

(D)   In view of the difficulties inherent in both the evolutionist and the state-bourgeoisie version of Greece's socio-economic developments in the 19th- and early 20th-century, Marxists have seen fit to adopt another interpretation of the transition from oligarchic to post-oligarchic rule. This is an anti-evolutionist stance that regards the 1909 military intervention and its consequences as a *failed* bourgeois revolution. In this version, the growing Greek middle classes before and after 1909 – unlike the 'conquering' Western bourgeoisies – failed to fulfil their true historic mission of building an autonomous industrial base and thoroughly transforming the pre-capitalist structures of 20th-century Greece. This failure was the consequence of their 'parasitic' and *comprador* character.[25]

Although the comparison and identification of qualitative differences between Greek and Western European development is a useful and much needed exercise, the notion of *failure* creates problems. It implies that conditions in early 20th-century Greece were in fact conducive to a Western type of development, and that it was only the peculiar character of the bourgeois classes that prevented them from grasping the opportunities that arose. This is a very dubious proposition – particularly if one remembers the strikingly different developmental trajectories of Greek and Western European societies. So, for instance, Greece, being a dependent province of the patrimonial Ottoman Empire, never experienced Western-type feudalism or absolutism; after its independence it occupied a very subordinate position within the international economy and polity; the country started to industrialise at least a century later than Western Europe and under extremely adverse conditions.

I do not mean to suggest that Greece's early 20th-century political and economic élites had no choice in the matter, that no alternative developmental routes were open to them.[26] All I want to point out is that a Western-type political and economic development was not and could not be one of those alternatives; and that, therefore, it is excessively voluntaristic and rather teleological to talk about the *failure* of the Greek bourgeoisie to steer the country into a Western-type capitalist economy and democratic polity – as if there had ever been any real possibility of doing so.

Finally, even if one ignores the methodological difficulties entailed in the concept of failure, to call the 1909 and subsequent developments a failed bourgeois revolution merely tells us what the 1909 transition was *not*, but very little about what actually happened, what kind of socio-political transformation the military intervention and the subsequent rise of Venizelos' Liberal Party brought about.

The question is, therefore: if we reject the Marxist structural explanations of the 1909 coup, explanations that focus primarily on the economy and class structure, are we then forced to accept the position of conventional historiography which, in reaction to Marxist fallacies, is suspicious of structural explanations *tout court*?[27] Must we, in other words, limit ourselves to mere descriptions, or to a 'great men' version of history? I think that the standard dilemma of Marxist structural analysis versus non-Marxist descriptive historiography is false. As already mentioned in chapters 1 and 3, it is both possible and necessary to identify not only economic but also political and cultural structures as generating constraints as well as opportunities for human conduct. In what follows I shall focus primarily on the polity, and particularly on the way in which its interrelated technological, appropriative, and ideological dimensions provide the basis for structural explanations that seriously take into account the specific logic and dynamic of political domination.

Ideally one should also pay attention to the cultural sphere, that is, to the complex technologies, relations of appropriation and ideologies that constitute the institutional orders of kinship, religion, and art, and their role in the 1909 transition. For several reasons this will not be done. *First*, my major aim is less to give a full account of the oligarchic/post-oligarchic transition in modern Greece, than to show in concrete fashion the limitations of class analysis and how non-economic structural explanations are possible that take into account some key elements of the Marxist paradigm. *Second*, a few exceptions apart, very little serious research has been done on the religious and kinship structures of late 19th- and early 20th-century Greece. *Third*, given the predominantly political nature of the 1909 transition, the polity and its complex relationship with the economy seem to me more fundamental than specifically cultural struggles and contradictions.[28]

3. PRE-CAPITALIST GREECE AND THE CONSOLIDATION OF OLIGARCHIC PARLIAMENTARISM: 1864–1909

3.1 The pre-capitalist economy

Despite its early integration into the world capitalist system, in terms of its internal structures of production, 19th-century Greece was clearly a pre-capitalist[29] social formation. After the spectacular development of England's industrial capitalism had destroyed early attempts at an industrial take-off in pre-independence Greece,[30] the indigenous Greek capital kept away from the spheres of both industrial and agricultural production. It oriented itself towards the much more lucrative and relatively risk-free commercial and financial investments. This tendency was reinforced, at least until the sixth decade of the 19th century, by the Greek state's liberal customs policies[31] that offered very little protection to local industries. It is not surprising, therefore, that despite a timid take-off of industrial production in the late 1860s and early 1870s, there were only 107 mechanised factories in Greece in 1875, employing on average 45 workers each.[32] Given that all the rest of the country's industrial establishments (constituting approximately 90 per cent of the total) were small family affairs, the extent to which capital kept shunning industrial production becomes all too clear.

The situation was a little better in the sphere of social overhead capital. Although road construction in the middle of the 19th century was still rudimentary (not exceeding 168 kilometres), the third quarter of the century saw some systematic attempts at building or repairing ports, at establishing telegraphic (1859) and postal services (1862), and the like.[33] Despite all this, however, and notwithstanding the relative importance of shipping,[34] the poor state of overland transport and the slow tempo of the commercialisation processes had not so far allowed the creation of a unified internal market. It is true that the commercialisation of agriculture, however slow and uneven, had meanwhile begun to generate a shift from the traditional autarchic economy to some market development. This can be seen by the growth of cereal and textile imports, and the beginnings of urbanisation. But these tendencies were rather weak and scanty. Apart from Athens, Piraeus and Hermoupolis, all the other so-called urban centres of the 1870s looked more like big villages – with a large proportion of their population still working in the primary sector.[35]

Concerning agriculture, finally, in the Peloponnese (as mentioned earlier) the small peasant landholding was dominant, especially after the 1871 distribution of the national lands. Although in Attica and Euboea big landed estates (the so-called *chifliks*) were rather more prevalent in terms of land tenure, production was organised mainly through various traditional and inefficient forms of share-cropping.[36]

In conclusion, the Greece of the first six decades of its independence (1821–80) was predominantly an agrarian, pre-capitalist society with rudimentary industry and a relatively inflated service sector. A large part of the latter consisted of a huge state apparatus absorbing into its ranks some of those who had left their villages and for whom a non-existent industry could not provide productive employment.

3.2 The oligarchic polity: the growth of administrative apparatuses

Moving now to the sphere of politics, the state apparatus was, of course, the main instrument through which a relatively national, unified political structure was gradually set up. During the protracted War of Independence (1821–28), as well as during the early years of the modern Greek state, nation-building was an exceedingly slow process. Territorial and market fragmentation was coupled with extreme political fragmentation, with large-scale brigandage,[37] as well as strongly entrenched regionalist interests systematically undermining all attempts at creating a unified national framework organised along Western principles of statecraft and administration.

The difficulties of the nation-building process become quite evident when it is remembered that before the War of Independence the bulk of the illiterate peasantry had no clear nationalist goals at all. A large number of them showed less interest in political independence than in a return to the 'good old days' when a strong Ottoman administration was able to resist the greed and rapaciousness of bandits, local landlords, and officials alike.[38] Such attitudes, even if they began to fade after independence, meant that the construction of national as distinct from ethnic identities[39] was extremely slow. In fact, the shift of loyalties from the local to the national level, the development of a sense of belonging to a social unit transcending kinship and village, took decades to mature. In that process of national maturation, the state apparatus played a crucial role, particularly once the internecine conflicts over the state form to be adopted were overcome. This point needs further clarification.

The years before, during as well as after the Greek War of Independence, were marked by a deep socio-political split between groups with a 'Westernising' and others with a 'traditionalist' orientation. The former, represented mainly by Western-educated intellectuals, diaspora merchants and financiers, and some of the Phanariote aristocracy,[40] wanted Greece to become a centralised state run along Western legal codes and principles of administration. The 'traditionalists', represented by the autochthonous military chieftains and primates, preferred to see the continuation of the kind of decentralisation that had prevailed during the centuries of Ottoman rule. They wanted the maintenance of customary law, and a sufficiently weak national army and executive to leave their local power and prerogatives intact.[41]

Given that the 'Westernisers' possessed administrative, diplomatic and legal skills that were indispensable for running the newly-created state, and given that they also enjoyed the support of the Great Powers (England, France, Russia) – whose intervention in 1827 had saved the Greek independence movement from total collapse – it was their vision of political rule that prevailed in the long run. But the 'traditionalists', being powerful at the local level, were able for quite a long time to put up an effective resistance to the centralising tendencies of the state.[42] When they finally realised that the decentralised confederation they were hoping for was not a viable proposition, they did their best to obtain control of the state apparatus from within and acquired whatever power and privileges went hand in hand with such control. From this point of view the democratic parliamentary institutions that were adopted initially, and reintroduced after a relatively short period of absolutist monarchical rule (1833–43), were used by the local military chieftains and other potentates as a means of both checking the absolutist tendencies of the throne, and of controlling their local voters/clients through a variety of legal and illegal expedients.[43]

With the gradual decline of regionalism, and with the state apparatus being systematically employed to provide jobs for political clients, the state administration quite soon attained spectacular proportions. It has been calculated that during the 1870s the number of civil servants per 10 000 of the population was approximately seven times higher in Greece than in the United Kingdom.[44] Another calculation for roughly the same period shows that a quarter of the non-agricultural labour force in Greece was being employed by the Greek state.[45]

This huge administrative growth becomes more extraordinary still if it is taken into account that the top state bureaucrats received salaries that compared favourably with the incomes of the economically dominant classes. So whereas the average annual income of the ten biggest landowners (before the annexation of Thessaly, which increased the proportion of big landed estates) did not exceed drachmae 20 000, and the largest Greek textile establishment had a profit of drs 5000 per annum, a state minister – in addition to obvious fringe benefits – received an annual salary of dr 10 000, and a general in the military dr 8300.[46] At this pre-capitalist stage, therefore, the importance of the state apparatus derived not only from its size, but also from the fact that, in the absence of a strong civil society, the top personnel syphoned off a significant part of the economic surplus.

Another important feature of the early Greek administrative apparatus was that it resembled more the patrimonial Ottoman administration in its declining phase than the legal-bureaucratic public administration systems of 19th- and 20th-century Western European polities. Not only was administrative action frequently disrupted by the persistence of large-scale brigandage, but the state apparatus itself was so pervious to pressures from political bosses and local interest groups that it was quite incapable of acting as a unified, corporate, collective body. Without secure tenure for civil servants, and without any criteria of merit for their recruitment, the position of every state employee high or low depended entirely on his political patron remaining in office, or on his connections with powerful bandits or influential notables.[47]

3.3 Relations of domination

(A) Having provided a sketchy outline of some of the structural features of the early Greek state's administrative apparatus, I shall now focus on how this apparatus was controlled – that is, on the prevailing relations of domination. From this point of view the two major institutional complexes directly relevant to the 'appropriative aspects' of the Greek polity were the throne and the political oligarchy's clientelistic networks.

During the period of King Otho's absolutist rule (1833–43) it was not only that the monarch, at least formally, was the exclusive master of the newly-created state apparatuses, but also that his Bavarian entourage occupied all the important state positions (at least up to the late 1930s). This did not mean, however, that the regional chiefs and their followers were without any political influence. The meagre resources of the young state's administrative and military apparatuses severely limited its capacity for reaching the political periphery and undermining the resistance of regionalist forces. Already in this early period, political parties (resulting from the various military and civilian forces that had fought in the War of Independence) were operating, setting themselves against the centralising and Western-ising tendencies of royal absolutism.[48] The fact that at this time as well as in the subsequent period of constitutional monarchy (1843–62) these parties were named after the three Great Powers (the Russian Party, the French Party, and the English Party) indicates the enormous influence that these countries had on Greek politics. In the pursuit of their fluctuating and often conflicting objectives, the Great Powers' resident representatives frequently supported their client-party's strategies against the King or against the other parties. In fact, the Great Powers' legations, by constituting poles around which Greek political life could revolve, contributed significantly to the early consolidation of the party system.[49]

If during the period of constitutional monarchy some of the crown's prerogatives were limited, *oligarchic parliamentarism* assumed its accomplished form from 1864 onwards – after the overthrow of the Bavarian dynasty, the enthronement of King George I, and the adoption of universal male suffrage. The new mode of domination entailed a balance of power between the throne and parliament (controlled to a large extent by the *tzakia* families). The throne was principally in control of the army and foreign affairs, leaving the other state functions to whatever part of the political oligarchy happened to be in power.[50]

Although universal male suffrage was introduced as early as 1864, the large majority of the population remained outside active politics. That is to say that the local chieftains and notables often had 'captive voters', or at least were powerful enough to control the political behaviour of their social subordinates, and so to keep a quasi-monopolistic control over the administrative apparatus.

Aside from more overt forms of coercion, this control was achieved and maintained by means of large-scale political patronage. Not only could the votes of the poor peasantry be easily bought, but a politician and his local bosses could also secure votes through rendering a battery of lesser or greater services to their clients – such as jobs in the state bureaucracy, better terms for agricultural loans, clemency in cases of brigandage and other criminal offences, cheap or free medical and legal services by professionals belonging to the same patronage network, and so on.[51] It was through such practices that politicans were building up *political capital* at the local and regional levels. Given the particularistic, personalistic character of these exchanges, clients were attached to the person of the patron rather than to his political programme (which was often non-existent). In these circumstances it is not really surprising that politicians could even switch from one party to another without losing their political clientele. Part of the reason for this state of affairs was that on the national level the political parties consisted of a very loose alliance of political barons lording it over extensive clientelistic networks. In other words, the 19th-century Greek political parties were mere coteries of notables, or rather a configuration of regionally based and hierarchically organised patronage networks.[52]

This being the situation at grass-roots level, the connection higher up between the parties and the state apparatus was one of mutual self-aggrandisement: politicians in charge of a ministry would endeavour to enlarge it in order to create more jobs for their clients, and so to enlarge and further consolidate their clientelistic networks. As a researcher of the 19th-century Greek polity put it:

> Patronage networks and the state bureaucracy, in invigorating and reproducing each other, came towards the end of the nineteenth century to constitute an indistinguishable and self-aggrandising system. The monstrous Greek state had reached its maturity.[53]
>
> [My translation]

This vertical, clientelistic mode of incorporation of the peasantry into the political system operated strongly not only during the 19th century, but also during the first four decades of the 20th. In the interwar period, at a time when Greece's Balkan neighbours developed strong peasant movements and parties, the Greek peasants, in their overwhelming majority, continued to be drawn into the clientelistic networks of the Venizelist and anti-Venizelist parties.[54]

(B)   In the foregoing it was argued that oligarchic relations of domination in Greece constituted a structural basis for the political division between rulers and ruled, between those who had relatively easy access to the means or technologies of domination and those who had not. It would be useful now to say a few words about the cleavages within the ruling groups, within the political oligarchy. Generally speaking, and particularly at the local level, political cleavages followed a strictly clientelistic, particularistic logic.

> Becoming a member of parliament or a minister was an end in itself, and each politican, and his local bosses, was prepared to go to any lengths to achieve this end... Politicians were only interested in their personal success and the satisfaction of their clients' demands, and ignored issues related to ideological consistency and collective action.[55]
>
> [My translation]

On the national level, however, the situation was more complex. During certain periods, criteria other than purely clientelistic ones played a role in shaping political cleavages.[56] So during the last quarter of the 19th century, Greek political life revolved around two parties that were each named after their leader: Trikoupis and Deliyiannis. The Trikoupis Party advocated political and economic modernisation as a necessary precondition for achieving Greece's irredentist projects, whereas the Deliyiannis Party considered modernisation as a peripheral issue,[57] and gave top priority to the country's geographical expansion. To some extent, the ideological differences between the Trikoupists and the Deliyiannists were the same as those that had split the 'Westernisers' and 'traditionalists' earlier. In different guises that split was to run through the whole of the 19th century.[58]

As mentioned previously, in the early years of independence the issue of modernisation versus tradition manifested itself in a struggle over the form of the state apparatus – Westernisers wanting a centralised state, traditionalists preferring a decentralised one that would leave their privileged positions intact. Centralisation prevailed. In the 1870s and 1880s, the period here under consideration, the struggle was more over the rationalisation of the state apparatuses. The traditionalists, represented primarily by the Deliyiannis Party, were quite content with the clientelistic status quo, whereas Trikoupis and his party made serious efforts at 'Westernisation', at bringing both the civilian and military branches of the state nearer the bureaucratic-legal model. Although in overall terms he did not succeed in eliminating the clientelistic and particularistic practices that were as much a feature of his own party as of his opponents', I shall try to show that his administrative reforms did have a marked impact on the late 19th-century Greek polity.

3.4 Political ideologies

(A)   Let us finally move to the ideological aspects of oligarchic parliamentarism. In this respect, two major orientations played a key role in cementing the political culture of 19th-century Greeks: the ideas of the Western European *Enlightenment* and, a little later, Western *Romanticism* with its glorification of nationalism and its focus on political messianism.

The Western European Enlightenment played a very crucial part in shaping the political ideologies of the early 19th-century Greek polity. Particularly its emphasis on political liberalism (with the ensuing ideas of freedom of speech, of association, and so forth), as well as its concern with classical antiquity, were key elements in the constitution of national-political identities in the Greek polity.[59] However, as had been the case with the importation of legal and political institutions, the Enlightenment ideas concerning human freedom and progress suffered something of a sea change, and operated very differently in Greece from the way they had done in the West.

To take political liberalism first, it is quite true that the first Greek constitutions, drafted during the turbulent years of the War of Independence, were clearly inspired by the French Revolution and could be used as important ideological weapons against Capodistria's (1828–31) and later King Otho's (1833–43) absolutist regimes. But once political liberalism had been implemented to some extent in the 1843–64 period, and more widely so after the institution of universal male suffrage in 1864, a gaping discrepancy remained between liberal, humanistic and universalistic values on the one hand, and the coercive and particularistic practices of Greece's political oligarchy on the other. This meant that political discourses were either highly abstract metaphysical ruminations on the concepts of freedom, of democracy, and so on; or, at the other extreme, they focused on purely personalistic differences over the distribution of political spoils.

Obviously the two levels, the formalistic/abstract and the personalistic/particularistic were nicely complementary. More often than not one could detect behind the high-flown abstractions and lofty democratic principles the narrow interests and ambitions of specific individuals. Furthermore, the combination of legalistic, abstract and personalistic, particularistic styles of discourse was an effective ideological mechanism for maintaining the political status quo. It contributed to the systematic exclusion from the political arena of more substantive issues – such as social betterment and political reform.[60]

(B) A similar distortion affected the other major component of the Enlightenment legacy: the concern with classical antiquity. In Western Europe ever since the Renaissance, the revival of classical studies had been a catalytic aspect of the overall movement that undermined the closed medieval community and reasserted Man's faith in reason, scientific exploration and progress. When these humanistic values were imported into 19th-century Greece, they were somehow turned into simply another ideological mechanism for underpinning the oligarchic status quo.

The fate that befell the work of Adamantios Koraïs, a diaspora Greek resident for most of his life in France, exemplifies this ideological distortion and obfuscation. Koraïs was the major representative of the Greek enlightenment. His profound political liberalism, humanism and admiration of the ancient Greek civilisation, together with his translations and commentaries on ancient Greek texts did more than anything else in disseminating French enlightenment culture in 19th-century Greece. On the other hand, his disciples or rather ex-disciples and opponents in Greece, finding themselves in a very different socio-political setting, disregarded Koraïs' liberal political ideas, so distorting his work as a whole. They also rejected his quite rational compromise solution to the burning controversy concerning the Greek language. In fact, the language problem and the way in which it was manipulated by political ideologues shows more clearly than anything else the effect that the West's fascination with ancient Greek culture had on post-independence Greece. As a prominent literary historian has put it:

> It was over language matters that disagreement first arose between the young scholars and Koraïs' teaching. The vision of the ancient world blinded linguistic theories to any consideration of practical experience or common sense. For the twenty years from about 1833 to 1853, and with Constantine Economou [one of Koraïs' disciples] as the main protagonist, one sees a gradual turning of the Greek language towards archaism... The arguments for this turning were mainly opportunistic: the use of ancient Greek would demonstrate the ancient origins of the new Greeks. This type of argument, consciously or unconsciously, suited both the wise and the foolish, it suited the spirit of the times.[61]

[My translation]

Distorted and impoverished, the so-called enlightenment that was allowed to take roots in 19th-century Greece elbowed aside the living cultural traditions and the language spoken by the people as the 'bastardised' heritage of four centuries of Ottoman yoke. The living culture was all but strangled by an obsessive archeolatry, and by the systematic attempt to create an artificial, 'pure' language (the so-called *katharevousa*) that, cleansed of all 'non-Greek' pollution, closely resembled its long-dead classical forebear. When this archaic, highly formal mode of speech and writing became the vehicle for all official discourses, it not only created vast linguistic confusion, but also exacerbated the relatively uneducated peasantry's alienation from the state bureaucracy. *Katharevousa*, scholasticism, and an indiscriminate idolatry of everything ancient came to be seen as expressions of the true heritage and patriotic spirit of the modern Hellenes.

(C) Moving now from the glorification of the past to grandiose visions of the future, it was a specific type of irredentism, particularly as shaped by the spread of romantic ideas during the middle of the 19th century,[62] that constituted the other main ideological component of Greece's oligarchic parliamentarism. Political romanticism, in reaction to the enlightenment ideas, put less emphasis on reason, scientific progress and personal liberty, than on patriotic feelings, religious sentiment, and above all on national unity. Such unity was believed necessary for the realisation of a nation's 'unique mission'. This new orientation rejected the Enlightenment's contempt for Byzantium as barbaric and obscurantist and, especially in Greece, saw Byzantine civilisation as the crucial link between ancient and modern Hellenism.

The major architect of this view of Greek history was Constantine Paparrigopoulos, the 19th-century 'national' historian *par excellence*, whose multi-volume magisterial *History of the Greek Nation*[63] attempts to refute theories like those of Fallmerayer, which deny any biological connection between ancient and modern Greeks[64]; as well as theories that do not consider Byzantium as the vital link between ancient and modern Greek civilisation.[65] For Paparrigopoulous, there can be no question of the unbroken continuity between ancient Greece, the Hellenistic empires, Byzantium, and finally the modern Greek state. Throughout the ages he detects the hand of Divine Providence, justifying the Greek 'ethnos' in

the unshakeable conviction that, just as in antiquity it had fulfilled a great historical mission; just as afterwards, during the Roman conquest, it was rescued by Divine intervention in order to fulfil a second great historic mission in the middle ages [that of Byzantium]; so later still it was rescued by God from Turkish dominance to fulfil a third, no less important historic mission in modern times.[66]

[My translation]

Teleology apart, this view of Hellenism's past achievements and future projects had a profound impact on Greece's late 19th-century political culture. It not only contributed to the shaping and consolidating the particular national identity that is dominant in Greece in our own day, but it also provided 19th-century Greek irredentism with a grandiose goal: the resurrection of the Byzantine Empire.

It is quite understandable that irredentism should have become the major orientation of all political actors in 19th-century Greece, particularly since prior to 1881 the Greek kingdom was restricted to the Peloponnese and parts of Continental Greece. Inevitably, the liberation of not only Thessaly and the islands but also of the northern territories of Epirus, Macedonia, and Thrace from the Turkish yoke were obvious targets of Greek nationalism. In fact, they became the dominant theme of every political discourse during the period under examination, especially since some of these objectives (for example, the annexation of the northern territories) clashed with the nationalist aspirations of Greece's Balkan neighbours.

Beyond these immediate and obvious targets, the aspirations for a Greater Greece looked for expansion not only north but also east, towards Asia Minor, where for centuries Greek communities had flourished economically and culturally, and from where many of the Ottoman administrative and entrepreneurial élites were recruited. Greece's nationalist ambitions went even further. Its most grandiose version, shaped by political romanticism and by a remarkable mid-19th-century revival of religious sentiment and concern with the Greek Orthodox Church, took the form of the *Megali Idea* (the 'Great Idea'). This aimed at nothing less than the revival of the Byzantine Empire and the reinstatement of Constantinople as the political and spiritual centre of modern Hellenism.

Now what I would like to point out here is that the romantically oriented Byzantium-centred vision of the *Megali Idea* – which partly superseded and partly merged with the earlier enlightenment ideology – operated among other things as a means of diverting public attention from the restrictive, oligarchic character of the relations of domination, and from the 'corrupt' and clientelistic practices they entailed. It was also a means of hiding the pitiful state of the public administration and the armed forces, where patronage flourished as rampantly as in all other branches of government.[67]

A brief recapitulation may be useful here. I have tried to delineate the technological, appropriative, and ideological aspects of the system of domination[68] that prevailed in 19th-century Greece, after its 1864 adoption of universal male suffrage. Although this mode of domination, which I have called *oligarchic parliamentarism*, was formally organised along Western legal codes and patterns of democratic government, it was in actual fact characterised by:

(1) a huge over-inflated administrative apparatus with marked 'Ottoman-Sultanistic'[69] patrimonial features;

(2) oligarchic relations of domination, which permitted effective access to state power only to the throne and to a set of notable families in charge of extensive clientelistic networks;

(3) political ideologies which, by focusing on grandiose irredentist visions as well as on the 'ancient Greek heritage', operated at least partly as displacement mechanisms to divert the citizens' attention from the regime's oligarchic and highly corrupt features.

3.5 Relations of production and relations of domination: a theoretical discussion

Oligarchic parliamentarism, its chronic governmental instability notwithstanding, showed a remarkable resilience: control of the means of domination by throne and oligarchy lasted for almost half a century (from the 1864 introduction of universal male suffrage to the 1909 military intervention). Before we examine the long-term process and the events that led up to the demise of oligarchic parliamentarism, a few words are needed about its relationship to the economy, that is, to the pre-capitalist modes of production that were dominant in both the agriculture and industry of 19th-century Greece.

(A) The major point to be stressed here is once again the *relative autonomy* of the political sphere from the prevailing economic division of labour and the ensuing class structure. To be more precise, there was no major overlap between the relations of domination and the relations of production. Political practices could not easily be derived from economic locations and practices. To repeat what has been said already concerning the *tzakia* families: it is not possible to relate the politically dominant groups in any systematic manner with landownership, or to find direct or exclusive links between political antagonisms and underlying class differences. This holds true for both the social origins of the *tzakia* families, and for the policies they saw fit to adopt over the period under examination.

True enough, the major political parties consisted of both

landowners and merchants, as well as a variety of individuals belonging to neither category. The one thing they all had in common was not so much economic as *political* capital: this is to say, they were able to build up and maintain political clienteles. That ability was based not only or predominantly on landownership or other forms of wealth, but also on charisma; on the occupancy of key positions within extended kinship networks; on possession of special legal, diplomatic or linguistic skills; on participation in key historical events such as the War of Independence, and so on. With regard to this last feature, as already mentioned, there is strong evidence that the political oligarchy which, together with the King, ruled Greece in the middle of the 19th century, was directly descended from the military and political cliques that had actively taken part in the protracted War of Independence.[70] Although the intra-Greek conflicts during the early stages of the war did tend to have a class character,[71] in the later phases class conflict gave way to conflicts between military and political cliques, or conflicts based on regionalist cleavages.[72] It was precisely the cliques that were formed on the basis of such cleavages that became the nucleus of the political oligarchy of 19th-century Greece.

It is worth quoting extensively from George Dertilis, whose research has contributed significantly to our knowledge of 19th-century economic and political structures, at this point:

> It is not by accident that during the national uprising and civil insurrections it was not only class divisions which played a crucial role but also single individuals as well as groups or cliques, whose unique *raison d'être* was not class antagonisms and projects at all but the acquisition of political power ... In the time to come the governance of the Greek state would be in the hands, not of a class-determined oligarchy but of a political élite. This élite was not an ensemble of class-based parties but an aggregate of the same political cliques that had played a leading role in the War of Independence – each clique including *chiflik*-owners, rich peasants, military chieftains, members of the indigenous bourgeoisie, diaspora Greeks, etc. – an ensemble of individuals from all classes addressing their political messages to all classes. Each of these cliques was a loose alliance, not of class-based groups but of personal and local clienteles. Their alliance was imposed by the same need for compromise that the Turkish threat and the pursuit of personal power entailed. Finally, at a higher level of organisation,

various configurations of cliques that had resulted from this same need for compromise would form the political parties.[73]

[My translation]

It could be argued of course that, even if one cannot identify a single class as the basis of the 19th-century political oligarchy, one may still use class analysis for identifying a number of *class fractions* or *factions* that were at its base. But this strategy will not do, particularly if it is seen to be sufficient in itself to account for all crucial structural cleavages on the political level. In so far as the basic split between dominant and dominated groups had a primarily *political* rather than economic base, to resort to an analysis of class fractions is not very helpful. In the same way that identifying the age groups of those active in antagonistic political parties does not necessarily make the conflict between them generational, so identifying the class composition of competing political groups does not necessarily make their antagonism one that is based on class conflict.

(B)   As a last-ditch defence, disciples of historic materialism may argue that, whatever the political oligarchy's social origins and policies and/or whatever its relative autonomy from class determinations, it was bound to operate within the *limiting framework* set by the material, economic base on the national level, and the interlinked world economy on the international level.

Taking the national level first, there is no convincing reason to make us see economic institutions and practices as limiting political ones, rather than the other way round. Why should one not, for instance, see the prevailing mode of domination as an ensemble of institutional structures and practices setting severe limits (as well as creating opportunities) to developments on the economic level? Why, for instance, should the unstoppable growth of the state apparatuses, and the systematic diversion of human and non-human resources from potentially productive to highly unproductive directions not be seen as following a logic that is less economic and more clearly political/clientelist? In respect of this specific example, in fact, I would argue that it is the mode of domination that is setting limits to the prevailing mode of production rather than vice versa. To put this slightly differently: it was the requirements of the extended reproduction of the political-patronage system that prevailed over the requirements of the extended reproduction of the economy.[74]

On the international level now, there is no doubt that the

19th-century world economy was indeed setting limits as well as creating opportunities to the newly-born Greek nation state. But there is also no doubt that the world polity,[75] and more particularly the direct political and diplomatic interventions of the three Great Powers in Greece's internal affairs, were equally, if not more, decisive in shaping the future of modern Greece. This was especially so since Greece, despite its protracted struggle against Ottoman rule, finally obtained its independence from 'above', that is, by the direct intervention of the Great Powers. After they had defeated the Turks at the Battle of Navarino (1827), they considered the Greece they had 'liberated' as under their guardianship. There is also no doubt at all that, at least up to the third quarter of the 19th century, the Western powers were trying, via their representatives and their indigenous political clients, to control developments in Greece through political, diplomatic, and ultimately military channels. Admittedly, after the 1873 world economic crisis and the massive influx of foreign and diaspora capital into the Greek mainland, tutelage in the economic sphere became rather more important than direct political guardianship. But this shift in emphasis only shows once again the necessity for rejecting dogmatic, *a priori* assertions about the primacy of this or that factor, and for adopting a flexible conceptual framework that poses the problem of 'dominance' as an empirical question rather than as a *passe-partout*.

These last considerations lead us to a brief analysis of the processes which, during the last quarter of the 19th century, gradually but surely undermined the political and economic structures on which oligarchic parliamentarism was built.

4. THE DEMISE OF OLIGARCHIC PARLIAMENTARISM

4.1 Transformations in the late 19th-century Greek economy

(A) I shall begin with listing some relevant developments on the level of the international economy. After the industrialisation of the Western European Continent had posed the first challenge ever to the industrial supremacy of England, Western nation states engaged in all-round competition for new markets and outlets in several peripheral and semi-peripheral countries. For the Balkan states this meant, as noted already, that the prevailing politico-military controls that the West had been exercising over them became more directly economic.[76] It was particularly after the 1873 world economic crisis, when Western capital needed to compensate for lower domestic profits, that it turned to the Balkan economies for quick and high gains. In Greece it was during the last quarter of the 19th century that foreign investments became not only more substantial[77] but also enjoyed the full backing of their respective governments.[78] This capital influx was considerably reinforced by Greek diaspora capital. Previously, Greek diaspora capitalists had thrived by acting as intermediaries between the metropolitan powers and their colonies or protectorates; after 1873, however, they not only felt the pinch of the economic crisis, but were also affected by the rise of nationalism (particularly in central and south-eastern Europe) that began to narrow their room for manoeuvre. A sizeable number of them, therefore, either relocated themselves in countries where British imperialism remained strong (for instance, Egypt and the Sudan), or took refuge in Greece itself.[79]

The relatively massive influx of foreign and diaspora capital mainly took the form of government loans and railway investments; the latter, having begun after the Crimean War, were much intensified in the post-1873 period. Foreign and diaspora capital was also directed into large-scale speculative financial operations, as well as to the purchase – after Greece's acquisition in 1881 of Thessaly and Etoloakarnania – of the ex-Turkish big landed estates.

On the national level these developments were accompanied by the state's attempt to abandon its 'night watchman' role and to intervene in the economy more systematically – mainly by developing the country's transport, communications, and banking systems, and by adopting protectionist measures for the growth of industry. All these events, in combination with the concomitant expansion of the Greek territory and population, set some of the necessary preconditions for the advance of industrial capitalism in the 20th century.

What should not be forgotten, however, is that until 1909, and even later, the organisation of economic production, both in agriculture and industry, retained its marked pre-capitalist character. With respect to agriculture, the ex-Turkish estates in the newly-annexed territories were acquired by rich diaspora Greeks under conditions that further increased the landowners' power *vis-à-vis* the direct producers. The reason for this was that, with the adoption of Roman law in post-independence Greece, the peasants working on the big estates under a variety of share-cropping agreements lost their traditional rights to cultivate the land. As in England, at the termination of the share-cropping contract the *chiflik* owner was legally entitled to evict the peasant. But unlike their English counterparts and more like East-European landlords, the *chiflik* owners did not use their enhanced powers for modernising agriculture. Thus agricultural productivity remained extremely low and with the population increase after 1881, Greek agriculture was unable to meet the country's needs in wheat, despite the newly-acquired wheat-growing Northern areas. Greece was therefore obliged to import large quantities of cereals, and this created severe balance-of-payment problems.[80]

In the Peloponnese (where since the 1871 agrarian reforms peasant smallholdings had been dominant) the situation was a little better. Due to the ruin of the French vineyards in the 1880s by an insect pest, international demand for Greek currants increased spectacularly, and this brought moderate prosperity for the direct producers and considerable riches for the merchants. But this economic boom lasted only until 1895, the year when external demand for currants dropped abruptly; a very severe crisis in the currant-producing areas followed. In these circumstances, and despite a certain degree of commercialisation in Greek agriculture during the late 19th and early 20th century, we see nowhere the emergence of large-scale capitalist enterprises using rural wage labour.

The situation was not more promising in industry. After a decade of relatively rapid growth (1865–75), Greek industry entered a period of stagnation and crisis that lasted until the late 1880s. In the last decade of the century it began to grow again, but even then without any marked technological improvements and without a fundamental transformation of its overall structure.[81] Late 19th-century conditions in Greece's secondary sector, therefore, hardly justify talk about the development of industrial capitalism on the scale of, for instance, Northern Italy or Spain. Despite the marked numerical increase of industrial establishments, the country's late 19th-century industry remained predominantly artisanal, non-capitalist in character since most of those industrial enterprises were small family businesses, employing very little or no wage labour.[82]

Given, finally, the weak linkages between Greek industry and railway construction, the country had to spend large amounts of foreign currency to import not only cereals but also railway and other industrial equipment. It is not surprising, therefore, that shortly before the turn of the century Greece was forced to declare bankruptcy.

It had to accept on its territory an international control commission (made up of representatives of foreign bond holders) which for a long time had an important say over the country's public finances.

In summary of the overall economic situation in late 19th-century Greece it may be said that infrastructural developments, the relative commercialisation of agriculture, and the hesitant steps towards industrialisation, although having diverse consequences for the rest of society, did not fundamentally change the prevailing relations of production in either agriculture or industry. Simple-commodity production remained the dominant form of organised production both in the secondary sector and in the currant-growing Southern part of the country; whereas various forms of share-cropping arrangements marked the cereal-producing, technologically backward *chiflik* areas of the North.

4.2 The rationalisation and further expansion of administrative, military and educational state apparatuses

With respect to the political sphere, the post-1880 period saw a number of crucial developments, some of them linked to the above-mentioned economic changes, some of them autonomous. These developments were gradually to undermine the social foundations of oligarchic parliamentarism.

(A) The first point to be noted in this context is the marked rationalisation or bureaucratisation of the means of administration. They were brought about in the 1880s and 1890s by Harilaos Trikoupis, the most prominent statesman of late 19th-century Greece. Trikoupis' administrative reforms somewhat attenuated the patrimonial aspects of the Greek State apparatus, by establishing a minimum educational standard for civil servants,[83] introducing measures that made the dismissal of State employees more difficult,[84] and creating specialised ministerial branches of government.

This administrative rationalisation was accompanied by an unprecedented expansion of the State budget, as State revenue and expenditure both rose dramatically. In contrast to the preceding period, the additional financial resources that the State managed to extract (through exorbitant, mainly indirect taxation, increased customs duties, and large-scale internal and external borrowing) were used not solely for the maintenance and expansion of the civil service; they also went to building up a more modern army and, as already mentioned, to developing the country's basic communication networks.[85]

These changes, as well as the previously mentioned economic ones, gradually sapped the structural basis of the prevailing relations of domination. The State apparatus not only grew larger in the post-1890 period, but as a result of the administrative reforms it also acquired a more corporate character as its personnel was less at the mercy of clientelistic bosses and patronage mongers.

Moreover, the expansion of the State apparatus as well as the multiplication of its functions affected not only the political centre, but also meant greater penetration of the periphery. It resulted in a considerable weakening of the hold of the local notables over the peasants, so freeing the latter to some extent from the former's patronage monopoly.

(B) If we now take a brief look at the military arm of the state, there too the 1880s showed developments that were quite similar to those occurring in the civilian State apparatuses. First of all, the armed forces experienced a large numerical increase, Trikoupis being very well aware that a larger and more modern army was a prerequisite for the realisation of some of Greece's irredentist projects. To that effect he introduced general conscription,[86] while at the same time making a systematic attempt at 'Westernising' the armed forces.[87] Like other Balkan societies, late 19th-century Greece witnessed a process of army modernisation and professionalisation under the guidance of West European military missions. So in 1884, a French military mission headed by General Victor Vosseur arrived in Greece, and during its three-year stay it endeavoured to pull the Greek armed forces into a more disciplined, bureaucratic, legal-rational shape.

This process of professionalisation was accompanied by a growing sense of *esprit de corps* among the officers, which resulted in their greater ability to articulate demands in more collective fashion. Whereas previously army officers had intervened in politics and negotiated with ministers and politicians on a more or less individual basis, by the turn of the century they were beginning to emerge as a distinct interest group, keen to promote (among other things) its professional interests.[88]

On the level of the military's rank and file too, the dramatic army expansion and the adoption of general conscription again operated as a force weakening parochial attitudes, and contributing to the creation of a more unified and centralised national-political arena. What in fact was happening was that the extended army organisation operated as a school for nationalist education, as a social space where the peasants' horizons could be broadened, and where the feeling could be forged of belonging to the nation-state rather than to the village community or the region.

(C) If the development of an *esprit de corps* and more bureaucratic structures in both the military and the civilian branches of government, as well as their quantitative growth, meant some relaxation (though by no means elimination) of the patrimonial control exercised over the state apparatus by the throne and political oligarchy, the oligarchic relations of domination were also undermined by a variety of other long-term processes. So, for instance, the phenomenal development of state education also contributed to the erosion of oligarchic rule. Given the potentially crucial role of public education as a mechanism for state-building, it was not surprising that the early Greek state made special efforts to create a nation-wide network of schools to instil its new generations with a proper sense of their national identity.

At the end of the War of Independence, the rudimentary schools that had existed lay in ruins, and the newly-founded state had to start from scratch. In spite of this, and in spite of the State's meagre resources, primary and then secondary and higher education establishments developed at an astonishingly rapid pace. Already in 1884, the percentage of children attending primary schools was not far removed from that of Western European countries,[89] and it was considerably higher in late 19th-century, pre-industrial Greece than it had been in the Western societies prior to their own large-scale industrialisation.[90] The situation was even more impressive in secondary education. So in 1890 and per 1000 of the population, 27 were attending secondary schools in Greece, 26 in France, 25 in Belgium, and 22 in Italy.[91] These figures explain why towards the end of the century illiteracy was much lower in Greece than in the rest of the Balkans, the Iberian peninsula, and several Eastern European countries.[92]

This impressive educational progress, which seems quite out of proportion to the country's financial resources, owed a very great deal to the financially formidable diaspora Greeks who were contributing substantially to the promotion of public education. Suffice to say that until 1870 the State-budget funds available for education kept lagging behind the donations for schools from rich Greeks living abroad.[93] Even when the State's expenditure for education generally, and for the development of the 'national spirit' in particular, increased by leaps and bounds – especially so during the accentuation of intra-Balkan rivalries over the Macedonian question[94] – the contribution of the Greek diaspora in terms of money, personnel and educational ideas continued to be significant throughout.

Another important feature of the 19th-century Greek educational system was its relatively open, non-elitist character. Not only was the proportion of school children from peasant families and the urban lower strata exceptionally high, but there were no 'streaming' techniques and, on the secondary level, no 'parallel' educational networks to cater for the lower and upper classes separately. If one takes into account that primary and later secondary education became free earlier than in most other European countries,[95] and that private education was very insignificant in the 19th century, one cannot help being impressed by the 'unidimensional' and in that sense 'democratic' character of the 19th-century Greek educational system.[96]

A third feature of the 19th-century educational set-up was the excessive amount of attention given to classical studies, and particularly to the teaching of ancient Greek. While teaching of any practical or technical skills was non-existent, towards the close of the century more than half of the hours taught at secondary-school level were devoted to Latin and ancient Greek.[97]

The above makes it clear that the rapid growth of education, its unidimensional character and its excessive focus on the ancient Greek heritage underscored its major function as a means for nation-state building. It underlines the state's intention of inculcating into the young a national identity based on the notion of an unbroken continuity between modern and ancient Greece. In other words, and contradicting what Marxist analyses would suggest, the public educational system in 19th-century Greece was not so much a means for legitimising the prevailing relations of production or of training subjects to accept and perform adequately their roles within the existing economic division of labour, as it was above all a formidable machinery for breaking down cultural and political localism, a tool for forging a particular type of national identity and for shifting loyalties and orientations from the local or regional periphery to the national centre.

4.3 Growing political contradictions, political protests and military intervention

(A) The development of the State's administrative, military, and educational technologies (particularly when seen in conjunction with Greece's late 19th-century rapid urbanisation and the development of communications) points very clearly to the gradual constitution of a *national political arena*. Within that context more general issues were able to emerge, such as those of modernisation or Westernisation, and this attenuated to some extent the strictly particularistic, clientelistic scramble for the spoils distributed by the State. The formation of a national political arena went hand in hand with the gradual appearance and consolidation of a national 'public opinion'; this became more and more significant as orientations and attachments began to shift from the periphery to the national centre.

Now all these developments were increasingly incongruent with the type of segmental, oligopolistic-clientelistic networks through which the political oligarchy controlled the predominantly rural electorate. To put this more in terms of the conceptual framework proposed here, the developing forces or technologies of domination, oriented as they were to the construction of centralised nation-state structures, and to the concomitant creation of specific national feelings and commitments, were in growing contradiction with the parochial, localistic oligarchic forms of political control.

It is possible, therefore, to identify a strictly political contradiction between the technologies and relations of domination,[98] a contradiction which, although related to economic contradictions and developments, had a specificity and a dynamic of its own. When such a specificity and dynamic are ignored, this can only lead to grossly elliptical or downright wrong accounts purporting to explain the demise of oligarchic politics in early 20th-century Greece.

(B) This fundamental contradiction was exacerbated by a series of conjunctural events. The most important of these was the military defeat of the badly organised Greek army in the Greco-Turkish War in 1897, which discredited both the throne and the political oligarchy. The pathetic inability of the Greek army to do justice to the grandeur of the *Megali Idea* meant that the latter could no longer be used as a displacement mechanism to divert attention from the inefficiency of the State's administrative and military apparatus, and from the clientelistic practices of the oligarchic parliamentary game.

At the level of social integration, all the above events resulted around the turn of the century in widespread popular disenchantment with the prevailing relations of domination. Anti-royalist feeling was running high, and there was general indignation with the corrupt practices of the oligarchic politicians and their inept handling of national affairs.

We have a number of concrete illustrations of this growing popular disillusionment with oligarchic parliamentarism at the beginning of the 20th century. An obvious one is the frequent references in the press concerning the deep-seated corruption of politicians and the urgent need for radical reform:

> During this period the daily press played an important function in the development of critical public opinion. The Greeks were avid newspaper readers and in Athens alone the average number of dailies hovered around ten from 1890 to 1910 ... In the 1905–1908 period some of the most prominent dailies spoke out against the old parties and called for a new spirit to transform the conduct of politics.[99]

Other instances that, on the level of agents, more or less directly reflected the growing incongruency between the oligarchic relations of domination and the emerging national political arena were:

 – student agitations demanding a clean-up in political life[100];
 – the mobilisation of various artisan-based associations, trade guilds and other interest groups to express their dissatisfaction with the political parties;
 – the spread of socialist ideas, and the creation in 1907 of the *Sociological Society* (a group of reform-minded, socialist-oriented, German-educated young men whose criticism of prevailing social and political structures were quite influential);
 – the emergence in parliament itself of a small but highly energetic group of reforming politicians setting themselves against the 'old parties' and demanding the regeneration of political life, and the rationalisation of public administration.

Concerning the members of this group,

> ... their pleas for reform, supported by several newspapers, aroused considerable publicity among the masses. Gavrielides of

the *Akropolis* [newspaper] dubbed them the 'Japan' party, paralleling their lofty goals to those of the dynamic leaders of Japan who transformed a formerly backward nation into the world power that defeated the Russians in 1905.[101]

(C) The growing disenchantment was, of course, felt most particularly in the armed forces which, as already mentioned, had become professionalised and were assuming a more collective identity and a distinct *esprit de corps*. Aside from the general malaise and discontent, many of the officers considered not only the political oligarchy but also the King and the Crown Prince (who had been in charge of two battalions in Thessaly during the Greco-Turkish War) as responsible for the military fiasco. Moreover, they disliked the way in which, after 1897, the throne attempted to reorganise the armed forces. They were especially opposed to a law voted by parliament in 1903 that gave supreme command of the armed forces – with extensive powers over matters of reorganisation, promotions, and so on – to Crown Prince Constantine. As a result of this law, a clique of royal favourites formed around the Crown Prince and his brothers. According to anti-royalist critics, this clique not only demoralised officers left out of the royal entourage, but also interfered with procedures of meritocratic promotion.

In addition to the bad management of military affairs by the Princes, legal provisos (introduced in 1908) destroying the promotional chances of non-commissioned officers further reinforced the frustration felt in the military.[102] Given the discontent with oligarchic politics in general, and the explosive situation within the armed forces in particular, it only needed the right kind of trigger to precipitate the military officers into action. This was provided by the Young Turks' Salonica revolt in 1908, which forced Sultan Abdul Hamid to restore the 1876 constitution in the Ottoman Empire. In May 1909 a number of young Greek officers created the Military League which, under threat of arms, demanded the removal of the Princes from army command, as well as a series of reforms for the reorganisation of the army structure, the public administration, the judiciary, education, and the like.[103]

The alacrity with which most navy and army officers approved of the military intervention, and the broad popular support for the coup (in Athens approximately 100 000 people demonstrated in favour, the largest popular gathering until then in modern Greek history)[104] were unmistakable indications of the extent to which the prevailing relations of domination were out of step with political and social reality in early 20th-century Greece.

(D)   Post-1909 developments make this dissonance even clearer. The politically quite inexperienced coup leaders, having failed in their hesitant and ineffective attempt to force the King and the political leadership to adopt a number of reforms, called the charismatic Cretan politician Eleftherios Venizelos to Athens to act as their political adviser. After some highly ingenious manoeuvres Venizelos – who did not have any strong connections with the old parties – managed to convene a national assembly for the revision of the Constitution, and to prepare the ground for elections in December 1910. In these elections his brand-new Liberal Party won 300 out of the 364 seats in parliament. This sudden, resounding electoral victory of a political outsider shows better than anything else how deeply alienated the Greek electorate had become from the old political parties and the oligarchic relations of domination that they represented.

However, although the old political leaders (the *paleo-kommatikoi* as they came to be called) were routed in the elections, they did not disappear from the political scene altogether. Yet, having irreversibly forfeited their oligopolistic control over the means of domination, they were obliged from that time onwards to share political power with the 'new men', with political upstarts.

With regard to the King, the decline of the *paleokommatikoi* entailed a decline in the power position of the throne, since the newcomers were less willing to accept that military and foreign affairs should be the exclusive preserve of the crown. This unwillingness was partly due to the fact that the post-1909 parties, although still clientelistic, were more broadly based and more centralised. This gave the party leaders tighter control over their cadres, and more bargaining power *vis-à-vis* the King. As party discipline became stricter, the throne grew less able to manipulate either the politicians or the elections.[105]

While it is difficult to provide any quantitative evidence for the relative decline of the monarchy's power position, it is rather easier to do so for the *tzakia* families. The post-1909 period saw a definite change in the composition of parliament, as hitherto political outsiders to a considerable extent took the place of the *ancien régime* political families.[106]

4.4 The 1909 military coup and the 'Rise of the Middle Classes' theory

(A)   This structural change has invariably been interpreted as the political expression of the 'rise of the middle classes' in late 19th and early 20th century Greek society. Although, as already mentioned, there are disputes over the nature of this rising class (whether it should be called an industrial, national or *comprador* bourgeoisie), there has been no disagreement at all about what these developments represent. They are agreed as pointing, *first*, to changes in the economic sphere that resulted in the emergence of new economic groups or classes, and *thereafter* to attempts by these groups to translate their newly-acquired economic importance or power into political terms; that is, their attempt to break the oligarchic control of the means of domination, and to broaden the system of political participation in such a way that they ceased being political outsiders. To repeat: economic transformation is seen as coming first, and subsequently, at some later stage, being reflected in the polity and bringing about its transformation. This image of the rising middle classes trying to enter the corridors of power has become so entrenched and seems so obvious and 'natural', that it has been adopted by all social scientists who have looked at the 1909 transition.[107] (It has also been adopted by theorists examining similar developments in other semi-peripheral parliamentary polities.[108])

I have no intention of denying the fact that changes in the late 19th-century Greek economy did generate new economic groups, and that these groups contributed to the decline of oligarchic parliamentarism. But I do propose to argue here that this interpretation only points to some (and not necessarily the most crucial) of the processes that contributed to the demise of the oligarchic mode of domination. The accepted image of the middle classes only seems so obvious and 'natural' if it is seen in a reductive conceptual framework that ignores the autonomous dynamic of the political sphere, and its importance for understanding the break-up of the political oligarchy's monopoly of power.

It seems to me that conceptualising a mode of domination as having its own technologies, appropriation arrangements, and ideologies, and as constituting with the economy two interrelated wholes portraying different logics and different rhythms or tempi of historical change, can help us realise that the 'rise of the middle classes' scheme is not as unproblematic as it appears at first sight. It can also help us pose in less one-sided fashion the issue of the demise of oligarchic parliamentarism and of the respective contributions to that demise by economic and political developments. More specifically, given that the oligarchic relations of domination were primarily based on economic and political localism, the question arises as to whether the weakening of *political localism* and the creation of a national political arena were preceded or followed by the demise of economic localism that led to the creation of national markets. In other words, was the move from localism to the creation of broader national networks of interdependence faster in the economy or in the polity?

(B)   Although the answer to such a question would require research which – for reasons that are by now obvious, I hope – has not yet begun, one could put forward the hypothesis that in late 19th-century Greece the tempo of political transformation leading to a national political arena was faster than the movement towards the creation of national markets. In fact, if we focus on the economy at the turn of the century, not only – as I mentioned earlier – were there no significant changes in the prevailing relations of production, but the transformations of the economic infrastructure (that is, of social overhead capital) were not as important as a superficial reference to the relevant statistics might indicate.

Let us, by way of example, look at railway construction, the infrastructural investment which, more than anything else, marked the decade of the 1880s. The initial project, adopted by Trikoupis, was to build a total network of 1600 kilometres over a five-year period. However, the work not only took much longer to realise (approximately 25 years), but was not strongly linked with Greece's industrial sector[109]; moreover, the income from this investment was extremely low, one main reason being the very slow growth of passenger and goods traffic. In other words, the demand for railway transport was much lower than the supply.

According to a student of the railway problem, in the late 19th century one sees in Greece

> socio-economic inertia typical of pre-capitalist economies: small familiy cultivation, self-sufficiency farming, limited exchange relations, low mobility. Movement from the village extends no further than the nearest semi-urban centre ... The transport of

passengers and merchandise remains steady or even declines as one moves deeper into the countryside. With the exception of export-able products, the merchandise carried by rail consists of few and often occasional surpluses and of basic necessities.[110]

[My translation]

The author goes on to argue that whereas in Western Europe railway construction met the growing demand for transportation by an already-formed national market and a rapidly growing capitalist economy, in Greece the absence of a national market and the relative immobility of its pre-capitalist economy meant that

the supply of a modern means of transport met a demand that was practically non-existent.[111]

Apart from the railways, shipping as another means of transport is also worth examining in this context. It is quite true that Greek shipping, after a prolonged period of crisis, rapidly began to develop again towards the end of the century. However, during this period control over shipping passed from the local shipowners of Ithaca, Galaxidi, and the Aegean islands to diaspora Greeks who gave it a more international orientation.[112] This disconnected it from the other sectors of the Greek economy, which did not profit much from its growth. Greece did not have

the stable and long-term connections that prevailed in nineteenth- and twentieth-century Norway, for instance, between shipping, commerce, oceanic fishing, and its related industries.[113]

[My translation]

In consequence, the development of shipping was, if for different reasons, as incapable as railroad construction of overcoming the economic localism and market fragmentation of Greece's 19th-century pre-capitalist economy.[114]

A similar situation obtained in respect of financial markets. It would seem that the influx of foreign and diaspora capital, and the relative development of the banking system during the last quarter of the 19th century, would have created favourable conditions for the creation of a national financial market. But even here market fragmentation was not overcome. Credit demand on the level of the village economy was met by the local usurer and merchant who, in turn, were connected with usurers and merchants higher up the financial hierarchy, at the top of which were the two major banks (the

National Bank and the Ionian Bank). These institutions preferred to lend to big merchants and usurers who could provide them with safe collateral, rather than directly to the small producers. So the various intermediaries were paid interest lying somewhere between the bank rate (6 to 10 per cent) and the exorbitant rates demanded from the peasantry (18 to 48 per cent).[115] According to Dertilis,

> this highly complex, hierarchical system of intermediaries was not conducive to the kind of competition that would eventually lower the cost of credit and eliminate the oligopolistic or monopolistic control that the usurer or merchant was exercising at village level. The local oligopolistic or monopolistic moneylender was not a competitor but a client of the moneylender higher up. The local market did not form an integrated, broader ensemble.[116]
>
> [My translation]

The reasons for the lack of integrated, national markets in 19th-century Greece become even more obvious if we also take into account that:

- the State's expenses for social overhead capital were extremely low during the 1878–97 period (which includes the Trikoupian 'golden age' of public investments), not exceeding 8 per cent of the overall state expenditure[117];
- the State's extensive and expensive borrowing, both internally and abroad, was used much more for its own maintenance and expansion than for economic investments;
- the diaspora capital was more interested in financial speculations and less in productive investments with transformative potential;
- the considerable profits of financial and merchant capital were, more often than not, either invested in real estate or exported abroad.[118]

(C)   Now if we compare the above with the situation in the political sphere (remembering the already mentioned rapid growth in the late 19th century of the State's administrative, educational and military apparatuses), it is not unreasonable to hypothesise that the pace of national-political integration was much faster than that of the economy; and that the decline of political localism preceded the decline of economic localism and the emergence of national markets. This hypothesis becomes the more plausible in view of the fact that the creation of a national political arena was not only helped by the spectacular growth of the State apparatuses, but also by the *internal dynamic* of the competitive party system itself.

I have already mentioned that in the late 1870s and the 1880s the party system took on a bipolar form, with the Trikoupis Party advocating modernisation before irredentism, and the opposition under Deliyiannis giving priority to the realisation of Greece's irredentist goals. While this party polarisation on a non-clientelist issue did not lead to the elimination of clientelism, it did lead to some party centralisation and to voters shifting orientations from the local periphery to the national centre. Concomitantly local politicians found it less easy to move from one party to the other in accordance with short-term, opportunistic calculations. As a study of 19th-century local politics in a Peloponnesian province puts it:

> From the 1880s onwards, the local party factions lost their influence, and alliances on the national level became more important in determining which politician would be elected.[119]

> [My translation]

This trend from traditional, decentralised to more centralised clientelistic parties became rather more strongly marked after 1909 and the rise of Venizelos' Liberal Party, but the tendency to party centralisation that initiated an incipient erosion of political localism had begun around the turn of the century.

Finally, it must also be noted here that the very logic of the oligarchic parliamentary game, particularly in a two-party system, creates centrifugal tendencies. For there is always the temptation for one of the two antagonists to attempt to acquire or maintain governmental power by wooing those voters who are relatively excluded from the political arena. After the removal in 1864 of formal legal restrictions to political participation (by men), appeals to the 'informally excluded' might be in the form of efforts by one of the parties to distribute more widely effective rights of citizenship; it might try to weaken local clientelistic practices through broadening the electoral districts; or profess a commitment to eliminate such chronically recurring malpractices as the buying of votes, electoral fraud, the use of the local gendarmerie for securing votes, and so forth. One could, in fact, see some of Trikoupis' reform efforts in this light.[120] Irrespective of whether such attempts are undertaken for idealistic or purely tactical reasons, they do tend to undermine the political oligarchy's control over the means of domination, and so lead to a broader system of political participation.

(D)   If the above is given due consideration, the one-sidedness of the 'rising middle classes → broadening of political participation' scheme becomes quite obvious. It also becomes obvious that, if we wish to explain the 1909 and subsequent events in Greece, we must focus not only on changes in the economic division of labour and the occupational structure, but also on changes in the *political* division of labour, where the ensuing transformations of political identities and affiliations create a potential for the emergence of new political constituencies, new political groups or quasi-groups.

Such political changes contributing to the demise of oligarchic parliamentarism may or may not be related to changes in the economy. It is perfectly well possible for certain processes undermining the oligarchic relations of domination to be generated *primarily* within the polity. Take, for instance, the penetration into the periphery of various state apparatuses (military, educational, administrative) and the subsequent weakening of the political monopoly that local notables had been enjoying over peasant votes. Proliferation and greater competition between patrons at village or regional level often entails more room for manoeuvre by the peasant clients, and so a weakening of oligarchic controls. The attitudes and political identities of the ruled might, therefore, change without any marked change in their economic situation.

Concerning the changes in political personnel that the spectacular rise of Venizelos' Liberal Party brought about, we know for certain that the number of the old political families who had been ruling 19th-century Greece in conjunction with the King was drastically reduced as new names, 'new men' gained access to the control of the means of domination.[121] We also know that in the post-1909 parliament professional men (particularly lawyers and doctors) were more numerous than in the *ancien régime* parliaments.[122] Moreover, the arrival and consolidation of the new political élite in the political arena was helped by the fact that in the post-oligarchic period it became easier to follow a political career without having a substantial fortune.[123]

All of the above makes the 'rise of the middle classes' scheme only partially plausible. One still needs to know whether the numerical growth in members of parliament from the professional classes was due primarily to these classes having become larger and economically more powerful in the late 19th century, or whether their increased importance was due more to their changed position *vis-à-vis* the means of domination. To put it differently: one still has to ask whether the displacement of the old political familes by the 'new men' was more the result of changing political rather than economic circumstances, these circumstances enabling a quasi-group of political aspirants (none of whom had a personal clientele under the old regime) to gain access to the means of domination. It could well be that the lawyers and merchants who had remained political outsiders in the late 19th century differed from the lawyers and merchants who were political insiders in the early 20th century in terms not of economic discrepancies but of *political capital*.

This hypothesis, stressing the primary importance of the political dynamic, is as plausible as the hypothesis of the 'rising middle classes'. Both deserve careful empirical investigation, since they imply different transformative processes and different types of interconnection between the economic and the political spheres.

More generally, the questions one should ask concerning the transition from oligarchic to post-oligarchic politics are:

(a)   to what extent was the rise of the 'new men' a result *primarily* of changes in the economic division of labour, and to what extent was it due *primarily* to changes in the political division of labour?;
(b)   if there was a two-way interaction (as is often the case), was it the political or the economic transformations that were more important in respect of both timing and causal weight?;
(c)   what degree of overlapping was there between the new political élites and rising economic groups resulting from a rapidly changing occupational structure?;
(d)   to what extent were the 'new men' influenced in their orientations and policies by group pressures or structural constraints emanating from the economy, and to what by those emanating from the polity?

It does seem to me that the above questions, which cannot be derived from a reductionist Marxist scheme, have to be tackled empirically if we want to further our knowledge of the demise of oligarchic parliamentarism in modern Greek history.

Of course, as I have already pointed out, Marxism can dismiss the above set of problems by arguing that class is not a strictly economic category, and that class practices are always the result of economic, political and ideological determinations. This attitude simplifies matters considerably, but at the price of reintroducing class reductionism, that is, by (wrongly) viewing all social groupings as classes or as class-derived entities.[124]

(E)   This brings me to another important point of this analysis, to the fact that the 1909 army intervention, the subsequent rise of Venizelism, and the decline of the *paleokommatikoi* indicate a structural transformation in the *relations of domination* rather than in the relations of production. As I said earlier, until 1909 there were no significant changes in the pre-capitalist relations of production, whether in agriculture or industry. It was only after 1909, that is, after the transformation of the oligarchic mode of domination that, particularly in the 1920s and 1930s, clear changes emerge in the relations of production. So in agriculture, for instance, the agrarian reform law voted in by the Venizelists in 1917 and seriously implemented in 1924,[125] irreversibly broke up the big *chiflik* estates and established petty-commodity production as the dominant mode in all parts of the country.

In industry, certain positive effects of the Balkan Wars and the First World War notwithstanding, it was mainly after Greece's defeat in the Graeco-Turkish war and the massive influx of Asia-Minor refugees in 1924 that industrial capitalism gained momentum. In fact, the settlement of great numbers of refugees in the main urban centres meant the availability of abundant cheap labour[126] and entrepreneurial skills,[127] at a time when Greece was experiencing a massive injection of foreign funds in the form of government loans, international aid to the refugees, private investments in public works, and so on.[128] With the favourable preconditions established in the four decades just past, the combination of entrepreneurial skills, cheap labour, and abundant capital gave a decisive boost to the development of Greek industry.

What was even more influential was the 1929 economic crisis which forced Greece, like many other Balkan and Latin American countries, radically to reorient its policies *vis-à-vis* the world market and the management of the economy. In fact, given the collapse of world trade and the incapacity of the Greek economy to export its traditional agricultural products, the State had to embark on a programme of import-substitution industrialisation by adoping a highly protectionist customs policy, by favouring industrial capital in a variety of ways, and more generally by becoming more involved with the management of the economy.

So in 1932 the Venizelos government initiated a series of legislative measures (the abolition of the free drachma convertibility into gold, quantitative restrictions on imports, bilateral forms of exchange not requiring the use of foreign currency, and so on)[129] which, in combination with earlier measures facilitating the development of industrial enterprises, provided a framework conducive to an effective breakthrough into the industrial sector. From 1923 to 1939, industrial production doubled its horsepower and value, and tripled its volume.[130]

Without any doubt, this period marks the decisive entrance of capital into the sphere of production. Prior to this, it was not only that the industrial sector as a whole remained relatively small, but the number of capitalist enterprises proper (that is, those using a large number of wage labourers) was insignificant. With the 1920s and 1930s came a considerable concentration of capital, as well as closer collaboration between banking and industrial capital – that is, the emergence of finance capital. This was the time of the multiplication of holding companies, trusts and cartels which, although they did not acquire the dimensions of their West European counterparts, were quite impressive by Balkan standards.[131]

This growth of finance and industrial capital came at a time when big landed property had virtually disappeared, and when merchant capital, in the wake of increasing state controls over the import-export trade and with the gradual deterioration of the international markets for currants and tobacco, was at a standstill.[132] From the 1930s onwards there is no doubt that the capitalist mode of production had become finally dominant in the industrial sector, to function as the dynamic pivot of the Greek economy – where dynamism is meant to imply not only high rates of growth, but also the systematic transfer of resources from the simple-commodity sector (prevalent in agriculture and small industry) to the industrial capitalist sector.

It was still the State, of course, that played the crucial role in creating and maintaining these transfer mechanisms that took the form of enormous state subsidies to big industry, scandalous credit facilities, indiscriminate tariff protection enabling highly inefficient firms to achieve quasi-monopolistic positions, the prevalence of indirect taxation which hit the small incomes very hard, and so on.[133]

The above points should make it quite clear that not only was there an increasingly close partnership between the State and industrial capital, but also that in this collaboration it was the State that was the major partner, in the sense that (as already mentioned) interwar industrial capital was to a great extent its creation: it had only come into existence because of the hot-house conditions that the State, forced by the world economic crisis, had created in its favour. The circumstances of this artificial or at any rate extremely dependent way in which capital had entered industrial production, and also the fact that the various private capitals did not manage to organise themselves at all coherently, easily disposes of the Marxist argument that tries to portray the interwar Greek state as a passive instrument of capital. This argument not only ignores the fragmentation and precarious position of interwar capital, but also underestimates the overriding power position that the Greek state occupied even before the dominance of the capitalist mode of production.

So even after the dominance of the capitalist mode of production in interwar Greece (despite the obviously closer links between class positions and political practices),[134] the logic and dynamic of the mode of domination tended to prevail over that of the dominant mode of production. It was not industrial capitalists that were shaping state structure and policies; instead, it was the State that for its own purposes both constituted and controlled industrial capitalists and even the industrial classes in general. Even if one looks at the industrial proletariat, there too – in contrast to developments in Western Europe – the interwar state managed to shape rather than be shaped by it. As in other Balkan and Latin American societies, the newly emerging Greek proletariat had to face an overdeveloped authoritarian state which, through a carrot-and-stick labour policy (that is, granting material and social benefits while at the same time preventing the growth of an autonomous trade union movement) managed to transform most trade union organisations into administrative extensions of the State.[135]

5.   CONCLUSION

I shall end this long chapter by summarising briefly the main points developed.

In the second half of the 19th-century Greece had a pre-capitalist economy and an oligarchic parliamentary polity marked by a huge, patrimonially organised state apparatus restrictively controlled by a small number of political families and the King. The ensuing oligarchic relations of domination were mainly legitimised by reference to the 'glorious ancient Greek past' and to ambitious irredentist projects.

During the last quarter of the 19th-century rapid processes of market, city and state expansion (linked to changes both to the world economy and polity) weakened the hold that local notables had over the predominantly rural population and these developments led to a growing political contradiction between: on the one hand the persisting oligarchic relations of domination and, on the other, the rapidly growing administrative, military and educational state apparatuses which were destroying political localism, shifting the political subjects' aspirations and allegiances from the rural periphery to the national centre. This basic incompatibility between the emergence of a national political arena and oligarchic controls led, at the beginning of this century to popular discontent and to a variety of political protests against the 'corrupt' political system, leading to the 1909 military intervention. The armed forces' intervention and the political events immediately following it mark the transition from oligarchic parliamentarism to a mode of domination based on a broadening of political participation, the entrance of 'new men' into politics and the relative decline of the *tzakia* and the throne.

Given that up to 1909 pre-capitalist relations of production were still dominant in both agriculture and industry, and given that the decline of political localism and the emergence of a national political arena preceded the decline of economic fragmentation and the development of truly national markets, one can argue that the major dynamic explaining 1909 came from the polity rather than the economy. Without denying the obvious interrelations between the two spheres, I have tentatively put forward the thesis that it makes more sense to view relatively autonomous political developments as having a transformative impact on the polity, rather than the other way round. In other terms 1909 cannot be understood as a 'bourgeois revolution' (if by this term we mean the early rise of an industrial or merchant bourgeoisie, or even a 'rising' middle class transforming the polity).[136] The 1909 intervention must be seen primarily as an essentially *politico-military* revolt which brought about an important change in the relations of domination, this change playing a crucial role in eventually transforming the relations of production a decade or more later.

It seems to me that however correct or incorrect one finds the interpretation of 1909 provided here, there is no doubt about the urgent need of a conceptual framework capable of raising such types of interpretation as hypotheses deserving empirical investigation. The mode of domination concept, by allowing the student to look at the complex relations between economy and polity in a systematic and at the same time non-aprioristic manner, can help him or her to overcome the various theoretical impasses discussed in Sections 1 and 2 of this chapter without abandoning the attempt at combining structural and conjunctural explanations of long-term historical developments – that is, without resorting to ad hoc or purely descriptive accounts of historical events. It allows for the *possibility* that, under certain conditions, the mode of domination may be more important than the dominant mode of production, either in terms of causal relations between political and economic agents, and/or in terms of functional relations between political and economic imperatives of reproduction.

Finally the conceptual framework proposed enables one to focus on the crucial significance of *timing* when examining the long-term relationship between economic and political trajectories. For it is obvious that Greece's developmental trajectory of capitalism and of democratic-parliamentary institutions has been radically different from that of most Western European societies. This difference has owed a great deal to *timing*, to the fact that in the West the development of the capitalist mode of production preceded the demise of oligarchic parliamentary politics, whereas in Greece it followed it. In other words, in the West, the opening up of the restrictive oligarchic system, and the transition from 'clubs of notables' to more centrally organised political parties, occurred *after* the large-scale development of industrial capitalism. This sequence of events helped the growth of a post-oligarchic state apparatus, the authoritarian tendencies of which were seriously checked by the existence and relatively autonomous organisation of both industrial workers and capitalists. In Greece, as in several other semi-peripheral capitalist societies with a long parliamentary tradition, oligarchic relations of domination gave way to broader forms of political participation before the dominance of the capitalist mode of production. This meant that the opening-up process took place in a pre-industrial context, where the industrial classes were weak in terms of both numbers and organisation, and where an overall weak civil society was unable to check the state's patrimonial-despotic features.

It seems to me that neither the conventional Marxist conceptual framework, which views political developments as the spatial and temporal extensions of the material base, nor Parsonian functionalism, which explains processes of political and economic differentiation as following the functional requirements of Society (with a capital S), can take seriously into account the complex relationship between the economy and the polity as delineated in this chapter.

NOTES

1. For a study which shows in considerable detail how the logic of politics frequently prevails over the market logic in the capitalist periphery see R. Bates, *Markets and States in Tropical Africa*, Berkeley: University of California Press, 1987.

2. See, for instance, J. Taylor, *From Modernisation to Modes of Production: A Critique of the Sociologies of Development and Underdevelopment*, London: Macmillan, 1979, pp. 220 ff.

3. See, for instance, H. Wolpe, 'The Theory of Internal Colonialism: The African Case', in I. Oxaal *et al.*, *Beyond the Sociology of Development*, London: Routledge & Kegan Paul, 1975; and S. Amin and K. Vergopoulos, *La Question Paysanne et le Capitalisme*, Paris: Anthropos, 1974.

4. See P. P. Rey, *Colonialisme, Néo-colonialisme et Transition au Capitalisme*, 3, Spring 1975.

5. Robert Wade, 'State Intervention in Outward-looking Development: Neo-classical Theory and Taiwanese Practice', in G. White and R. Wade (eds), *Developmental States in East Asia*, mimeo, p. 78; see also R. Wade, 'Dirigisme Taiwan-style', *IDS Bulletin*, Vol. 15, No. 2, 1984, Institute of Development Studies, Sussex.

6. See, for instance, I. Wallerstein, *The Modern World System: Capitalist Agriculture and the Origins of the European World-Economy in the sixteenth century*, New York: Academic Press, 1974; *The Modern World-System II: Mercantilism and the Consolidation of the European World-Economy 1600–1750*, 1980 and *The Modern World-System III: The Second Era of Great Expansion of the Capitalist World-Economy 1730–1840s*, 1989.

7. See, for instance, A. G. Frank, *Capitalism and Under-development in Latin America*, London: Monthly Review, 1967 and *Dependent Accumulation and Under-development*, London: Macmillan, 1978. For a balanced criticism of Gunder Frank's work see D. Booth, 'André Gunder Frank: An introduction and appreciation', in I. Oxaal *et al.*, *Beyond the Sociology of Development*, Routledge & Kegan Paul, London, 1975.

8. For an elaboration of these points see N. Mouzelis, 'Sociology of Development: Reflections on the Present Crisis', *Sociology*, Vol. 22, February 1988.

9. See, for instance, T. Vournas, *Goudi: The Military Coup of 1909*, (in Greek), Athens: Tolidis, 1957; and his *History of Modern Greece from the 1821 Revolution until the Goudi Military Intervention*, (in Greek), Athens: Tolidis, 1974. For a critical treatment of Marxist views of the 1909 coup see G. Dertilis, *Social Transformation and Military Intervention: 1880–1909*, (in Greek), Athens: Exantas, 1977, pp. 196 ff; and P. N. Tzermias, *Marxism and Historiography in Greece: A Critical Examination*, (in Greek), Athens: Evroekdotiki, 1987, pp. 204 ff.

10. One finds this kind of evolutionism in some of Marx's writings on Third-World countries, as well as in the early strategies and manifestos of several Third-World communist countries. See S. Avineri, *Karl*

Marx on Colonialism and Modernisation, New York: Anchor Books, 1969.

11.   See J. M. Maguire, *Marx's Theory of Politics*, Cambridge: Cambridge University Press, 1978.

12.   For a development of this point see N. Mouzelis, *Politics in the Semi-Periphery: Early Parliamentarism and Late Industrialisation in the Balkans and Latin America*, London: Macmillan, 1986.

13.   This was more true, of course, in England and in the Scandinavian countries, and less so in France and Germany. For the impact of the industrial classes on the decline of oligarchic and/or clientelistic politics in the West, see for instance R. Alford, *Party and Society*, London: John Murray, 1964, pp. 33 ff; and O. Kircheimer, 'The Transformation of European Political Parties', in J. Lapalombara and M. Weiner (eds), *Political Parties and Political Development*, Princeton, N.J.: Princeton University Press, 1966; W. L. Langel, *Political and Social Upheaval 1832–1852*, New York: Harper & Row, 1969; and J. R. Kurth, 'Industrial Change and Political Change: A European Perspective', in D. Collier (ed.), *The New Authoritarianism in Latin America*, Princeton, N.J.: Princeton University Press, 1979.

14.   For the concept of patrimonialism see M. Weber, *Economy and Society*, edited by G. Roth and C. Wittich, Berkeley: University of California Press, Vol. 2, pp. 1006 ff.

15.   See M. Dobb, *Studies in the Development of Capitalism*, New York: International Publishers, 1968.

16.   See G. Dertilis, *Social Transformation*, op. cit., pp. 85 ff.

17.   See on this J. Petropoulos, *Politics and Statecraft in the Kingdom of Greece, 1833–1843*, Princeton, N.J.: Princeton University Press, 1968, pp. 236–8.

18.   In this first land reform, 662 500 acres were distributed in 357 217 individual lots. Since at this time the agricultural population numbered 254 000 families, one may conclude that after 1871 the majority of Greek peasants had acquired some landed property of their own. See N. Vernicos, *L'évolution et les Structures de la Production Agricole en Grèce*, Dossier de Recherche, Université de Paris VIII, 1973; and D. Vergopoulos, *The Agrarian Problem in Greece: The Issue of the Social Incorporation of Agriculture*, (in Greek), Athens: Exantas, 1975.

19.   According to George Dertilis, in the late 19th-century two-thirds of the big landowners were diaspora Greeks. See his *Social Transformation*, op. cit., p. 86.

20.   G. Mavrogordatos, *Stillborn Republic: Social Conditions and Party Strategies in Greece 1922–1936*, Berkeley, Los Angeles and London: University of California Press, 1983, p. 123.

21.   This does not mean, of course, that there were no landowners at all among the political oligarchy. It simply means that they were by no means dominant, and that the fundamental base of the *tzakia* families was more political than economic. This becomes clearer if one takes into account the relative continuity between the pre-independence and post-independence Greek élites, and the fact that the former had derived their economic power *politically* by managing to acquire

special privileges (such as the right to collect taxes) from the Ottoman state. See on this point G. Dertilis, 'Réseaux de Crédit et Stratégies du Capital' in G. Dertilis (ed.), *Banquiers, Usuriers et Paysans: Réseaux de Crédit et Stratégies du Capital en Grèce 1780–1930*, Paris: Editions La Découverte, 1988, pp. 41 ff.

22. Following R. Dahrendorf, I mean by quasi-group 'any collectivity of individuals sharing positions with identical latent interests without having organised themselves as such'. See his *Class and Class Conflict in Industrial Society*, London: Routledge & Kegan Paul, 1959, pp. 237–8.

23. See, for instance, C. Tsoukalas, *Social Development and the State*, (in Greek), Athens: Themelio, 1981, pp. 259 ff; see also Mavrogordatos, *Stillborn Republic*, op. cit., pp. 123 ff.

24. See above, chapter 3, section 4C.

25. The concept of a failed bourgeois revolution is employed by Marxist-influenced thinkers to characterise both the 1821 and the 1909 revolutions in Greece. For a critical review of this type of literature see T. Tzermias, *Marxism and Historiography in Greece*, op. cit., pp. 189 ff.

26. For instance, the State's economic policy during the last quarter of the 19th-century focused on building railways rather than encouraging shipping. This, according to George Dertilis, was a fundamental mistake:

> In 1875, just after the end of the world economic boom, Greece, this formerly great maritime country, had only 28 steamships totalling 13,000 tons. Thus, Greece failing to invest in shipping in the 1850s and investing in railroads instead, is as if Belgium had failed to invest in industry between 1850 and 1870 and trying desperately to create a commercial fleet in the 1880s. G. Dertilis, *Social Transformation*, op. cit., p. 80.

> [My translation]

27. For such an approach see S. V. Papacosmas, *The Military in Greek Politics: The 1909 Coup D'État*, Kent, Ohio: The Kent University Press, 1977.

28. This is, of course, only a hypothesis which needs empirical verification.

29. Capitalism in this text should be defined in its narrow sense, as referring to a mode of production characterised by the use of wage labour, and hence by the direct producers being divorced from the means of production. With this definition, the integration of the economy into a world capitalist market, or the commercialisation of some of its sectors, do not automatically make this economy capitalist. See M. Dobb, *Studies in the Development of Capitalism*, New York: International Publishers, 1968, pp. 1–32. For a debate on the concept of capitalism and the relevance of diverging definitions in explaining the transition from feudalism to capitalism, see R. Hilton (ed.), *The Transition from Feudalism to Capitalism*, London: New Left Books, 1976; and E. Laclau, 'Feudalism and Capitalism in Latin America', *New Left Review*, May–June 1971.

30. During the middle of the 18th-century Greek merchant capital had started quite successfully to enter shipbuilding and textile production.

This promising early start was cut short at the beginning of the 19th century when both these sectors fell into a rapid decline. See V. Kremmidas, *Introduction to the History of Modern Greek Society, 1700–1821*, (in Greek), Athens: Exantas, 1976.

31.   See S. Gregoriadis, *Economic History of Modern Greece*, (in Greek), Athens: 1975, pp. 24 ff.

32.   See on this C. Agriantoni, *The Beginnings of Industrialisation in Nineteenth-Century Greece*, (in Greek), Athens: Historical Register of the National Bank of Greece, 1986, pp. 207–9. See also A. Mansolas, *Survey of the Steam-operated Industrial Establishments in Greece*, (in Greek), Athens, 1876.

33.   See N. Svoronos, *Review of Modern Greek History*, Athens: Themelio, 1976, pp. 89 ff.

34.   The tonnage of Greek shipping increased from 85 502 in 1838, to 268 600 in 1858, and 404 000 in 1870. But the introduction of steam created a severe crisis: by 1875 the tonnage had dropped to 262 032. See Svoronos, op. cit., p. 90.

35.   See on all these points, C. Agriantoni, *The Beginnings of Industrialisation*, op. cit., pp. 129 ff.

36.   For a detailed analysis of land tenure conditions in 19th-century Greece see W. W. McGrew, *Land and Revolution in Modern Greece: 1800–1881: The Transition in the Tenure and Exploitation of Land from the Ottoman Rule to Independence*, Kent, Ohio: Kent State University Press, 1985.

37.   On the problem of brigandage in 19th-century Greece see J. Koliopoulous, *Bandits*, (in Greek), Athens: Hermes, 1988.

38.   See on this point L. S. Stavrianos, *The Balkans since 1453*, New York: Holt, Rinehart & Winston, 1958, pp. 144 ff; see also his 'Antecedents of the Balkan Revolution of the Nineteenth Century', *Journal of Modern History*, 1959, pp. 335 ff.

39.   For a discussion of the national-ethnic distinction see A. D. Smith, *The Ethnic Origins of Nations*, Oxford: Blackwell, 1986.

40.   The Phanariote Greeks were a sort of *noblesse de robe* of the Ottoman Empire. Their organisational skills, their knowledge of languages, and their urban sophistication made them indispensable advisers of the *Porte*. For generations they managed not only to occupy and maintain key positions in the Ottoman administration, but a handful of them, through their political influence, played an important role in banking and finance.

41.   See on this point N. Diamandouros, *Political Modernisation, Social Conflict and Cultural Cleavage in the Formation of the Modern Greek State 1821–1828*, PhD Thesis, Columbia University, 1972.

42.   The long-term policy of King Otho (1833–62) was to eliminate or reduce the powers of the various regional potentates, and to create a society of small peasants ruled by a centralised monarchical bureaucracy. See P. Pipinelis, *The Monarchy in Greece* (in Greek), Athens, 1932.

43.   On the strength of the particularistic, clientelistic political networks during the early rule of King Otho see J. Petropoulos, *Politics and Statecraft in the Kingdom of Greece 1833–1843*, op. cit.

44. See G. Dertilis, *Social Change and Military Intervention in Politics: Greece 1881–1928*, PhD Thesis, University of Sheffield, 1976, Table XIV.
45. See C. Tsoukalas, 'The Reforms of Trikoupis', in *History of the Greek Nation: Modern Hellenism 1881–1913* (in Greek), Athens: Ekdotoki Athinon, 1977, p. 13.
46. C. Tsoukalas, 'The Reforms of Trikoupis', op. cit., p. 13.
47. See on these points C. Tsoukalas, *Social Development and the State*, op. cit., pp. 37 ff.
48. See on this J. Petropoulos, *Politics and Statecraft*, op. cit.
49. One should not, however, forget that during this early period each of the three parties was a very loose confederation of relatively autonomous factions, often fighting one another as much as the other two parties. See on this point J. Petropoulous, 'The Greek State from 1833 to 1862' in *History of the Greek Nation* (in Greek), Athens: Ekdotiki Athinon, 1977, Vol. 13, p. 87.
50. According to the 1864 constitution, the monarch was supposed merely to reign, not to rule. In practice, however, the King considered not only the army and foreign affairs as falling under his personal responsibility, but also that he had the right to appoint Cabinets even from parties that did not enjoy a majority in parliament. This meant of course that the King's powers of interfering directly and influencing political developments even beyond the spheres of military and foreign affairs were considerable. This particular source of conflict was removed in 1875 when the King accepted the principle that a government had to have a majority of votes to enjoy the confidence of parliament. The post-1875 balance between the throne and parliament survived until 1909.
51. See on this G. Dertilis, *Social Transformation*, op. cit., pp. 140 ff.
52. Conceptualising clientelistic party institutions as pertaining to the relations rather than forces of domination might seem confusing, since parties as well as state apparatuses can be seen as instruments/ technologies of domination. However, it seems to me that in the case of parties the appropriation dimension is stronger than the instrumental/technological one, whereas in the case of the state apparatuses the opposite is true. In other words, party institutions, together with the parliament and throne were the major instruments through which the state apparatuses were controlled; as such they occupied a place analogous to property institutions on the level of the economy.

   My distinction between the technological and the appropriative dimensions of the State is quite similar to, though not identical with, Michael Mann's distinction between the State's *infrastructural* and *despotic* powers. The former comprise the breadth and depth of penetration of the State apparatuses; the latter indicate the degree to which the State élites can operate without constraints from civil-society groups. See M. Mann, 'The autonomous power of the state: Its origins, meanings and results', *Archives Européennes de Sociologie*, 1984, XXV, pp. 185–203.

53.   See G. Dertilis, *Social Transformation* op. cit., p. 140.

54.   For some of the reasons that explain the non-appearance of a strong peasant party in interwar Greece, see N. Mouzelis, 'Greek and Bulgarian Peasants: Aspects of their Socio-political Situation during the Inter-war Period', *Comparative Studies in Society and History*, January 1975.

55.   See C. Lyrintzis, *Politics and Society in Achaïa in the Nineteenth Century*, (in Greek), mimeo.

56.   For instance, before as well as during the first decade of the Othonian constitutional monarchy (1844–54), a major although not unique feature differentiating the three parties (the English, Russian and French) was their respective allegiance to one of the Great Powers. After the blockade of Piraeus by the Powers in 1854, party differentiation in terms of loyalty to a foreign power, as well as with respect to other ideological differences, faded out and clientelism became the all-important factor. See N. Diamandouros, *Political Clientelism and Political Modernisation of Nineteenth-Century Greece*, mimeo, pp. 59 ff.

57.   Concerning internal policies, Deliyiannis can be said to have been Greece's 19th-century precursor with respect to the idea of the welfare state. In contrast to Trikoupis' liberal orientations, he advocated notions of 'social co-operation' and of the necessity to protect the small producers and the landless workers from the vagaries of the capitalist market. See on this point N. Economou, 'Greek political tendencies before Venizelos', in R. Veremis and O. Dimitrakopoulos (eds), *Studies on Venizelos and his Time*, (in Greek), Athens: Philippotis, 1980.

58.   See N. Diamandorous, *Political Modernisation*, op. cit.

59.   See on this point P. Kitromilides, 'Ideological Currents and Political Demands: Perspectives from the Greek nineteenth century', in D. Tsaoussis (ed.), *Aspects of Nineteenth-Century Greek society*, Athens: Estia, 1984. For the more philosophical aspects of the Greek en-lightenment see P. Kondilis, *Neohellenic Enlightenment: The Philosophical Ideas* (in Greek), Athens: Themelio, 1988.

60.   For an elaboration of this point see N. Mouzelis, *Modern Greece*, op. cit., pp. 134–48.

61.   D. Dimaras, 'The Greek Enlightenment' in his *Hellenism under Foreign Rule: 1669–1821* (in Greek), Athens: Ekdotiki Athinon, 1975, p. 359.

62.   See C. Dimaras, *Greek Romanticism* (in Greek), Athens: Hermes, 1985.

63.   K. Paparrigopoulos, *History of the Greek Nation: From Ancient Times till the reign of George I* (in Greek), Athens: Eleftheroudakis, 1925, Vols. 1–6.

64.   According to Fallmerayer, Slav invasions during the middle ages completely destroyed any ancient Greek cultural trace and thereafter mainland Greece was inhabited by Slavs who were eventually hellen-ised by the Byzantines. He therefore saw modern Greeks as basically hellenised Slavs. The rejection of Fallmerayer's thesis, and the estab-

lishment of an unbroken biological and cultural continuity of Hellenism has been the theme of numerous writings since, and has absorbed the energies of many historians and men of letters. See G. Veloudis, *Jacob Philip Fallmerayer and the Birth of Greek Historicism* (in Greek), Athens: 1982.

65. For instance, Rizos Neroulos, the president of the Greek Archaeological Society, argued that after the defeat of the Greeks by King Philip of Macedonia, the Greek spirit was stone dead, since the Hellenistic empires and Byzantium had very little real connection with ancient Greek civilisation. (See K. T. Dimaras, *K. Paparrigopoulos* (in Greek), Athens: Educational Institute of the National Bank of Greece, 1986, pp. 70–1.) This negative view of Byzantium became peripheral among men of letters after the spread of Romanticism in the middle of the 19th-century.

66. Quoted in Dimaras, *K. Paparrigopoulos*, op. cit., p. 183.

67. I do not, of course, wish to imply that ideological dissimulation was the *Megali Idea*'s only function. But there can be no doubt that it provided an excellent escape mechanism for all those who were unwilling or unable to cope with those highly intractable problems of modernisation (especially on the politico-military level) with which 19th-century Greece was faced.

68. A possible objection to the conceptualisation of the Greek polity in terms of its technological, appropriative and ideological dimensions is that these three categories are hardly sufficient to deal with the complexities of the concrete situation. Although I do not deny the possibility, or even necessity, of further conceptual elaboration, I think that, because they focus on what I consider the most important features of the political system, these three dimensions are particularly useful for looking at its overall constitution and its long-term transformation.

69. For the concept of *Sultanism* as an extreme form of patrimonial administration, see M. Weber, *Economy and Society*, op. cit., Vol. I, p. 231.

70. Landowners and the high clergy, having more to lose, were slow in participating in the early phases of the national struggle. They did so only when they realised that the revolutionary process was irreversible. See D. Tsakonas, *The Sociology of Modern Greek Culture* (in Greek), Athens: 1968, pp. 99–103. For a comparison with other Balkan countries see T. Stoianovich, 'The social foundations of Balkan politics', in D. and B. Jelavich (eds), *The Balkans in Transition*, Berkeley: 1963, pp. 297–345.

71. See on this C. Stamatopoulos, *The Internal Struggle before and after the 1821 Revolution* (in Greek), Athens: Kalvos, 1971, Vol. I, pp. 54–69. Even if one does not entirely accept what Stamatopoulos says about the pre-revolutionary struggles between *Cotsabassides* (notables) and Greek *klepthes* (bandits, Greece's primitive rebels) and the re-emergence of that type of conflict in the early years of the revolution – there is no doubt that land distribution was a real issue during that early period.

72.   See J. Petropoulos, *Politics and Statecraft*, op. cit., pp. 62 ff.
73.   See G. Dertilis, *Social Transformation*, op. cit., pp. 106–7.
74.   Of course, there is also, by way of ultimate defence of historic material-ism, the 'determination in the last instance' argument (see L. Althusser, *For Marx*, London: Penguin, 1969, pp. 117 ff). But its casuistic and teleological character does not warrant its serious examination.
75.   As on the level of the social formation, Marxist-oriented writers focusing on the world system have the tendency to reduce the political into the economic. Thus not only classical and modern Marxist theories of imperialism but even 'World-System' theories (influenced by Wallerstein's scholarly work) systematically view nation states and their interrelations in terms of the functions they perform for the capitalist world economy. Therefore the problem of how the relatively autonomous dynamic of geopolitical struggles among nation-states affects world capitalist development is not tackled.
76.   See L. S. Stavrianos, *The Balkans since 1453*, op. cit., pp. 513–44.
77.   A recent calculation puts the influx of foreign capital into Greece between 1879 and 1893 (arriving in various forms including state loans, private investments and so on) at the considerable amount of 750 million gold francs. Figures taken from M. Nikolinakos, *Studies on Greek Capitalism* (in Greek), Athens: Nea Smyrna, 1976, p. 38.
78.   See Stavrianos, *The Balkans since 1453*, op. cit., pp. 416 ff.
79.   See C. Tsoukalas, *Dependence and Reproduction: The Social Role of Educational Mechanisms in Greece (1830–1922)* (in Greek), Athens: Themelio, 1977, pp. 267 ff.
80.   See C. Agriantoni, *The Beginnings of Industrialisation*, op. cit., pp. 281 ff.
81.   Ibid., pp. 340 ff.
82.   As late as 1920, out of 2905 industrial establishments only 492 employed more than 25 workers. See G. Dertilis, *Social Transforma-tion*, op. cit., Tables X and XI. The difference between capitalist and non-capitalist economic units is not always clear-cut, of course. For Marx, for example, capital production really begins only when

> Each individual capitalist employs simultaneously a large number of labourers; when consequently the labour process is carried out on an extensive scale and yields relatively large quantities of products. A greater number of labourers working together, at the same time, in one place (or, if you will, in the same field of labour), in order to produce the same sort of commodity under the mastership of one capitalist, constitutes both historically and logically the starting point of capitalist production.

(Capital, New York: International Publishers, 1967, Vol. I, p. 322).

83.   In 1883 Trikoupis instituted the country's first system of examinations for the recruitment of civil servants. At the same time the gymnasium diploma became a precondition for access to certain bureaucratic posts. See on this C. Vergopoulos, 'Governmental policies and problems from 1881 to 1895', in *History of the Greek Nation*, Athens: Ekdotiki Athinon, 1977, Vol. 14, p. 46.

84.   Although civil servants did not acquire tenure until 1911, Trikoupis' administrative reforms limited the right of ministers to arbitrarily dismiss civil servants. They also made it more difficult to transfer civil servants from one area to another for clientelistic pupoces, or to withhold payment of their salaries. See Vergopoulos, ibid., p. 46.
85.   See C. Tsoukalas, *Social Development and the State*, op. cit., pp. 58–71.
86.   The law was introduced in 1878 but only came into effect in 1880. This tendency became more apparent in the 20th-century. See T. Veremis, 'The Regular Army in Nineteenth-Century Greece', in D. Tsaoussis, *Aspects of Greek Society*, op. cit., pp. 165–91; see also his *The Greek Army in Politics*, PhD Thesis, Trinity College, Oxford, 1974.
87.   For some of the measures that Trikoupis' government took in order to modernise the army and navy, see C. Vergopoulos, 'Governmental Policy and Problems', op. cit., pp. 48–50.
88.   See N. Mouzelis, *Modern Greece*, op. cit., pp. 105 ff.
89.   See C. Tsoukalas, *Dependence and Reproduction*, op. cit., p. 396.
90.   See N. Mouzelis, *Politics in the Semi-Periphery*, op. cit., pp. 12–13.
91.   See C. Tsoukalas, *Dependence and Reproduction*, op. cit., p. 398.
92.   Ibid., p. 394.
93.   Ibid., pp. 483 ff.
94.   See on this J. Campbell and P. Sherrard, *Modern Greece*, London: Ernest Benn, 1969, p. 106.
95.   See C. Tsoukalas, *Dependence and Reproduction*, op. cit., p. 504.
96.   Ibid., pp. 503–10.
97.   The fact that vocational training was very rudimentary indicates the degree to which the educational system was focused on non-practical or non-technical areas (see C. Tsoukalas, *Dependence and Reproduction*, op. cit., p. 556). It should be mentioned, however, that Trikoupis' educational reforms in the 1880s managed to shift the emphasis of the curriculum from ancient Greek and religion to the natural sciences. He also strove to encourage vocational schools (see Vergopoulos, 'Governmental policy . . .', op. cit., pp. 52–4).
98.   A systemic contradiction between forces and relations of domination implies, as mentioned in the previous chapter, an incompatibility between the organising principles underlying the technologies of domination, and those underlying the ways in which such technologies are appropriated or controlled.
99.   S. V. Papacosmas, *The Military in Greek Politics*, op. cit., pp. 31–2.
100.   See G. Dertilis, *Social Transformation*, op. cit., p. 204.
101.   S. V. Papacosmas, *The Military in Greek Politics*, op. cit., pp. 32.
102.   See G. Dertilis, *Social Transformation*, op. cit., p. 188.
103.   Agrarian reform did not have high priority on the military's list of demands. In fact, the break-up of the big landed estates was never an important subject in the negotiations between the Military League and the King or the political leadership (see on this point G. Dertilis, *Social Transformation*, op. cit., pp. 196 ff). This is hardly surprising in view of the peasantry's failure to organise in a less vertical, more horizontal, class manner.

104. Ibid., p. 205.
105. It had been very easy for King George in 1868 to dismiss Prime Minister Koumoundouros (who, despite his overwhelming majority in parliament, gave in without a protest) over a disagreement on the Cretan question. It was much less easy for King Constantine to get rid of Venizelos in 1915 over their disagreement on Greece's participation in the First World War.
106. See D. Kitsikis, 'L'évolution de l'élite politique Grèque', in M. B. Kiray (ed.), *Social Stratification and Development in the Mediterranean Basin*, Paris: 1973; see also K. Legg, *Politics in Modern Greece*, Stanford, California: Stanford University Press, 1969, Chapter 5.
107. Even historians who tend to avoid any type of structural or class analysis have adopted the 'rise of the middle classes → political transformation' scheme. See for instance G. Vendiris, *Greece 1910– 1920*, (in Greek), Athens: Ikaros, 1930, 2 vols; and G. Dafnis, *Greece between the Two Wars: 1923–1940* (in Greek), Athens: Ikaros, 1955, 2 vols.
108. For Argentina, for example, where the passage from oligarchic parliamentarism to a broader form of political participation occurred at approximately the same time as in Greece (in 1916), see D. Rock, *Politics in Argentina 1880–1930: The Rise and Fall of Radicalism*, Cambridge: Cambridge University Press, 1975; and A. A. Borón, *The Formation and Crisis of the Liberal State in Argentina 1880–1930*, PhD Thesis, Harvard University, 1976.
109. See G. Dertilis, *Social Transformation*, op. cit., pp. 80 ff.
110. See E. Papayiannakis, 'The Greek Railways: 1880–1910', in D. Tsaoussis (ed.), *Aspects of Nineteenth-Century Greek Society*, op. cit., p. 119; and Papayiannakis' *The Greek Railways*, Education Department of the National Bank of Greece, Athens, 1982.
111. Ibid., p. 120.
112. See G. Dertilis, *The Greek Economy and the Industrial Revolution: 1830–1910* (in Greek), Athens: Sakkoulas, 1984, pp. 31 ff.
113. Ibid., pp. 35–6.
114. A similiar point can be made about mining, a sector that was not organically linked to the industrial one. See C. Agriantoni, *The Beginnings of Industrialisation*, op. cit., p. 262.
115. Ibid., p. 85.
116. Ibid., p. 83. It was only with the creation by the State of the Agricultural Bank during the interwar period that we see a clear move towards a unified market – as far as agricultural credit is concerned. See on this point G. Dertilis, 'Réseaux de crédit...', op. cit., p. 68.
117. This percentage was much lower before as well as after the 1878–97 period. See G. Dertilis, Ibid., p. 89.
118. On all these points see G. Dertilis, *Social Transformation*, op. cit., p. 40 ff.
119. C. Lyrintzis, *Politics and Society in Achaïa*, op. cit., p. 55.
120. See N. Diamandouros, *Political Clientelism and Political Modernisation*, op. cit., p. 64 ff.

121. See D. Kitsikis, 'L'évolution de l'élite', op. cit.
122. See K. Legg, *Politics in Modern Greece*, op. cit., pp. 303 ff.
123. C. Lyrintzis, *Politics and Society in Achaïa*, op. cit.
124. On this point see Appendix I.
125. After Greece's defeat by Turkey in 1924, more than a million refugees from Asia Minor settled in mainland Greece. This massive influx of refugees dramatically accelerated the agrarian reform programme.
126. The abrupt restriction at approximately this time of migration to America increased the labour availability even further.
127. The fact that even as late as 1961 a quarter of Greek industrialists originated from outside Greece, mostly from Turkey, demonstrates the crucial contribution of Asia Minor refugees with regard to entrepreneurial skills. See A. Alexander, *Greek Industrialists*, Athens: Research Monograph Series of the Centre of Planning and Economic Research, 1964, p. 128.
128. From 1923 to 1930, imported foreign capital amounted to 1162.8 million gold francs. Considering the short period during which this capital came into the country, it was an unprecedented influx in modern Greek history. See M. Nikolinakos, *Studies in Greek Capitalism*, op. cit., p. 55.
129. For a detailed examination of these measures see C. Vergopoulos, 'The Greek Economy from 1926 to 1935', in *History of the Greek Nation: The New Hellenism 1913–1941*, op. cit.
130. S. Gregoriadis, *Economic History of Modern Greece*, op. cit., p. 48.
131. At the same time there was a marked differentiation of banking capital, as some of the functions previously performed by the all-pervasive and all-powerful National Bank of Greece were spread over several specialised institutions: the Bank of Greece (founded in 1927) which became responsible for currency issuing, the Real Estate bank (1927), and the Agricultural Bank (1931). Particularly the creation of the Bank of Greece which – after great resistance from vested interests – took over the prerogative of currency control from the National Bank, was a significant move in the State's attempt to establish a firmer hold over the economy.
132. Since the main Greek exports were luxury goods for which international demand was relatively inelastic, Greek exporters became more and more dependent on foreign buyers. See M. Serafetinidi, *The Breakdown of Parliamentary Institutions in Greece*, PhD Thesis, London School of Economics, 1976.
133. A close analysis of how these mechanisms link small-commodity agricultural production to industry is given in Vergopoulos' *The Agrarian Problem in Greece*, op. cit., pp. 176 ff. A more theoretical treatment is contained in S. Amin and C. Vergopoulos, *La Question Paysanne*, op. cit.
134. See on this point G. Mavrogordatos and C. Hadjiiosiph, *Venizelism and Bourgeois Transformation* (in Greek), Heraklion: Cretan University Publications, 1988, pp. 11 ff; see also N. Mouzelis, 'Class and Clientelistic Politics', *Sociological Review*, November 1978.

135. For the development of the Greek trade union movement see T. Katsanevas, *The Industrial Relations System in Greece: Historical Development and Present Structure*, PhD Thesis, London School of Economics, 1980; and D. Dertouzos, *The Greek Labour Movement*, PhD Thesis, Rutgers University, 1962.

136. One can argue, of course, that the 1909 revolt was 'bourgeois' in its *consequences* – in that it triggered developments which contributed to the growth and dominance of industrial capitalism in the 1920s and 1930s. But this interpretation not only reads history backwards, it also fails to tell us anything significant about the nature of the 1909 revolt or about the major reasons that brought it about.

5 Conclusion

In this work I have tried to deal with what I consider the major weakness of Marxism, namely its economistic orientation. I have focused especially on the methodological and conceptual problems of economic reductionism which, as I have argued, cannot be overcome without abandoning some of the fundamental presuppositions of historic materialism and creating new analytical tools for the study of the political and cultural orders. My major argument has been that the Marxist conception of the technological, appropriative and ideological dimensions of social life can – if seen not in terms of the material-base/superstructure dichotomy but as constitutive elements of a differentiated society's every major institutional order – help us greatly to understand how these orders are constructed, reproduced and transformed.

The technological dimension helps the student to look at social macro-realities as entities that are neither simply given (like Durkheim's collective consciousness), nor the mere result of inter-subjective understandings (as some interpretive micro-sociologies would imply). Although intersubjectivity is always involved, it is too restrictive a concept to account for the complex technological appar-atuses – that always compromise a varied mixture of material tools, organisational arrangements, and knowledge about such tools and arrangements – by means of which economic, political and cultural macro-orders are constituted and reproduced.

The appropriative dimension, on the other hand, through stressing the differential control of technologies by social groups, leads away from neutralist, purely systemic conceptions of the social (as does Parsonian functionalism), and provides an excellent bridge for view-ing social wholes in both agency and systemic terms: that is, both as a set of actors struggling over the control of technologies, and as a configuration of institutions whose organising principles may contra-dict each other.

The ideological dimension of an institutional order, finally, by asking questions about the discursive and non-discursive means through which the actual control of technical apparatuses is legiti-mised, enhances the critical, demystifying aspects of social analysis.

If the above is accepted, then technologies, their mode of control or appropriation, and the ideological legitimation of such controls can be seen in terms of not only a mode of economic production, but also in terms of modes of domination and cultural production.

Acutely aware that the type of theory developed here can only make sense if seen as a set of conceptual tools with greater or lesser usefulness in the course of empirical investigations, I have tried to demonstrate its utility by showing how it helps to solve some of the methodological problems Marxist historiography encounters when trying to explain socio-political transitions in late 19th- and early 20th-century Greek society.

I am quite aware, of course, that the above conceptualisation of what I consider the basic dimensions of all major institutional orders represents a by no means highly cohesive framework. Not only have I not dealt seriously with the technological, appropriative and ideological aspects of cultural modes of production, but I have given only a very loose and tentative indication of the possible interconnections between these three dimensions within a specific institutional order, as well as of the overall interrelationships between modes of economic, political and cultural production in a specific social formation and in broader international contexts.

There are two reasons for the unfinished, tentative and open-ended character of the proposed conceptual framework. The first, as already explained, arises out of my conviction that conceptual frameworks are in the nature of heuristic propositions about ways of looking at social life, rather than substantive statements that reveal its hidden, unknown qualities. I do believe that conceptual frameworks should be seen more as flexible, malleable kinds of scaffolding than as finished, rigid structures with fixed functions and built-in furniture. From this point of view what I tried to do is to develop very tentatively an interrelated number of conceptual tools geared to deal with a very specific problem: that of avoiding economic reductionism, while retaining such useful features of Marxism as its holistic orientation and its balanced agency/institutional structure approach to the study of societal transformations. Given this, the way to assess the conceptual tools presented here is to see to what extent they manage to deal in a more satisfactory manner than pre-existing tools with the research problems and dilemmas examined in chapter 4.

The second reason for the looseness of conceptualisation lies in the fact that in this work I only examined issues of reductionism related to 'horizontal' linkages between economic and political orders on the macro-level of analysis. A companion volume[1] will examine the more 'vertical' types of reductionism that relate to linkages between more and less inclusive social units, that is, social units operating at different levels of analysis. Although this type of reductive analysis is present also within Marxism, it is much more prevalent in the non-Marxist social sciences, where the ongoing debate between adherents of 'macro' and of 'micro' sociologies continues unabated. I am thinking here of attempts that entail the reduction of macro-institutional orders into the micro-worlds of interacting actors, and vice versa. I also have in mind the interrelated, but analytically distinct, problem of the relations between agency and institutional structure which, for reasons that I have explained in chapters 2 and 3, creates more acute problems within the non-Marxist social sciences.

With respect to differentiating between Marxist and non-Marxist social sciences, and although I have myself often done so in my work, I hope that the present book and its companion will help in some measure to bring about the eventual abolition of this distinction. Although in actual empirical research the boundaries between Marxist and non-Marxist approaches have frequently been successfully transcended, on the theoretical level the distinction is still very much alive.

The conceptual framework proposed here brings together elements drawn from Marxist political economy and from Weber's political sociology. I call it post-Marxist rather than post-Weberian, because I arrived at it after attempting for a number of years to use Marxist tools flexibly for understanding the long-term socio-political developments of a set of late industrialising parliamentary democracies. It was while struggling with the intractable theoretical and research problems created by Marxist class analysis that I concluded that something more drastic was needed than the mere distinction between vulgar/mechanistic and non-vulgar/humanistic Marxism, or even a more liberal interpretation of the basic texts. I also realised just how much effort and other resources are wasted by the compartmentalisation of the social sciences into Marxist and non-Marxist.

The above will have explained the reasoning behind the title of this volume. My use of *post-Marxist* implies, among other things, that it is high time to transcend the Marxist/non-Marxist cleavage in the social sciences; and by *alternatives* I mean that those who reject historic materialism in all its versions need not, and should not, adopt the type of post-Marxism which denies Marxism all useful contribution to the social sciences. There is indeed a post-Marxist alternative or rather alternatives that neither deny nor stop using the profound insights that Marxism has still to offer to those who are interested in how whole societies are reproduced and transformed.

Needless to say, the conceptual framework presented in this book does not claim to be the *only* constructive alternative to the wholesale rejection of Marxism. There are, obviously, many other ways of retrieving valid and/or useful elements from the long tradition of Marxist writings.

The strategy of retrieval developed here, however limited and tentative, suggests at least the possibility and desirability of seeking constructive alternatives to the total rejection of Marxism. It also suggests that it is premature and unjustified to declare the death of Marx or Marxism. Marx is definitely not dead but neither is he alive as the privileged or exclusive holder of all social wisdom and knowledge. He is as alive or as dead as the other major founding fathers of the social sciences. As far as sociology is concerned, given the nature of its project, its founding fathers have not and cannot be buried and forgotten as easily as those in the natural sciences.

Finally, as far as the dimensions of technology, appropriation and ideology (elaborated in chapter 3 and applied in chapter 4) are concerned, given that non-Marxist social science paradigms do not deal seriously or successfully with them, and given that these three dimensions are indispensable for the study of long-term societal transformations – any total rejection of Marxism deprives the student of macro-societal changes with conceptual tools necessary for his or her investigations. Therefore, if Marxism is rejected *in toto* – as it seems to be nowadays in France and elsewhere – one shall have, sooner or later, to reinvent some of its fundamental insights in any serious, non-empiricist attempt to explain how total societies persist and change.

NOTES

1.   See N. Mouzelis, *Back to Sociological Theory: Bridging the Micro-Macro Gap*, London: Macmillan, forthcoming.

Appendix I

TYPES OF REDUCTIONISM IN MARXIST THEORY*

Most Marxists would agree that two of Marxism's most lasting contributions to the methodology of the social sciences are: (1) its holistic orientation – its unwillingness to examine social phenomena in a compartmentalised fashion; and (2) its portrayal of collective agents in a dialectical relationship to their social environment – with economic, political and ideological structures setting limits to collective action, while at the same time collective agents (classes, social movements and so on) react to these limitations and try, more or less systematically, either to change or maintain them. In other words, Marxist methodology shows human beings as both the producers and the products of their social world.[1]

On the other hand, Marx's emphasis on the primacy of the economic sphere and his disciples' innumerable attempts to formulate this primacy in rigorous theoretical terms has led to various forms of reductionist tendencies which have diluted the dialectical and holistic character of Marxist thought. Thus the various mechanistic and a priori attempts to derive cultural and political institutional forms and practices from the structure and functioning of the economic base have repeatedly impaired the usefulness of Marxism as a holistic conceptual framework – by consistently neglecting the specificity and relatively autonomous dynamics of political and cultural phenomena. Furthermore, the subject-social environment or agent-structure dialectic has been jeopardised by either an ultra-voluntarism which sees social classes as omnipotent and omniscient anthropomorphic entitites; or, at the other extreme, by emphasising systemic/structural constraints and possibilities to the extent of portraying agents as mere puppets of a complex articulation of economic, political and ideological structures.

One of the chief foci of analysis in the marked rivival of Marxist theory has been criticism of the economic reductionism which was so prevalent a feature of the 'orthodox'/dogmatic Marxism of the Stalinist era. The debates on Marxist theory of the capitalist State – both in this country and on the Continent – demonstrate a common and abiding preoccupation with how to forge conceptual tools for going beyond economistic/reductionist explanations of the political

157

sphere; hence the centrality of such concepts as the relative autonomy of the State, the specificity of the political instance and the like. Despite this growing preoccupation, however, little has been done to clearly define the above concepts and to distinguish, for instance, between different types of reductionism or of 'relative autonomy'. Let us take a very simple example.

To argue that the action of political agents can be reduced to the action of economically dominant groups is a proposition very different from arguing that those agents' policies can be fully understood in terms of the reproduction requirements of the capitalist mode of production.

The first type of reductionism implies an agent→agent relationship; the second, insofar as the main focus of explanation is not a socio-economic group but the capitalist system's functional requirements, implies an institutional structure→agent relationship.[2] Furthermore, the idea that the political system as a whole, or the constitutional framework of the State (rather than the policies of its personnel), can be completely understood in terms of the 'logic' of capital accumulation leads to a third type of reductionism, one implying a structure→structure relationship. This variant in turn must be differentiated from a fourth, which tries to explain political institutions as the direct result of the conspirational machinations of economically dominant groups (an agent→structure relationship).

The distinction, therefore, between (institutional) structures and agents (in non-Marxist sociology: the system-action or the system integration-social integration distinction)[3] is a useful basis for establishing four different types of relationship: (1) agent→agent, (2) agent→structure, (3) structure→agent, and (4) structure→structure. If we limit our analysis of reductionism to attempts at reducing the political to the economic sphere, we obtain the following diagram:

	political agents	political structures
Primacy of economic agents	voluntaristic variants of reductionism	
Primacy of economic structures	structuralist variants	

This typology (with the help of which I shall attempt a critique of some of the recent debates on the relationship between the economic and the political instances in capitalist social formations) may be useful for identifying the quite distinct theoretical practices grouped under the economic reductionist umbrella, and for becoming aware of the variety of reductionist traps which exist in Marxist theory.

(1) Voluntaristic Types of Reductionism

Since these reductionist variants are quite straightforward and have been very common in recent Marxist debates on the relationship between the economic and the political, they will be discussed only very briefly.

(A) Agent→Agent (A→A) reductionism

A→A reductionism typifies all those theories which contend that the actions and policies of those directly exercising State power are invariably subjected to the pressures of an omnipotent bourgeoisie constantly pulling the strings behind the backs of politicians or the military. Here the class-State relationship is viewed as one between economic groups on the one side, and political groups or agents on the other, in a situation where the political groups are the passive instruments of the economic ones.

The conceptualisation of the economic-political relationship as a relationship of agents involved in a zero-sum power game allows for an either 'economistic' or 'politicist' reductionism of the agent→agent kind. As Poulantzas puts it, in the former case 'the dominant class absorbs the State by emptying it of its own powers, in the latter case the State imposes "its" will (that of the bureaucracy and political elites) on the divergent and rival interests of civil society'.[4] As this essay is mainly concerned with economistic forms of reductionism, the former is what is of interest here. In this case a category of State agents is conceived as the passive tool in the service of economically powerful groups.

This 'instrumentalist' view of the State is a characteristic feature of 'vulgar' Marxism, and in less caricatured form it can be found in the writings of C. W. Mills and of Miliband, for instance.[5] However, it can be argued that the stand taken in these writings is not reductionist in the strict sense of the word, since it does not a priori reduce political to economic practices; since the establishment of links between political and economic agents (either in terms of an analysis of the class origins of State personnel, or in terms of linkages between economic, political and military élites) is based on empirical research. Their analysis would be truly reductionist only if the relationship between economic interests and State personnel were established a priori, that is, in a manner ruling out any possibility of seeing the relationship as variable, problematic and open to empirical investigation. Such exclusion of crucial problem areas from empirical investigation is indeed a major characteristic of economic reductionism.

On the other hand, Poulantzas has already pointed out that the conceptual framework underlying the writings of Miliband and Mills focuses predominantly on agent→agent relationship. As such it evades the study of the structural/institutional context of economic, political and ideological constraints and possibilities which both set limits and create opportunities for political and economic agents.[6]

It might be useful, therefore, to distinguish between 'strong' and 'weak' forms of A→A reductionist practices. In the strong type, the reduction of political to economic practices tends to be of a mechanistic, a-prioristic character substituting ready-made formulae for empirical investigation; the weak type of reductionism results from a conceptual framework focusing exclusively on problems of social rather than system integration, on social conflict rather than structural constraints/opportunities and systemic contradictions.

In other words, if the 'strong' version of reductionism eliminates problem areas through a-prioristic/dogmatic assumptions as to the total lack of autonomy of certain phenomena (for example, political groups), the 'weak' version of reductionism eliminates problem areas by default, so to speak – by using a conceptual framework which, though it makes no dogmatic reductions, fails to draw the student's attention to such phenomena.

It goes without saying that no reductionist orientation is implied where economic primacy is established (either in the form of the overriding importance of agents, or institutions, or both) not as a *universal* postulate in the conceptual framework itself, but as the result of theorisation and empirical investigation of specific cases, or even specific types of social formation. To argue, for instance, that the relationship between class locations and political practices tends to be more direct in capitalist than in pre-capitalist formations, and that in consequence political struggles based on economic cleavages are more important in the former, does not involve any reductionist connotations, strong or weak.[7]

(B) Agent→Structure (A→S) reductionism
The A→S type of reductionism is another version of instrumental voluntarism, but here the State as an instrument is seen in terms of its

institutional structure rather than in terms of its personnel. Here the bourgeoisie does not control and guide the political decision-making process by constant lobbying, but instead by creating an institutional framework which itself will ensure that the State personnel (irrespective of their social origins or interest-group connections) will generate policies which safeguard and promote bourgeois interests. This type of reductionism too can take more sophisticated forms, as for instance when political institutions are seen as not only the result of bourgeois machinations, but as the intended or unintended long-term outcomes of class struggles.[8]

Of course, the two types of reductionism examined so far (A→A and A→S) can be and often are combined, resulting in the type of ultra-voluntarism which portrays dominant classes as omnipotent and omniscient entities controlling all groups and shaping all institutions within a given social formation. Such types of theory, although quite discredited among scholars, still exercise a powerful influence as ideological weapons in the political arena. On that level, when it is not the bourgeoisie as a whole which is portrayed as running the day-to-day management of the capitalist world, it is usually such all-powerful agencies as the Pentagon or the CIA which are said to implement its wishes.[9]

It could be argued that the distinction between the above two voluntaristic variants of reductionism is spurious, that there can be no differentiation between the autonomy or lack of autonomy of agents on the one hand and institutions on the other and that, for instance, autonomy of political groups implies autonomy of political institutions and vice versa. Now it is perfectly true that in most concrete situations the distinction between the relative autonomy of groups, on the one hand, and that of the institutions, on the other, is quite difficult to draw in any but purely analytical terms. However, where for instance, due to conjunctural circumstances, a politically dominant group exercises an inordinate amount of power without this power having yet been institutionalised into stable 'authority' structures, their group autonomy and institutional autonomy do not coincide.[10]

This is merely another way of saying that just as systemic or structural contradictions do not necessarily overlap with social conflict,[11] so structural/systemic constraints do not always overlap with group pressures. Claus Offe provides a good example of systemic constraints and group pressures not necessarily overlapping. He argues that in early capitalism, before the advent of universal suffrage, the State was much more an instrument of the dominant classes – that is, that in its policy-making it was much more compliant to pressures from the dominant classes. Universal suffrage at a later stage of capitalist development brought with it a reduction of 'class' domination and the growth of 'capitalist system' domination. In Poulantzas' formulation, the State became increasingly preoccupied with the overall reproduction of the capitalist system – that is, it became much more exposed to systemic 'demands'.[12]

(2) Structuralist Types of Reductionism

In the voluntaristic variants of reductionism, the major linkages between the economic and the political instances are in terms of actions, strategies or practices of groups or quasi-groups which, more or less deliberately, shape political institutions or directly control the political decision-making process. The anthropomorphism and voluntarism of these types of reductionism contrast sharply with the structure→structure (S→S), and structure→agent (S→A) variants, which must now be examined.

In structuralist reductionist explanations, agents are no longer central to the analysis. Either they disappear altogether, or they play a very peripheral role as the passive products of structural determinations. As anthropomorphic voluntarism gives way to functionalist linkages between the economic and the political institutional spheres, so 'strategy' concepts such as policies, intended/unintended consequences, group pressures and class struggles are replaced by systemic concepts such as functional requirements, structural constraints, tendential laws and contradictions. Another way of putting the difference is to say that, whereas in voluntarism social processes are viewed in terms of the actors, in functionalism the same social processes are seen in terms of the institutional system and the requirements for its persistence/reproduction.

If the voluntaristic types of reductionism have been out of fashion for some time now, the spectacular development of Althusserian Marxism has invested the functionalist/structuralist variants with a high degree of popularity and intellectual respectability. It is quite appropriate, therefore, to examine them rather more closely.

2.1) *Structure→Structure (S→S) reductionism*
In this variant, the institutional features of the political system are derived from, or reduced to, economic structural constraints, or to the 'laws of motion' of the capitalist mode of production.

(A)   The crudest form of S→S reductionism conceptualises the institutional structure of the State or the overall political system as an epiphenomenon, as a mere reflection of the infrastructure. This epiphenomenalist view of the State and the political sphere allows neither voluntaristic mechanisms (group pressures, policies, strategies) nor functionalist ones (systemic constraints, functional requirements) as linkages of the economic and political; the political sphere simply reflects the economic one and, diachronically, whenever changes occur in the infrastructure, they sooner or later make themselves felt, in more less autonomatic fashion, on the superstructural level.

This type of epiphenomenalism is also out of fashion, although there are vestiges of it in, for instance, Offe's early writings on the State. Offe starts by criticising both 'instrumentalist/influence' and 'systemic constraints' theories of the State as these are expounded in Miliband's and Poulantzas' work respectively. In Offe's view, neither theory succeeds in proving the class character of the bourgeois State, since they both focus on external pressure or constraints, rather than on its internal structure – that is, on those administrative mechanisms which transform the general interests of capital into public policy.

In fact, for Offe the State is a *capitalist* State rather than a State within capitalism, because its internal structure includes various selective mechanisms which ensure;

(a)   the elimination of all policies representing non-capitalist interests;
(b)   that the 'proper' decisions (from the point of view of the general interests of capital) are taken for the further accumulation of capital;
(c)   that the State policies in favour of capital are presented as favouring the general interest of all classes.[13]

Now assuming that such a complicated 'filter system' exists which, irrespective of group influences or systemic constraints, ensures that decisions are produced which are right for capital, how does Offe explain its emergence and persistence?

Since he does not choose to show in *historico-genetic* manner how such a filter system comes about, he has only two options left: *either* to demonstrate by teleological means that these three selective mechanisms exist as the result of certain systemic constraints in the economy; *or* to show that these mechanisms 'reflect' on the level of the State's internal structure the *complementarity* between the

structure of the economy and the structure of the polity – a complementarity which ensures that the requirements of the one system
must correspond to those of the other and vice versa.

In fact, as Offe avoids dealing systematically with group influences
and systemic constraints external to the State, he comes very close to
the second line of reasoning. Sardei-Diermann *et al.*, have argued
that 'Offe's reasons for focusing on the State alone are based on the
assumption that the relationship State-economy is *reflected* in the
internal structures of the political system. While there is no doubt
that the analysis of the structures of the State is important and a
widely neglected field, their development has to be examined in a
socio-historic context. A priori a full correspondence between the
structures of the relationship State-economy and the internal structures of the State cannot be assumed. Even if such a correspondence
does exist at one stage of the development, this very fact might
impede the development of such a correspondence at a later stage'.[14]

(B)   Most variants of S→S reductionism avoid the reflectionist
conceptualisation by establishing functionalist linkages between the
economic and the political instances. So Suzanne Brunhoff's study of
State-capital relationships[15] elaborates a theme which has become
widely accepted among Marxist theorists of the State. This is that,
contrary to *laissez faire* liberal ideologies about the bourgeois State,
intervention of the State in the capitalist economy (even during its
competitive stage) is not the 'external' intervention of an autonomous
subject in an already constituted, self-regulating economic system;
rather, as well as being external (given the differentiation between
the economic and the political spheres in capitalism and the relative
autonomy of the latter), it is also innate to the economy. State
intervention is seen as playing a *constitutive* role in the reproduction
of the money-commodities-money (M-C-M) circuit.

Brunhoff tries to establish this by examining the M-C-M circuit of
two specific commodities in capitalism: labour and money. She
argues, for instance, that without State intervention the M-C-M
circuit cannot, on a purely capitalist basis, ensure the long-term
reproduction of labour power. For insofar as the price of labour
power tends to cover only the cost of its day-to-day reproduction
('*reproduction quotidienne du travail*'), the costs necessary for its
long-term reproduction (which would involve such things as coverage
against illness, unemployment, accidents at work and so forth) must
be met in a non-capitalist manner – namely, by State intervention.

With respect to labour power, therefore, the M-C-M circuits are not conceivable in the long run without State intervention; hence State intervention does not play a merely corrective role *vis-à-vis* capitalism, but is present in its very constitution.

Brunhoff allows that in economies where the capitalist mode of production has not expanded very widely, the long-term reproduction of labour power can be ensured by the large non-capitalist sectors with minimum State intervention. But as capitalism expands more and more, State intervention too has to become more extensive – hence the shift from mere State 'assistance' to the full-blown 'social security' welfare institutions of advanced capitalism. This shift from minimal to large-scale State intervention in the field of labour legislation is due not so much to class struggles or the development of class consciousness and class organisation among the workers, as much more so to the long-term reproduction requirements of monopoly capitalism. In other words, this type of reductionism conceives the increasingly welfaristic character of the contemporary capitalist State as primarily a necessary condition for the existence of advanced capitalism.

It is not, of course, only labour which cannot reproduce itself through purely capitalist means. The reproduction of capital encounters similar problems. Thus, according to the German 'logic of capital' school of the State,[16] the interest differences between fractions of capital would, if left to their own devices, tend to create an anarchic state of affairs where fierce competition, cut-throat inter-capital fights and the ensuing over-exploitation of labour would actually jeopardise the very reproduction of the capitalist mode of production. It is this which necessitates State intervention to safeguard the interests of capital as a whole by regulating competition, controlling labour-capital conflicts, and generally providing the bourgeois legal framework which is a fundamental prerequisite for the reproduction of capitalism. So here too the basic institutional features of the contemporary capitalist State are derived from the 'logic of capital', namely, the reproduction requirements of the capitalist mode of production.

(C)   This type of reasoning is not, of course, used only in the context of the study of the capitalist State. Godelier, for instance, employs it to explain the political institutions of the Mbuti pygmies, a society of hunters and food-gatherers in equatorial Congo.[17] Their system of production (mainly hunting in bands, with the women and children driving the game into nets held by the men) generates three fundamental constraints which express the 'social conditions for the reproduction of the productive process: (1) the *dispersion constraint*, which refers to the fact that for the system to operate effectively, the band members cannot be above or below a certain number; (2) the *co-operation constraint*, which emphasises the need for collaboration of all members in the productive process according to sex and age; and (3) the *fluidity* or *non-closure constraint*, which is the band's need to be in 'permanent flux', that is, in frequent movement of members from one band to another.

These three constraints form a system which 'is the origin of a certain number of *simultaneous* structural effects of *all* other instances of the Mbuti's social organisations'.[18] For example, on the political level, Mbuti society is characterised by relative equality among band members, and by a remarkable lack of aggression among bands. Why is band warfare rare in Mbuti society? According to Godelier, because it 'is incompatible with the mode-of-production constraints [1], [2] and [3] taken separately and in their reciprocal relations'. How can one explain the role of the 'fool' within the band? By the fact that the fool, by means of certain institutionalised practices, defuses conflict between tribal members and thus enhances the co-operation which is a prerequisite for the reproduction of the system.

Thus there are similar norms of co-operation in all instances of the Mbuti social formation; and this *isomorphism* between instances is 'generated by the fact that they are all different aspects of the *same cause* (i.e. the system of the three constraints) which acts simultaneously on all societal levels'.[19] In other words, Godelier sees political structures as directly derived from economic ones, or rather political institutional forms as the direct result of the economic system's reproduction requirements.

(D)   J. Hirsch's work, although in many ways similar to the above-mentioned approaches, presents two interesting features which set it apart.

(1)   *Surface and depth analysis.*   More so than any other member of the German school, Hirsch is very critical of theorists like Poulantzas who – starting from the idea of the relative autonomy of the political instance – either study political structures in isolation from the underlying economic ones; or examine the State-economy relationship by limiting their analytical focus to the epiphenomenal forms of

economic and political structures. In so doing they, like non-Marxist social scientists, take the given institutional forms of the State and the economy at face value, and neglect a deeper study of the hidden laws of motion of capital which, in the final analysis, provides the explanation of both economic and political institutional forms.

Hirsch argues that it is not by the establishment of direct superficial links between economic and political institutions, but only by means of these capitalist laws as formulated by Marx and elaborated by his successors (labour theory of value, tendency for the rate of profit to fall, and so on), that a solid basis can be laid for the proper understanding of not merely the structure of the capitalist State, but also of the institutional structure of present-day capitalist economies.

Thus for him:

> it is with respect to the still major contradiction of the capitalist mode of production as expressed by the tendential law of the falling rate of profit that one can understand the increasingly interventionist character of the contemporary capitalist State – such intervention being necessary in order to counteract the falling profit rate by a radical restructuring of the economy.[20]

The distinction Hirsch draws between depth and surface analysis does not make his approach any the less reductionist, however. It simply replaces a surface structure→structure reductionism with a more complicated reductionism which takes the form of

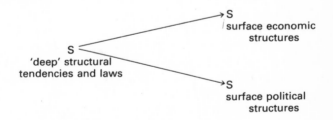

In other words, in this case it is not the functional requirements of the epiphenomenal economic institutions which shape the institutional structure of the State, but instead both these surface structures can be derived from the 'hidden' laws of motion of capital.

(2) *Structural and historical analysis.* Another distinctive feature of Hirsch's work which at first sight attenuates his S→S reductionism, is his insistence that the type of a-historical structuralist and purely logical analysis which characterises the German school must be

complemented by historical analysis of the class struggles which at any specific moment can explain the concrete forms taken by State intervention. He contends that since the laws of motion of capital are not iron laws but structural tendencies, often neutralised or weakened by counter-tendencies, it is the outcome of specific class struggles which will determine their structural efficacy. For instance, a trade-union victory over wages can reinforce the tendency of the profit rate to fall, whereas a defeat would reinforce counter-tendencies and attenuate capitalist crises.

In other words, Hirsch makes the general point that the type of logico-deductive structural analysis developed by the German school (identifying the necessary conditions for the existence and repro-duction of monopoly capitalism) should not take the place of, but rather go hand in hand with a historico-genetic analysis of specific class struggles in the light of the more abstract propositions about the tendential laws of the capitalist mode of production.[21]

Unfortunately, despite these programmatic utterances, Hirsch's work contains no serious historical analysis of class struggles, neither is there a serious theoretical attempt at integrating the structural analysis of tendential laws and contradictions with a historical analy-sis of class struggles. In fact, the concept of class struggles, although repeatedly brought up both in his own writings and in those of other members of the German school, plays a purely decorative role. It is used as a *deus ex machina* to save the analysis from the circular formalism and teleological tendencies necessarily entailed in S→S reductionism.

It has frequently been pointed out that to list the functional requirements for the maintenance and reproduction of an economic system, and then to say that certain institutional features of the State seem to fulfil these requirements, does not suffice as an explanation of the specific form taken by these institutional features or of how they came about. The attempt of many structuralist theorists to do so by using terms such as structural determination, determination in the last instance, and so on, is simply to illegitimately transform functional consequences or functional requirements into causes – a teleological type of explanation which both non-Marxists and more recently also Marxist theorists have criticised and rejected.[22]

Given the deeply ingrained teleological bias of all S→S reductionist explanations, paying lip service to the concept of class struggles can by no means redress the balance between structuralist and historical analysis. Drawing up, as Hirsch does, long lists of structural tendencies and counter-tendencies, and then at the very end invoking class struggle as the ultimate arbiter in the balance of the two, is hardly the way to integrate the logico-deductive/structuralist with the historical/ class-struggle approach. It is simply an ad hoc use of concepts of the latter as a smokescreen for the theoretical impasses which are an unavoidable consequence of the former.

2.2)   Structure→Agent (S→A) reductionism

If the S→S type of reductionism derives the main features of political institutions from the functional requirements or constraints imposed on it by the economy, S→A reductionism uses similar terms to try to explain political *practices*. An area where this type of reductionism emerges very clearly is in the debates on the structural determination of classes in capitalist societies.

A useful starting point would be Poulantzas' distinction between class 'places' and class 'positions'. The first is basically a concept referring to the 'objective' location of agents in the technical and social division of labour; the second is a 'strategy concept' referring to such things as the political organisations or agencies representing a class, the strategies ('positions') and policies it formulates in a concrete conjuncture, and so on. 'What one means by "class consciousness" proper and by an autonomous political organisation – i.e. from the point of view of the working class, a revolutionary proletarian ideology and an autonomous party – refer to *class positions* and to the *conjuncture*, they constitute the conditions for the intervention of classes as *social forces*'.[23] (Since in English the term 'position' often refers to what Poulantzas calls 'places', I shall be using the term 'practices' or 'strategies' here instead of 'positions'.) Once Poulantzas' distinction is accepted, the question arises of what linkages there are between class places and class practices.

A straightforward reductionist explanation would involve the establishment of direct one-way linkages between the two: class practices and strategies on the political level are derived and understood in terms of the objective class structure, that is, in terms of the objective places alloted to agents by the capitalist division of labour on the level of the economy.

Now given that, as I shall argue below, it is very difficult, if not impossible in many instances, to establish *direct* links between objective class places and political practices, there are two distinct strategies which can be used to cope with the problems created by an S→A type of reductionism.

(A)   The first strategy is to argue that, whenever political conflicts are not directly on class cleavages but on for instance regional, ethnic, racial, religious or clientelistic ones, then the latter are *epiphen menal*, and going beyond appearances will soon make it evident that it is in fact class divisions which are at the root of such conflicts.

To take a concrete example: Luciano Li Causi has criticised anthropologists who study Mediterranean politics purely in terms of patronage, and who consequently tend to neglect the class structures underlying clientelistic practices.[24] Although he is right in insisting that clientelistic practices should be linked with the class structure, I think he slips into an S→A type of reductionism when he argues that clientelism is an epiphenomenon, a mere ideology useful for concealing the underlying structures of exploitation. According to him, in the rural areas of Italy, for instance, there are always exploiting landlords behind the patrons, and exploited peasants behind the clients. From a theoretical point of view, therefore, the problem of patronage ceases to exist for him.

By dismissing clientelism in this cavalier fashion, Li Causi eliminates a crucial problem in Mediterranean politics: the examination of the intricate shifting relationships between clientelistic and class/political organisations during the process of capital accumulation. His reduction of clientelistic practices to class locations does not allow for the study of those conditions where the dominant political cleavages are closely connected with objective class divisions (that is, where they take the form of exploiters versus exploited), and those conditions where they are not (namely, where major conflicts take the form of one clientelistic or regionally-based exploiter/exploited alliance against another).

Moreover, Li Causi's reductionist position totally misses the fundamental point that political conflicts along clientelist 'vertical' lines often cut across and inhibit the political organisation of the exploited classes along 'horizontal' class lines[25]; as well as the fact that in many peripheral capitalist formations a variety of vertical and horizontal political organisations coexist and alternate in importance according to the political conjuncture.[26]

(B)   The S→A reductionism examined above either sees political practices as the direct effect of class locations, or whenever this does not seem to be so, that is, whenever political practices do not appear to be founded on class divisions, the importance of class locations is reasserted by dismissing as epiphenomenal the clientelistic, ethnic, regional basis of such practices. In other words, there is a refusal to accept that institutional structures other than economic ones (regional, ethnic) may have an important impact on political practices.

A more sophisticated form of S→A reductionism, such as Poulantzas' for example, would accept the obvious fact that political practices cannot be entirely understood or explained by focusing on economic structures alone. Let us look in more detail at how he deals with the class place/class practice relationship.

Poulantzas begins by admitting that it is not possible to establish a one-to-one relationship between class places and practices. For instance, he argues that in terms of class places, the 'labour aristocracy' belongs to the proletariat, although this category of workers often adopts 'bourgeois' strategies which are incongruent with its objective interests.[27]

How then can this incongruency be explained? According to Poulantzas, by the fact that class practices are not determined simply by the economic instance, but by the overall structuralist matrix which consists of a complex articulation of economic, political and ideological structures. It is precisely because political and ideological structures, in addition to the economic ones, have pertinent 'effects' on class practices, that there can be no one-to-one correspondence between class places and practices.

This, of course, avoids the crude class reductionism of a direct place-practice correspondence, but merely replaces it with a more general structural determinism which portrays political agents and their practices as the passive product of a complex articulation of institutional structures at the level of the overall social formation. Of course, like Hirsch, Poulantzas constantly talks about class struggles which, he says, constitute the primary motive force for reproducing the relations of production and the whole matrix of structures. But, again like Hirsch, his analysis uses the concept of class struggles as an ad hoc formula which has no serious theoretical connections with the rest of his conceptual framework – a framework which in any case does not allow for any real effectiveness of class struggles.[28] Poulantzas defines the concept of social classes as 'a concept which indicates the effects of all the structures of a mode-of-production matrix or of a social formation on the agents who constitute the supports: this concept indicates therefore the effects of the global structure in the sphere of social relations'.[29]

So classes are seen here as the 'effects' rather than the 'causes' of structures, and agents are simply 'supports' of structures. In fact, Poulantzas' determining relationships always develop from the structure to the agents, rather than the other way round. We are constantly told how complex structural determinations shape the agents' practices; we are never shown how the latter, especially in the form of such collective agencies as political movements, parties and the like, can in their turn have an impact, can maintain or transform the overall structural configurations.

Given this particular conceptualisation of classes and the place→ agent relationship, it is obvious why the concept of class struggles does not fit at all into Poulantzas' structuralism. For if classes are the effects of the overall matrix of institutional structures, then struggles between 'bearers of structures' are just as much the effects of structural determinations as everything else.

In conclusion, the serious integration of the concept of class struggle into Poulantzas' overall theory would have necessitated a drastic alteration of the author's rigid S→A reductionism. It would have necessitated the conceptualisation of classes and class struggles not merely as 'effects' of structural determinations, but as relatively autonomous collective agencies, as social forces which are not simply the products of structural constraints, but which at the same time continuously produce, reproduce and transform institutional structures. Since this is not done, the ritualistic incantation of the class struggle can not in any way mitigate Poulantzas' S→A reductionism.

So finally Poulantzas' – notwithstanding his useful distinction between class places and practices, and despite his other efforts to differentiate his class theory from that of Althusser – does not manage to break away from the latter's obsessive structural reductionism which argues that 'the real subject of all partial history is the *combination* under the dependence of which are the elements and their relationships, that is to say, something which is *not a subject*. So it could be said that the chief problem of a scientific history, a theoretical history, is identifying the combination on which depend the elements that are to be analysed'.[30]

It is in this way that Althusserians, in violent reaction to the crude voluntaristic reductionism found both in the Marxist and the non-Marxist traditions, ended up at the other extreme: with an S→A reductionism which denies all possibility of any autonomous collective action, an ultra-structuralism which reduces all social analysis to the a-historical identification of a number of invariant elements and the study of their intricate articulation and combination.

CONCLUSION

The four types of reductionism that have here been examined, either separately or in various combinations, all neutralise the most fruitful aspects of the Marxist framework: its dialectical and holistic character. Insofar as they suggest that it is possible systematically to derive political practices and institutional structures from the 'laws' or functional requirements of the capitalist mode of production or the machinations of an all-powerful bourgeoisie, they discourage serious study of the complicated and more or less indirect linkages between the economic and the political instances. Moreover, insofar as they portray collective agents as omnipotent, anthropomorphic entities or, at the other extreme, as mere 'effects' of structural determinations, they lead either to an ultra-voluntarism or to a structural determinism – both extremes emasculating Marxism's dialectical character, that is, its portrayal of collective agents in a constantly changing relationship with a social environment which both constructs actors' identities and presents them with a more or less large number of alternatives.

Is it possible then, given this state of affairs, to theorise the relationship between the economic and the non-economic spheres, or between institutional structures and agents' practices without falling into any of the reductionist traps mentioned above? Of course, it is beyond the scope of this essay to give an answer to this complex question. One thing is clear, however. The problem of reductionism cannot be solved by merely proclaiming the 'specificity' or 'relative autonomy' of the non-economic sphere. For if the idea of 'relative autonomy' is going to be something more than an empty phrase, one has to construct conceptual tools which can actually lead to the relatively autonomous study of political and cultural phenomena. For the moment such tools do not exist in Marxist theory. When Marxists analyse the non-economic spheres (political parties, religious organisations, kinship or educational institutions, and the like) they do so in terms of concepts derived from the economy, that is, in terms of class or the reproductive requirements of modes of production. Of course, there is nothing wrong in examining the intricate inter-relationships between economic and non-economic spheres or more precisely, the contributions of the latter to the reproduction of the former. But to argue, as many Marxists do, that political or cultural institutions are 'nothing but' the conditions of existence of the economy or the dominant mode of production, tells us less about such institutions and more about the conceptual poverty of present day Marxist theory.

The point is that for the moment, despite ritualistic statements about the relative autonomy or specificity of the 'political' or the 'ideological', that Marxism does not provide concepts which can help the student to take seriously into account the specific dynamic and 'history' of non-economic spheres. Or to put it in another way, there are no theories of politics and culture which are both Marxist and non-reductionist. Therefore the choice of the student is either reductionism or an ad hoc, empiricist treatment of such areas of study as law, education, the family and so on.

Exactly the same argument applies if one tries to overcome the type of reductionism which portrays actors and their practices as mere 'effects' of structural determinations (whether on the economic, political or cultural level). It is not enough to proclaim in a highly abstract manner that it is misleading to conceptualise agents or classes as the 'bearers of structures'. One has to construct specific concepts which can provide systematic guidance as to how structural constraints/possibilities articulate with collective agents' strategies and struggles, or how a 'logico-deductive' structuralist approach can be integrated with a 'historical-genetic' class analysis.

It seems to me that the present crisis of Marxism as a theory is to a great extent linked with its failure to provide adequate conceptual tools to the two areas mentioned above. It remains to be seen to what extent theorists within the Marxist tradition will be able to fill these two 'gaps' in theory and to overcome the varieties of reductionism discussed here without diluting the specificity of the Marxian paradigm.

NOTES

* A modified version of this essay was published in *TELOS*, Fall, 1980. This essay does not attempt an exhaustive review of the vast literature on the Marxist theories of the capitalist state. Moreover, given the date of its initial publication, more recent developments in this literature are not taken into account. However, the above limitations do not affect the major arguments developed here – since the major aim is to use examples from the state literature as illustrations of the different types of reductionism that one finds within Marxism.

1. For an elaboration of this view of dialectics of G. Lukacs, *History and Class Consciousness. Studies in Marxist Dialectics*, London: Merlin Press, 1971.

2. This is the distinction behind the Poulantzas-Miliband debate; see E. Laclau's 'The Specificity of the Political: The Poulantzas-Miliband Debate', *Economy and Society*, Vol. IV, No. 1, pp. 87–110.

3. For a discussion of the system-social integration or system-action distinction cf. D. Lockwood, 'Social Integration and System Integration', in G. K. Zollschan and Hirsch (eds), *Explorations in Social Change*, London: Routledge, 1964, pp. 244–56; see also N. Mouzelis, 'Social and System Integration: Some Reflections on a Fundamental Distinction', *British Journal of Sociology*, XXI(2), 1979, pp. 207–18. For the distinction between structures and practices cf. N. Poultanzas, *Social Power and Social Classes*, London: New Left Books, 1975, p. 85 ff. Cf. also M. Castells, *La Question Urbaine*, Paris, Maspèro, 1972.

    It should be emphasised that both Marxist and non-Marxist theorists who use the structure(system)-agent(actor) distinction see it as an *analytical* one. To use Poulantzas' expression, the distinction does not refer to 'ontologically different domains', but to two different ways of looking at the same social processes.

    Finally, given that I am here concerned with *institutional* structures, the concept of structure does not have the connotation that one finds in the work of Levi-Strauss or in Giddens' theory of structuration. (As far as Giddens is concerned, my institutional structures/action dichotomy could roughly correspond to his distinction between an analysis on the level of institutions and one on the level of what he calls *strategic conduct* – see his *Central Problems in Sociological Theory*, Macmillan, 1979.)

    Of course, one could argue that when Marxists, especially Althusserian Marxists, use the concepts of structure and structural determinations, their use of the term is closer to Levi-Strauss' than to Parsons' idea of structure. Although in theory this might be so, in practice all of the Marxist theorists discussed below (including Poulantzas and Godelier) use the concept of structure and structural determination in the more conventional functionalist manner. That is to say, structure is seen as a system concept which leads to the view of social processes from the point of view of the social whole's reproductive or functional requirements.

4. N. Poulantzas, *State, Power, Socialism*, New Left Books, 1978, p. 14.

5. C. W. Mills, *The Power Elite*, 1956, and R. Miliband, *The State in Capitalist Society*, London: Weidenfeld & Nicolson, 1969.

6. Cf. N. Poulantzas, 'The Problem of the Capitalist State', *New Left Review*, No. 58, Nov.-Dec. 1969. The debate on this issue continued in subsequent numbers of the same journal (Nos 59, 82, 95). Cf. also E. Laclau, 'The Specificity of the Political: Around the Poulantzas-Miliband Debate', *Economy and Society*, Vol. 5, No. 1, February 1975.

7. For an elaboration of this argument cf. N. Mouzelis, 'Class and

Clientelist Politics: The Case of Greece', *Sociological Review*, August 1978.

8. Cf. J. Holloway and S. Picciotto, 'Capital, Crisis and State', in *Capital and Class*, Summer 1977, pp. 58 ff.

9. To take an example I am quite familiar with, in Greek political debates the CIA is often presented as an all-powerful deity regulating and controlling everything and everybody on the social and political scene. Even price fluctuations and global economic crises have been regarded as the direct result of sinister CIA machinations. Cf. for instance John Katris, *The Birth of Neo-Fascism* (in Greek), Geneva, 1971. For a critique of this approach, as far as Greece is concerned, cf. N. Mouzelis, 'The Rise and Fall of the Greek Dictatorship', *New Left Review*, March-April, 1976.

10. The 1967 Greek military coup provides a good example of the non-correspondence of group and institutional autonomy. The coup did give a group of officers the opportunity to exercise an inordinate amount of power for a limited period of time. But because of their failure to legitimise army rule on a long-term basis, *military institutions* in Greece did not acquire the degree of salience and relative autonomy which they have in neighbouring Turkey, for instance. There, given the crucial role that Kemal Atatürk's army played in founding the Republic, military institutions exercise a dominance which persists throughout the various political conjunctures and regime changes.

11. Cf. D. Lockwood, op. cit.

12. Cf. Claus Offe, 'Political Authority and Class Structures', in P. Connerton (ed.), *Critical Sociology*, London: Penguin, 1976.

13. Ibid.

14. Cf. S. Sardei-Dierman *et al.*, 'Class Domination and the Political System: A Critical Interpretation of a Recent Contribution by Claus Offe', *Kapitalistate*, 2/1973, p. 68 (italics mine).

15. *Etat et Capital*, Presses Universitaires de Grenoble, 1978.

16. An exposition and presentation of some representative articles in this intellectual tradition is to be found in J. Holloway and S. Picciotto, *State and Capital: A Marxist Debate*, London: Edward Arnold, 1978.

17. *Horizons, Trajets Marxists en Anthropologie*, Paris: Maspero, 1973, pp. 13–82.

18. Ibid., p. 68.

19. Ibid., p. 72 (translation and emphasis mine).

20. T. Hirsch, 'The State Apparatus and Social Reproduction: Elements of a Theory of the Bourgeois State', in J. Holloway and S. Picciotto, op. cit., pp. 57–167.

21. Ibid., pp. 81 ff.

22. Cf. for instance R. K. Merton, *Social Theory and Social Structure*, Glencoe: Social Press, 1963, pp. 60–4; R. Dore, 'Function and Cause', *American Sociological Review*, 1961
     Criticism very similar to that used by the above sociologists against teleological functionalist explanations has recently been rediscovered by Marxist theorists who, with great panache, employ similar arguments though dressed up in a different terminology. (The term

'functional requirements' is replaced by 'necessary condition of exist-ence' – the argument being that it is one thing to logically identify the necessary conditions of existence of an institutional system, and quite another to explain the specific forms these conditions take in a concrete social situation.) Cf. A. Cutler, B. Hindess, P. Hirst and A. Hussain, *Marx's Capital and Capitalism Today*, Vol. 1, London: Routledge, 1977.

23.   *Les Classes Sociales dans le Capitalisme d'Aujourd'hui*, Paris: Seuil, 1974, p. 10.

24.   'Anthropology and Ideology: The Case of Patronage in Mediterranean Societies', *Radical Science Journal*, No. 1, 1975; for a similar approach cf. M. Gilsenan, 'Against Patron-Client Relations', in E. Gellner and J. Waterbury (eds), *Patrons and Clients in Mediterranean Societies*, London: Duckworth, 1977. For a reduction of the caste system to the class structure, cf. C. Meillassoux, 'Are there Castes in India?', *Economy and Society*, February 1973; concerning class reductionism *vis-à-vis* racial conflict, see the critical article of G. Ben-Tovim, 'The Struggle Against Racism: Theoretical and Strategic Perspectives', *Marxism Today*, July 1978; cf. also J. Gabriel and G. Ben-Tovim, 'Marxism and the Concept of Racism', *Economy and Society*, May 1978.

25.   For the concepts of 'horizontal' and 'vertical' organisations cf. E. Wolf, *Peasants*, Englewood Cliffs, N.Y.: Prentice Hall, 1966, pp. 81–6.

26.   For an elaboration of these points cf. N. Mouzelis, 'Class and Clientelist Politics: The Case of Greece', op. cit., and also 'Ideology and Class Politics', *New Left Review*, November-December 1978.

27.   *Les Classes Sociales dans le Capitalisme d'Aujourd'hui*, op. cit., p. 17.

28.   For such a critique of Poulantzas' use of the class-struggle concept cf. Terry Johnson, 'What is to be Done? The Structural Determination of Social Class', *Economy and Society*, Vol. VI, No. 2, May 1977.

29.   Cf. his *Pouvoir Politique et Classes Sociales*, Paris: Maspero, 1968, p. 66. Furthermore, referring to the distinction between places and agents, Poulantzas expressly states that 'the analysis made here of the relations of production according to the phases of present-day mono-poly capitalism, concerns the *place* of capital and its functions. Another [question] is the problem of *agents* who exercise its powers, i.e. those who occupy this place or who depend on it directly . . . in the last analysis they (the agents) are simply an effect of the modification of the relations of production', *Les Classes Sociales*, op. cit., p. 32.

30.   *Lire le Capital*, Vol. II, p. 146.

Appendix II

IDEOLOGY AND CLASS POLITICS: A CRITIQUE OF
ERNESTO LACLAU*

Ernesto Laclau's *Politics and Ideology in Marxist Theory* contains
four interconnected, but relatively self-contained essays.[1] Two of
these had already been published and had been quite influential.
Laclau's critique of Gunder Frank's theory of underdevelopment,
and especially of his definition of capitalism in market rather than
production terms, has for several years now been a standard reference in the sociology of development, and has contributed considerably to the current emphasis on 'mode of production' analysis in
studies of Third-World countries.[2] His intervention in the well-
known Poulantzas-Miliband debate on the capitalist state not only
clarified some of the misunderstandings arising out of this controversy,
but provided a penetrating critique of some aspects of Althusserian
Marxism at a time when the French philosopher's sway over left
intellectuals in the English-speaking countries was very considerable.[3] Since both these essays are quite well known and have been
widely discussed, I shall focus my analysis on the two lengthy
unpublished chapters which actually constitute the bulk of the book.
In these, Laclau does not limit himself to criticising theories put
forward by others. He tries, on the basis of Althusser's concept of
ideological interpellations, first to provide the elements for a reformulation of the Marxist theory of ideology; secondly, to build a
general theory of populism applicable not only to populist movements in Third-World countries, but also to European fascism.

1 Poulantzas and Fascism

Laclau starts with a critique of Poulantzas' theory of ideology, as
developed in his book *Fascism and Dictatorship*.[4] Although he sees
Poulantzas' work as a great advance over purely descriptive, empiricist analyses of fascism, since it offers a variety of theoretical
insights into the complex contradictions which led to the rise of
Hitler's and Mussolini's regimes, he criticises Poulantzas for not
giving an adequate account of the ideological crisis which constitutes
the keystone for an adequate explanation of these developments.

According to Laclau, this failure is principally due to the fact that Poulantzas seeks in too reductionist a manner to establish necessary links between discrete ideological elements and specific social classes. Thus for Poulantzas during the competitive phase of capitalism, Marxism-Leninism is the ideology of the working class and liberalism that of the bourgeoisie. Poulantzas is quite aware, of course, that in actual historical situations specific class ideologies are an amalgam of ideological elements; that, for example, the dominant bourgeois ideology contains within its discourse both working-class and petty bourgeois ideological themes. But this realisation does not prevent him from the unwarranted assumption that, within a specific ideological discourse, it is always possible to identify the class basis of each specific ideological elements, both during the formative growth of this discourse and in its eventual transformation.

Laclau does not agree that liberalism should necessarily be attributed to the bourgeoisie, since the same ideology was and is still being used by quasi-feudal landlords in the Latin American context. Nor does he see militarism as an essentially feudal ideological element, seeing that it has played a central role in the ideologies both of the bourgeoisie and of Third-World anti-imperialist movements. In other words, for Laclau there are no such things as paradigmatic or pure ideologies with determinate class connotations. Ideological themes such as nationalism or democracy are in themselves neutral and not the monopoly of any one class. They can be articulated with the ideological discourse of a vareity of contradictory interests. It is, therefore, only by looking at the overall structure of an ideology, that is, at the way in which it combines its constituent elements, that its class connotations can be established.

2 The Concept of Interpellation

Laclau begins his own analysis of ideological discourses by adopting Althusser's concept of *interpellation*: according to the latter, the factor common to all ideologies is the portrayal of individuals (which, in reality, are mere 'bearers of structures') as autonomous subjects. This inversion, by which the determinate is falsely presented as the determinant, takes place through a process of 'hailing' or 'interpellating' individuals as subjects. 'If, therefore, the basic function of all ideology is to constitute individuals as subjects, and if through interpellation individuals live their conditions of existence as if they were the autonomous principle of the latter ... it is clear that the unity of the distinct aspects of an ideological system is given by the specific interpellation which forms the axis and organizing principle of all ideologies.'[5] On the basis of the above, Laclau makes a fundamental distinction between class and popular interpellations. Class interpellations, insofar as they address individuals as class subjects, arise out of contradictions related to a specific mode of production, whereas popular/democratic interpellations (hailing or addressing agents as 'people') are related to the people/'power-bloc' contradiction – a contradiction which becomes intelligible if one focuses on the *political and ideological* relations of domination.

So what is the relationship of these two types of ideological interpellations with the contradictions to which they correspond? Popular-democratic interpellations do not have a determinate class content; they are an abstract – or rather neutral – ideological raw material, which can be fitted into the ideological discourses of a variety of classes. This precisely is why popular interpellations are the 'domain of ideological struggle par excellence'[6]: the ideological battleground in which antagonistic classes try to appropriate popular beliefs and use them for the promotion of their own interests. It is the strategy of the dominant classes to articulate popular interpellations into their class discourse in such a way that antagonistic interests are neutralised and presented as mere differences. Whenever they succeed in this, they achieve ideological hegemony – since a hegemonic ideology does not imply the uniform imposition of the *Weltanschauung* of the ruling class on the rest of the population, but the presentation of different views of the world in such a way that their antagonistic contradictions are either hidden or neutralised. If the dominated classes, on the other hand, manage to disarticulate popular-democratic elements from the discourse of the ruling class, and succeed in articulating them antagonistically into their own discourse, then they present a serious challenge to the hegemonic position of the power-bloc.

In this way, 'class' and 'people' are both constituent elements of ideological discourses. Class contradictions are related to popular contradictions through *articulation*, not by *reduction*. But although popular contradictions cannot be reduced to class contradictions, the latter do determine the articulating principle of that discourse. In other words, the people/power-bloc contraction, although relatively autonomous, is determined in the last instance by class contradictions and class struggles. This priority of class struggle over popular-democratic struggle is obvious, according to Laclau, 'since the latter takes place only at the ideological and political level (the "people" do not obviously, exist at the level of production relations)'.[7] Clearly, therefore, the major mechanism which transforms ideologies is the class struggle, as classes fight over the articulation/disarticulation of popular-democratic elements.

3 Laclau's Theory of Populism

This conceptualisation provides the basis for an analysis of European fascism, as well as for a more general theory of populism. Starting with the latter, for Laclau the most essential characteristic of populism is its antagonistic articulation of popular-democratic interpellations: '*Our thesis is that populism consists in the presentation of popular-democratic interpellations as a synthetic-antagonistic complex with respect to the dominant ideology*'.[8] In an ideological crisis of the hegemonic class (expressed as a failure to 'neutralise' popular-democratic interpellations, or as a failure of 'transformist' policies), the possibility exists for an antagonistic articulation of popular-democratic elements by either the dominated classes or class fractions of the fragmented power-bloc. In the former case, the working classes may, for instance, articulate popular interpellations into their discourse so as to achieve the 'maximum fusion of popular democratic ideology and socialist ideology'.[9] In the latter case, fractions of the dominant classes seek mass support by the antagonistic use of popular-democratic interpellations, in order to restructure the power-bloc to their own advantage.

Of course, the populism of the dominant classes has the difficult task of both mobilising the masses and at the same time making sure that this mobilisation does not lead to socialist solutions. Hence the need for both the antagonistic articulation of popular interpellations and the 'neutralisation' of the populist movement, by keeping it within 'safe' boundaries. In the fascist variant of populism, this neutralisation is achieved by directing the mass movement towards racialism, and by attempting ideological homogenisation through the imposition of totalitarian forms of repression and indoctrination. In the 'Bonapartist' variant, neutralisation is achieved by the use of State power in such a way that, by means of a complex process of mediations, a delicate balance is struck between various antagonistic social forces. It becomes obvious, therefore, that for Laclau the various types of 'populism' (from Hitler's via Peron's to those of Mao or Tito) do not share a common class basis or express similar class interests, but are instead united by a specific (that is, antagonistic) ideological articulation of popular-democratic elements.

This brings us to Laclau's theory of fascism. He views European, and especially German fascism primarily as the result of a double ideological crisis – affecting both the hegemonic class and the working classes. The ideological crisis in the ruling bloc stemmed from the resistance of the dominant landowning fraction within it to the reforms which the advent of monopoly capitalism was making imperative. This resistance led to a serious fragmentation within the power-bloc, with the monopoly capital fraction unable 'to impose its hegemony within the existing institutional framework – as it had done in England and France'.[10] The working classes, on the other hand, were divided into an 'opportunist' wing with a trade-unionist, re-formist orientation; and a sectarian, revolutionary wing with a 'class reductionist' orientation – an orientation which, instead of getting the party to articulate popular interpellations into its revolutionary discourse, made it drive a wedge between class and popular inter-pellations and stress the need for a 'pure' class party and a strictly working-class ideology, uncontaminated by so-called bourgeois nationalist or populist elements.

Given this failure of the working classes to take advantage of the ideological crisis in the dominant class, the road lay wide open for monopoly capital to use popular interpellations in a manner antagon-istic to the dominant ideology, and so to create a mass movement based on the petty bourgeoisie and part of the working classes. For Laclau, therefore, the development of European fascism is directly related to the failure of the working class to articulate into its discourse popular-democratic interpellations, and so establish a hege-monic ideology which would have enabled it to present itself as the leader and founder of a new social order: 'Our thesis is that if fascism was possible, it was because the working class, both in its reformist and its revolutionary sectors, had abandoned the arena of popular-democratic struggles'.[11]

4   Class, Ideology and Organisation

The idea that a variety of classes may draw their ideological themes from a common intellectual pool and manipulate them in different ways for the promotion of mutually incompatible interests is not, of course, a novel one. The great ease with which nationalism or highly complex religions such as Christianity or Islam can be manipulated for the achievement of antagonistic goals is a recurrent idea in most treatises on ideology. But Laclau's formulation has the undeniable merit of seeking to develop this idea in a more systematic and theoretical fashion, via his use of the concept of interpellation, and his attempt to distinguish between class and 'popular' interpellations and to link these with different types of structural contradictions. Moreover, Laclau's insistence that there can be no one-to-one correspondence between ideological elements and class locations; that the people/power-bloc contradiction cannot be reduced to class contradictions; and that it is only when one looks at the overall complex articulation of interpellations that an ideological discourse can be related to a specific class – all these elements constitute a definite theoretical advance and a valuable corrective to the ever-present reductionist tendencies in Marxist theory. Also, by relating the structure of ideologies to the dynamic of class struggles, Laclau avoids treating the subject statically and draws attention to the constantly changing and dialectical character of ideological discourses. However, a number of serious problems arise both in the author's formulation of what populism is, and in his explanations of how and why it comes about.

Probably the most serious of these difficulties concerns the way in which Laclau's analysis moves directly from structural contradictions (of the 'class' or 'people'/'power-bloc' type) to ideological practices, without ever taking into serious account the political organisations which, after all, provide the actual setting in which the processes of articulation and disarticulation of interpellations take place. True enough, as Laclau says, there is no necessary correspondence between political groups and classes. Moreover, populism for Laclau is not a movement, but an ideology which can be adopted by a variety of movements with very different class bases.[12] But even if one were to accept Laclau's definition of populism, there would be no valid reason for dismissing the study of the varied political groups and organisational structures associated with populist ideologies – on the contrary, there would be a very good reason for putting them at the centre of the analysis. This is particularly so if one wants to avoid – as Laclau claims he does – a purely descriptive examination of populist ideologies, and intends to show 'the role played by the strictly populist element in a determinate social formation'.[13]

Indeed, I believe that if one means to demonstrate how populist interpellations relate to all the other dimensions of a social formation, it is not possible to avoid focusing on the complex political-organisational processes which mediate between structural contradictions, on the one hand, and ideological discourse, on the other. Class and popular interpellations do not, after all, articulate or disarticulate on their own. Neither are they constituted into ideological discourses, in an anthropomorphic way, by 'the bourgeoisie' or 'the proletariat'. It is quite true, as Laclau points out, that class struggles are at the root of ideological transformation. But if the concept of class struggle is not specified in more detail – if it is not shown how such struggle relates to political organisations, which finally are the concrete agencies which *do* the actual articulating and disarticulating – then it is left hanging in the air, so to speak. It only has a decorative role in the theory: it establishes (to use Laclau's terminology) formal or 'connotative', rather than theoretical, linkages between the key concepts of the discourse.

5 The Defects of Laclau's Theory of Populism

This gap between real contradictions and ideologies has serious consequences for Laclau's theory of populism. As we have seen, Laclau defines populism as the antagonistic articulation of popular-democratic interpellations *vis-à-vis* the dominant ideology. If, on the one hand, this definition stresses the fact that populism can take a variety of forms; on the other, given the indeterminancy of the concept of antagonism and the lack of any attempt to relate ideological discourses to organisational forms, the term becomes so vague and malleable that it loses much of its analytic utility.

Take, for instance, Laclau's contention that the Italian Communist Party, in attempting to become a hegemonic party through the antagonistic articulation of popular-democratic elements in the ideology, is a populist party. To decide whether the PCI, or any other party for that matter, is populist, the criterion of 'articulation of popular elements in an antagonistic manner' is hardly enough. One would certainly have to look at the organisation of its cadres; at the relationships between rank-and-file and leadership; at what complex articulations exist between the party's ideology, long-term policies and day-to-day organisational practices; and so on.

To illustrate this, let us concentrate for a moment on the question of organisation. Populist parties tend to have a fluid, protean organisational structure. Even populist movements with a strong grass-roots organisational base are characterised by directness in the relationship between leader and led which tends to weaken the structuring of intermediary administrative levels between the top leadership and the rank-and-file. Any intermediaries, whether of the clientelistic or the more bureaucratic type, are distrusted. They seem as preventing the direct, immediate *rapport* between the populist leader and 'his people'. This intensely 'plebiscitary' element in populist organisations differentiates their structure both from purely clientelistic parties (whether the oligarchic or the more 'modern' type)[14] and from Western European socialist and communist parties (which in turn differ from each other). The latter – irrespective of their degree of sectarianism, reformism or radicalism, and irrespective of the degree to which they have antagonistically articulated popular-democratic elements into their discourse – have much more solid and autonomous intermediary organisational structures between leaders and led. Even if Robert Michels was partly right in arguing that West European socialist parties have oligarchic rather than pluralistic systems of internal control, there is not the slightest doubt that these parties exhibit organisational features which differentiate them from both populist and purely clientelistic parties. For the 'internal plebiscitarianism' of the former, and the dyadic patron-client relationships resulting in personal clienteles of the latter, are not dominant. Although, of course, such elements exist in all party structures, they only play a peripheral role in the organisation of Western European socialist and communist parties. From this point of view, I believe it is possible to speak of common organisational features of populist movements without falling into class reductionism – that is, without directly linking populist organisational elements to a determinate class basis. For this 'gelatinous' character can be found in populist movements of both the conservative and socialist type.

Finally, it is precisely because of the collapse of any organisational autonomy and the close identification of the entire movement with the person of the populist leader, that many socialists mistrust populism. This mistrust, which Laclau considers too as misguided[15] does not stem simply from a sectarian insistence on keeping working-class parties as 'pure' class parties. It stems rather from a well-justified suspicion of movements where it is the leader, rather than strongly rooted administrative structures and practices, from whom emanates the main integrative and directing force – a situation which frequently leads to the type of 'adventurist' tendencies which are so prevalent a feature of the so-called socialist populist movements of the Third World.

If this is accepted, then the PCI (Italian Communist Party) can by no means be seen as a populist party, and it is highly misleading to put it in that category. Neither its highly articulated organisational structure in the North, nor its contrasting clientelist networks in the South, come anywhere near the organisational structures of, for instance, Latin American populist movements. The organisational fluidity and the populist immediacy of the relationship between leader and led are quite absent: in the North, due to the long tradition of strong local and provincial cadre organisation; in the South, because of the traditional patronage structures. What is interesting, indeed, in the South is that when the PCI sought to abandon the strict Leninist model of party organisation in order to broaden its popular base, the result was not a populist, but a predominantly clientelistic type of organisational structure.[16]

Laclau might, of course, argue that if his definition of populism is adopted, the organisational dimension of populism becomes unimportant; and conversely, since populist ideologies can be based on a variety of organisational structures, these are irrelevant in trying to define the specific characteristic of populism. However, on the one hand, it still remains to be demonstrated that populist ideologies, as defined by Laclau, are in fact compatible with all types of political organisational structures. On the other hand, if they are not – as I would argue – then it is necessary to show the specific *organisational implications* of the articulation of popular interpellations in a manner antagonistic to the dominant ideology. Thus, whatever stand is taken on the organisational implications of a populist ideology, it is clearly not possible to show the 'role played by the strictly populist element in a determinate social formation' without *some* theorisation of the politico-organisational structures which mediate between class contradictions, on the one hand, and ideological discourses on the other. If this crucial dimension is not conceptualised, the result must be either a presentation of classes as anthropomorphic entities, mysteriously articulating and disarticulating ideological elements, or – at the other extreme – an idealist treatment of ideologies as self-unfolding essences. Certainly Laclau would in principle reject either alternative; but the point is that in practice his inadequate conceptualisation does not allow him to do this.

Hence, in a certain way, Laclau's attempt to correct Poulantzas' class reductionism leads him to the other extreme: to the portrayal of ideological themes as highly malleable and free-floating – classes being capable of articulating and disarticulating ideological interpellations at will. What this position tends to forget is that when classes are conceptualised, not in an abstract, anthropomorphic manner, but in terms of their internal fragmentation, their political organisation and their complex alliances and links with other organised interests, then it becomes obvious that there are strict limits to the types of content that their ideological discourse can have. Given such limits, which it is true are not always easy to define, one cannot argue that, so far as ideological manipulation is concerned, anything goes. For instance, certain ideological themes (whether 'popular' or not) can be so incongruent with the structural and organisational realities of a class that they cannot become dominant in its discourse. In other terms, if there is no one-to-one correspondence between class and ideological themes, neither is there a completely arbitrary relationship between the two. The non-arbitrary linkages between classes and the content of their ideological discourse is obvious when one looks not only at the historical genesis of specific ideologies, but also at the ways in which such ideologies develop subsequently. For although the class basis of ideological themes can change from one social formation to another, once an ideological discourse takes a specific place and form within a concrete social formation, then it too becomes organised and relatively fixed within limits imposed both by the internal organisation of a class and by the overall socio-political context. For example, it is inconceivable that the European feudal aristocracy could have created liberal political ideology, or that the South African ruling class today could decide to deploy a socialist programme.

Given Laclau's unsatisfactory conceptualisation of populism, it is not surprising that his attempt to identify the basic conditions for its emergence are not very successful either. According to him, the emergence of populism 'is historically linked to a crisis of the dominant ideological discourse which is in turn part of a more general social crisis. This crisis can either be the result of a fracture in the power-bloc, in which a class or class fraction needs, in order to assert its hegemony, to appeal to the "people" against established ideology as a whole; or of a crisis in the ability of the system to neutralise the dominated sectors – that is to say, a crisis of transformation'. [17] But such causes or preconditions for the emergence of populism derive from the definition automatically. If populism is to be defined by the articulation of popular elements in antagonism to the dominant ideology, and if this type of articulation can come either from the dominant or the dominated classes, then a populism of the dominant classes automatically implies an ideological crisis and a fragmentation of the power-bloc; and a populism of the dominated classes is then the logical outcome of a failure of 'transformism'.

This is a good example of a purely rationalist discourse, such as the author himself has rightly criticised in the introduction to his book: that is to say, a discourse where the logical properties of concepts form the only principle relating them to one another, so that one 'could pass from one to the other by a purely deductive process'.[18] The same purely deductive reasoning is to be found in Laclau's explanation of the emergence of European fascism. As mentioned already, the rise of fascism is explained in terms of a dual crisis: '(a) a crisis of the power-bloc, which was unable to absorb and neutralise its contradictions with the popular sectors through traditional channels; (b) a crisis of the working class, which was unable to hegemonise popular struggles and fuse popular-democratic ideology and its revolutionary class objectives into a coherent political ideological practice'.[19] But again, given the definition of Nazism as a populist movement of the dominant classes, both (a) and (b) must follow logically. The rise and success of a right-wing populist movement implies both a crisis of the power-bloc, and the failure of the dominated classes to take advantage of this crisis to themselves articulate popular-democratic elements in an antagonistic manner.

6 Alternative Theories of Populism

Given the lack of substance in Laclau's own explanation of populism, he is perhaps rather harsh in his criticism of alternative theories, such as, for instance, those of Germani and Di Tella.[20] Of course, Laclau is right in criticising these for their use of the tradition-modernity dichotomy which has played such a misleading role in the sociology of development. On the other hand, he is too quick to reject a number of insights contained in these theories which, if 'disarticulated' from the tradition/modernity neo-evolutionist discourse and 're-articulated' into a mode-of-production discourse, could prove extremely useful for the study of Third-World populism. Laclau is perfectly right, for example, when he stresses that populism is not a phenomenon specifically linked to import-substitution industrialisation, or to Third-World underdevelopment more generally, and that it can also occur in developed capitalist social formations. But this is no argument against building a more limited, *context-bound* theory of, say, Latin American populism in particular. In fact, it is precisely this limitation which makes Germani's and Di Tella's theories – for all their shortcomings – less vacuous than Laclau's own. As Laclau himself admits, populism, occurs more frequently in peripheral capitalist social formations. Why is this so?

Again, the crucial concept of political mobilisation, and Germani's and Di Tella's ideas about the abrupt way in which the masses have entered the political arena in many Latin American countries (especially if this is compared to similar processes of political mobilisation and integration in West European development) cannot be so easily dismissed. It is perfectly possible to use such ideas without introducing into the analysis neo-evolutionist, teleological notions of 'modernisation', or moralistic, Euro-centric considerations about the political immaturity of Latin American working-class movements and so on. For instance, one can easily explain the more rapid entry – as compared to Europe – of both rural and urban working people into active politics in Latin America, by taking into account the different ways in which capitalism has developed in the two continents.

At the risk of over-generalisation, it might be argued that Western capitalism, being a slower and more indigenous process, not only managed to expand more widely throughout the economy, but also became articulated with non-capitalist modes of production in such a way that the results of technological advances in the capitalist sector spread to the rest of the economy with relatively positive effects on productivity and on wealth and income differentials.[21] In the case of Latin American capitalism, on the other hand, a variety of reasons (which cannot be explained here) prevented the capitalist mode of production from expanding so widely, so that it instead took a more restricted form, failing to destroy non-capitalist modes of production to the same extent as had occurred in Europe. Moreover, the fact that it articulated more 'negatively' with the very large surviving non-capitalist sectors goes a long way to explain the huge productivity differentials between capitalist and non-capitalist sectors, the ever-growing inequalities and, more generally, the unprecedented disruptions that capital accumulation generates in these countries.[22] And since such processes engender large-scale political mobilisation and an unavoidable abrupt entry of the majority of the working population into active politics, it is understandable why the oligarchic-clientelistic parties are not easily able to readjust their structures to accommodate the new entrants, and at the same time why the socio-economic context is unfavourable for the emergence of strongly organised, non-personalistic mass parties on the West European pattern.[23] This is what explains the proliferation of (and frequent changes in) modes of political integration in which paternalistic/ 'plebiscitary' leadership (rather than intricate patronage networks of well-articulated, multi-level administrative structures) plays the dominant role.[24]

The above rather unsystematic remarks do not pretend to formulate an alternative theory of populism. They are simply suggestions of how some of Germani's and Di Tella's ideas, and more generally concepts such as political mobilisation and integration, can and should be taken into account in a Marxist theory of Third-World populism. Laclau does not do this. In fact, he manages the remarkable feat of developing a theory of populism without dealing at all seriously with the concept of political mobilisation. He could argue, of course, that the concept of 'articulation of popular interpellations in a manner antagonistic to the dominant ideology' itself implies the idea of mass mobilisation. However, the theme of 'antagonism' is not made at all clear in his theory. Either the concept of antagonistic articulation of popular interpellations need not necessarily imply that this type of discourse has any effectiveness so far as popular mobilisation is concerned – in which case it can also refer to 'ineffective' anti-establishment ideas with no popular impact. Or else antagonistic articulation always implies mobilisation, in which case the crucial problem of the intricate relationships between the ideological content of a discourse and its political impact on mass mobilisation is being swept under the carpet.

Of course, as Laclau points out, the concept of political mobilisation has been developed mainly by political scientists like Nettl, Apter and Deutsch.[25] Thus, the suggestion that one should bring into Marxism concepts predominantly derived from functionalist sociology might be dismissed outright as mere 'bourgeois' eclecticism. However, one should in fact stay clear of two equally unacceptable extreme positions: first, an *ad hoc* eclecticism which brings together concepts derived from different paradigms *without any serious attempt at theoretical reworking and reconceptualisation*; second, a paradigmatic purism or sectarianism which insists that one should never 'contaminate' the Marxist discourse with so-called 'bourgeois' concepts. The latter position, moreover, is based on the dubious assumption that competing paradigms in any one field of study are utterly disconnected from each other, exhibiting a high degree of internal unity and coherence. Although it is not possible to discuss this epistemological problem here, examination of the dominant paradigms, at least in the social sciences, makes it immediately obvious that they are not totally self-contained, but in fact interpenetrate in a variety of ways. This is strongly confirmed when one remembers the extreme fragmentation and proliferation of sub-paradigms, both within Marxism and in non-Marxist social sciences.

I feel impelled, therefore, to draw a parallel between the fact that popular interpellations can be articulated into a variety of different ideological discourses, with radically different political consequences, and the fact that crucial concepts such as political mobilisation and integration can be articulated into a variety of different theoretical discourses with very different theoretical effects. From this point of view, Laclau's theory would have been more successful if he had not dismissed the valuable insights and concepts of earlier theories of populism in quite such a cavalier fashion.

7 Class and People

Moving now from the theory of populism to a more abstract level, and considering how Laclau conceptualises class and popular interpellations, certain difficulties are encountered here too. We have seen that, for Laclau, class and popular interpellations arise out of different structural contradictions: the former out of mode-of-production contradictions, and the latter, on a more concrete level of analysis, out of the 'complex of political and ideological relations of domination constituting a determinate social formation.'[26] To begin with, I do not see by what logic Laclau equates the concept of a social formation with the political and ideological level (according to him, agents as 'people' do not – by definition – exist at the level of production, since popular struggles take place on the superstructural level). While it is true that the concepts of both mode of production and social formation are interpreted and used in a variety of ways among Marxists, it is almost unanimously agreed that the social-formation concept implies (1) the notion of totality, referring to *both* the economic and the politico-ideological level, and (2) the notion of concreteness, in contrast to the more analytic mode-of-production concept. Now Laclau is obviously wrong so far as (1) is concerned, since as I have said he seems precisely to equate a social formation with the political and ideological level. He is also very confusing with regard to (2), since he seems to make the following connections: mode of production (more analytic level) – class contradiction – class interpellations; social formations (more concrete level) – people/power-bloc contradictions – popular interpellations.[27]

This type of conceptualisation can easily lead to the strange conclusion that political conflict on the 'concrete' politico-ideological/social formation level has very little to do with class divisions and struggles; and that politics invariably means 'populist' politics, that is, politics has to do with the 'people' rather than with 'classes'. Such misleading connotations derive from some strictly logical inconsistencies in Laclau's formulations. For, according to him, the people/power-bloc contradictions and popular interpellations are situated on the concrete, social formation/politico-ideological level of analysis. But given that a concrete populist ideology (for example, Peronism) contains both class and popular interpellations, why are popular interpellations and the related contradictions situated on the more concrete social-formation level? I would have thought the 'concreteness' of the social-formation concept would correspond not simply to popular interpellations, but to a whole populist ideological discourse consisting of an articulation of both class and popular interpellations, and resulting from both economic and politico-ideological contradictions. Although Laclau's 'structuralist' logic is dubious, if one were to carry it through in a rigorous manner, the connections should take the following form:

- mode of production (analytical level) – class contradictions – class interpellations;
- politico-ideological relations of domination (analytic level) – people/power-bloc contradictions – popular interpellations;
- social formation (more concrete level) – economic, political and ideological practices (the latter referring to concrete ideological discourses as well).

Such a conceptualisation would at least avoid the absurd position of conflating popular themes and movements with politics in general.

Given these difficulties, Laclau's theorisation does not solve many of the problems created by Poulantzas' theory of ideology. True, Poulantzas' analysis of fascism tries to link discrete ideological elements to specific classes, which as Laclau rightly points out is an untenable class-reductionist position. But in Poulantzas' more theoretical works, one can find elements which provide a more coherent solution to the type of class-reductionist problem referred to by Laclau. As is well known, Poulantzas stresses that there is no one-to-one correspondence between structurally determined, objective class places and class practices (such as concrete ideologies, strategies of specific parties, and so on). This is because it is not simply structural relationships and contradictions arising from within the economic sphere which determine class practices, but also contradictions and relations located in the political and ideological spheres. As the latter contradictions cannot be reduced to the former, they exercise an autonomous effect on class practices. And it is precisely because a concrete ideological discourse is the result of an overall structural matrix, consisting of economic, political and ideological determinations, that it is impossible to deduce class practices from objective class places.[28]

This position is not incompatible with Laclau's useful idea that it is impossible to establish to which class discrete ideological elements belong. Thus, on a theoretical level, Poulantzas avoids class reductionism; and he does allow for the relative autonomy of contradictions arising on the superstructural level. If in practice he is not always consistent in his meta-theoretical pronouncements, that is another matter. A more appropriate criticism of Poulantzas on the theoretical level, therefore, would be that, although he avoids the type of class reductionism that Laclau deals with, he falls into an overall structural determinism which always portrays class practices as the effects of structural determinations on the economic and politico-ideological level. In other words, in line with Althusser's general position, he portrays classes in a passive, puppet-like manner as mere 'bearers of structures'; structural determinations always work from structures to the agents, never the other way round; collective agents such as parties, movements or social forces are always the effects, never the causes, of structures. Given this passive portrayal of collective agencies, the structural 'matrix', that is, the complex articulation of economic, political and ideological structures, remains, of course, as unexplained as Durkheim's *conscience collective*. So it is not surprising that, although Poulantzas constantly invokes the class struggle, he does not integrate this concept theoretically into his discourse: it is left to play the role of *deus ex machina*. If classes and class practices are effects of structural determinations, then struggles between bearers of structures cannot have any autonomous effectiveness either.[29]

8 The Problem of Theory

Finally, since Laclau – both in the introduction and throughout his book – deals extensively with problems related to the structure and

types of theoretical discourse, a brief comment is needed on his
general epistemological position. Laclau holds that there are two
major theoretical obstacles to the advance of Marxism: (1) an
empiricist orientation which leads to the establishment of connotative
articulations between concepts – that is, articulations based on
common-sense knowledge and on formal principles extraneous to the
logical nature of the concepts involved; (2) at the other extreme, an
orientation which destroys connotative articulations, only to replace
them by purely rationalist ones – that is, articulations which transform concepts into essential paradigms, the logical properties of
which are the only principles relating them to each other. In this
manner, theoretical discourse is reduced to a purely deductivist
exercise, to the 'self-unfolding of an essence', as concepts are
logically and necessarily derived from other concepts. For Laclau, a
successful theory would have to avoid both connotative and purely
rationalist articulations of concepts, and establish *theoretical* articulations. How do theoretical articulations or determinants differ from
purely rationalist ones? Laclau does not give us a clear answer to this
crucial question. The nearest he comes to it is the following: 'Any
approximation to the concept presupposes increasingly *complex
conceptual articulations* and not the mere exposition of the logical
properties of a simple conceptual whole. Consequently, the more
concrete is the analysis, the more theoretical determinations must be
included in it; and since theoretical determinations are not necessary
moments in the self-unfolding of an essence but discrete conceptual
formations, the precondition of any theoretical approximation to the
concrete comprises a progressive process of abstraction which frees
concepts from their connotative articulations'.[30] This quotation
makes it clear that Laclau's definition of theoretical determinations is
wholly negative: that is, theoretical determinations are those which
are not purely rationalist ('not necessary moments in the self-
unfolding of an essence, but discrete conceptual formations') and not
empiricist either (comprising 'a progressive process of abstraction
which frees concepts from their connotative articulations'). Beyond
this type of circular definition, all we learn about theoretical articulations is that they are 'more complex'; but to characterise them as such
without specifying the type of complexity involved is hardly adequate.

   A similar unease and difficulty in distinguishing between a rationalist and a theoretical/scientific discourse is found in the author's
discussion of problems arising out of the 'empirical validity of a
theory'. Laclau rightly argues that what is wrong with the empiricist

emphasis on the necessity to confront theories with 'concrete facts' is the fallacy that somehow these facts are real objects, totally outside the theoretical discourse: 'If however the "concrete" facts are produced by the theory or problematic itself – as modern epistemology asserts – then the problems of logical consistency and empirical validity are not substantially different'.[31] And 'assuming that the area of empirical confrontation of a theory's system of propositions is not external, but internal to the theory (in that the problematic creates its own objects), the *'empirical' verification*, insofar as it disproves the theoretical propositions, demonstrates the internal contradictions of the *theoretical system*'.[32] Now, that empirical verification is not external to the theory, and that the style and conditions of the empirical verification are always dictated by the theoretical discourse itself, is perfectly true, though hardly original.[33] But to argue that logical consistency and empirical validity are not substantially different problems is a more dubious proposition. For although all weaknesses of a theory do take the form of 'internal contradictions of the theoretical system', there are *different types of internal contradictions*, some more and some less directly derived from purely logical inconsistencies.

Let me give an example derived from Laclau's own book. The author, in criticising certain aspects of Poulantzas' work, states: 'At one moment a class can only be considered as distinctive and autonomous if it exercises "pertinent effects", i.e. a decisive impact; next moment, these "pertinent effects" may be "ineffectual".'[34] Here, I think, one has an excellent example of purely logical inconsistency: an 'internal contradiction' which derives from the fact that fundamental concepts are given different, contradictory definitions within the same discourse. But the above internal contradiction is radically different from another type of 'internal' contradiction, resulting from conflicts 'between the sphere of "empirical" confrontation and the theoretical system in question'.

Let us suppose a theory which tries to analyse the development of capitalism in a specific Latin American formation; whose problematic leads to an examination of wealth and income inequalities in this formation; and which leads to the conclusion that income inequalities are rapidly decreasing. Now even if this conclusion is incorrect, following Laclau, one can still talk about an 'internal contradiction'. In this sense, the issue of income differentials becomes a 'problem' to be investigated because of its relevance to certain features of the theory itself – as Laclau puts it, the theoretical 'problematic creates its own objects'. But whether one calls the above contradiction internal or external, the point is that it differs radically from the Poulantzas-type contradiction mentioned earlier, in that the theoretical procedures required for demonstrating its 'contradictory' character are different. In Poulantzas' case, a purely armchair demonstration of definitional inconsistencies suffices, in the other it certainly does not. There are, therefore, fundamental differences between purely logical contradictions and those more directly derived from the sphere of 'empirical confrontation'. To try to conflate the two, as do Laclau and many Althusserians, too easily leads to the type of sterile, purely deductionist theorising which has become so fashionable in French and German Marxism.[35]

If I have concentrated on the more problematic aspects of Laclau's essays, this must be understood as a criticism of the gaps and incompletenesses of his theoretical framework (that is, his omission of the political-organisational dimensions of populism), rather than as a dismissal of his work as a whole. There are, both in his previously published articles and in his essays on populism, a number of seminal ideas which, if further and more adequately elaborated, can be of great value to the development of Marxist theory. Thus the four essays, viewed as a whole, constitute a stimulating theoretical introduction to some of contemporary Marxism's most crucial debates.

NOTES

*   This essay appeared, in a slightly modified form, in *New Left Review*, No. 112, November-December 1978.
1. Ernesto Laclau, *Politics and Ideology in Marxist Theory*, London: NLB, 1977.
2. The essay first appeared in *New Left Review*, 67, May-June 1971.
3. Laclau's article on the Miliband-Poulantzas debate was first published in *Economy and Society*, No. 1, 1975.
4. Nicos Poulantzas, *Fascism and Dictatorship*, London: NLB, 1974.
5. *Politics and Ideology*, p. 101.
6. Ibid., p. 159.
7. Ibid., p. 108.
8. Ibid., p. 173.
9. Ibid., p. 174.
10. Ibid., p. 173.
11. Ibid., p. 124.

12. Laclau, in his critique of populist theories, briefly mentions – with seeming approval – one which conceptualises populism not as a movement but as an ideology (containing such elements as hostility to the *status quo*, mistrust of traditional politicians, appeal to the people not classes, and so on) which can be adopted by a variety of movements each with a different class basis. The only criticism he makes of this kind of theory is that '(a) the characteristic features of populist ideology are presented in a purely descriptive manner . . . (b) nothing is said of the role played by the strictly populist element in a determinate social formation' (*Politics and Ideology*, p. 147). It is precisely in these two directions that Laclau's own efforts are turned.

13. *Politics and Ideology*, p. 147.

14. For an account of the structural differences between these two types of clientelistic parties, see E. Gellner and J. Waterbury (eds), *Patrons and Clients* (especially the articles by P. Loizos, Sabri Sayari, Samir Khalaf), London, 1977; and S. W. Schmidt *et al.*, (eds), *Friends, Followers and Factions*, Berkeley, 1977.

15. *Politics and Ideology*, p. 196.

16. Sidney Tarrow, *Peasant Communism in Southern Italy*, New Haven, 1967. Just as the Italian Communist Party cannot be considered populist, a similar argument applies in the case of fascist parties. Given the profound organisational and overall structural differences between fascist and conservative populist parties of, say, the Latin American type (and some of these, as we have seen, Laclau himself points out), it is highly misleading to lump them together under the same label. It is Laclau's failure to distinguish populist ideologies from populist movements which leads him to this type of gross categorisation.

17. *Politics and Ideology*, p. 175.

18. Ibid., p. 10.

19. Ibid., p. 115.

20. Gino Germani, *Politica y Sociedad en una Epoca de Transicion*, Buenos Aires, 1965. Torcuato Di Tella, 'Populism and Reform in Latin America', in Claudio Veliz (ed.), *Obstacles to Change in Latin America*, London, 1970.

21. See, for instance, Celso Furtado, *Development and Underdevelopment*, Berkeley, 1967.

22. On the concept of negative linkages or disarticulation, see Samir Amin, *Accumulation on a World Scale*, Hassocks, 1976; also his *Unequal Development*, London, 1978. On the lack of expansion of the capitalist mode of production in underdeveloped countries, see Geoff Kay, *Development and Underdevelopment: a Marxist Analysis*, London, 1975.

23. For a development of this argument in relation to a specific case, see Nicos Mouzelis, 'Class and Clientelist Politics: the Case of Greece', *Sociological Review*, August 1978.

24. This does not imply that clientelistic and populist forms of organisation must be incompatible. Given that, in the form of elements or principles of organisation, they are present in most political structures, the point is to see which element is dominant and in what way it articulates with peripheral elements.

25.　*Politics and Ideology*, p. 148. The works in question are P. Nettl, *Political Mobilisation. A Sociological Analysis of Methods and Concepts*, London, 1967; D. Apter, *The Politics of Modernisation*, London, 1969; and K. Deutsch, 'Social Mobilisation and Political Developments', in Eckstein and Apter (eds), *Comparative Politics*, New York, 1963.

26.　Ibid., p. 166.

27.　Another difficulty with Laclau's definition of popular interpellations, and with his notion of the people/power-bloc contradictions, is the very loose manner in which he uses the term 'popular'. For instance, very often the terms 'national' and 'democratic' are used interchangeably with 'popular' or 'populist'. This is not the place to discuss the complex problems of the relationship between nationalism, populism and 'democracy', and the further connections between these notions and that of socialism. However, the fact that Laclau does not tackle seriously the problem of nationalism and its relationship to working-class movements, and the fact that he often conflates national and popular interpellations, is another indication of the 'blanket' character of his definition of populism.

28.　See Nicos Poulantzas, *Classes in Contemporary Capitalism*, London: NLB, 1975.

29.　For an elaboration of this argument, see Nicos Mouzelis, *Modern Greece: Facets of Underdevelopment*, London, 1978, pp. 46 ff.

30.　*Politics and Ideology*, p. 10 (italics added).

31.　Ibid., p. 59.

32.　Ibid., p. 61.

33.　In fact, the point was made with less fuss and far greater clarity long before the Althusserian anti-empiricist vogue. See, for instance, R. B. Braithwaite, *Scientific Explanations*, Cambridge, 1914, pp. 76–8; G. Ryle, *Dilemas*, London, 1962, pp. 89–92.

34.　*Politics and Ideology*, p. 71.

35.　A good example of this type of purely rationalist discourse is the attempt to derive the basic features of the capitalist state from the 'logic of capital': from the systemic constraints that the reproduction of the capitalist mode of production imposes on the political system. For a representative sample of such works in English, see John Holloway and Sol Picciotto, *State and Capital: a Marxist Debate*, London, 1978.

Index